August 1994 —

Judy – I hope this
helps feed your love of
beauty.
Best of everything to you —
always. You deserve it.
Phyllis W.

DANCE IN AMERICA

DANCE IN AMERICA

· ROBERT COE ·

· E. P. DUTTON   NEW YORK ·

To Elisa, for faith and unstinting effort

Published in the United States by E. P. Dutton, a division of New American Library, 2 Park Avenue, New York, N.Y. 10016

Library of Congress Cataloging in Publication Data

Coe, Robert.
  Dance in America.

  Bibliography: p.
  Includes index.
  1. Dancing—United States—History. 2. Ballet—United States—History. 3. Modern dance—United States—History.
I. Title.
GV1623.C64 1985   793.3'1973   85-10431

ISBN: 0-525-24325-9
Published simultaneously in Canada by Fitzhenry & Whiteside Limited, Toronto

10 9 8 7 6 5 4 3 2 1

World

First Edition

Color insert printed by Reprocolor Llovet, S.A., Barcelona, Spain.

ONTENTS

Color insert follows page 120

ACKNOWLEDGMENTS

I want to salute the choreographers and dancers whose artistry is the heart of the *Dance in America* public television series on which this book is based. Tribute should also be paid, on behalf of the viewers of the series and the readers of this book, to the farsighted funders who made the programs possible: The National Endowment for the Arts, the Exxon Corporation, and the Corporation for Public Broadcasting. I wish personally to thank Parmenia Ekstrom, Elizabeth Kendall, Amanda Smith, Sally Sommer, and David Vaughan for their advice on various chapters of this book, portions of which were published in other forms by *The New York Times Magazine, Vanity Fair,* and *The Soho Weekly News.* I am also indebted to the instructive writings of Arlene Croce, Lincoln Kirstein, Marcia Siegel, and the late Edwin Denby, as well as to the staff of the Dance Collection, New York City Public Library at Lincoln Center, for help during the two years I worked on this book. Thanks also to Don Cutler, who initiated the project, and to Leonard Mayhew at WNET/New York, as well as to producers Judy Kinberg and Emile Ardolino and Merrill Brockway at *Dance in America.* Mary Whitney, my photo editor, aided tremendously in collecting and sorting through a vast number of photos, as did Judith Aminoff early in the life of the project. I am also grateful to the staff at E. P. Dutton: Jack Macrae, who first undertook the book; Elisa Petrini, who helped me develop it; Nancy P. Danahy, who designed it; Jerret Engle and William Whitehead, who supported and sustained it; and finally Jennifer Josephy, who came on board during the final stages. Seymour Barofsky provided invaluable editorial assistance as well. And special thanks to JoAnne, who bore with me through it all.

DANCE IN AMERICA

DANCE IN AMERICA

· A COMING OF AGE ·

As the oldest human art, dance has been an essential part of culture in North America since people first set foot on the continent. The dances of native Americans—the Navaho, the Iroquois, the Sioux—held the universe in balance, binding the individual to the customs and beliefs of the tribe, and weaving together the course of human life with an image of the cosmos for five hundred centuries before Columbus. This primeval experience did not inspire the dominant American concert dance of today. Three hundred and fifty years ago, America was reborn as the dream of European civilization, heir to the customs and beliefs of another place and time. Nevertheless, as a distinctly American culture grew through the experience of immigrants from Africa, Latin America, and Asia, as well as Europe, men and women instinctively renewed the primal kinship between the spirit of place and the human impulse to move.

Indeed, almost as swiftly as they arrived from the Old World, dances began to express in exuberant cadences the restless innocence of an emerging American character. Jigs and hornpipes from the British Isles were recast in a livelier vein, invading the popular stage by the late eighteenth century; moving from boxwood gardens to wide-open prairies, English country dances were transformed into the square dances of the American West. Much of the originality of American dance, as well as its music, came from peoples from Africa and the Caribbean who arrived in North America in terror and sorrow—black slaves and their descendants, who combined Scotch-Irish clog dances with their own ancestral shapes and rhythms to fashion the earliest American native dancing, the origins of modern tap-dance styles.

Americans have always danced among themselves, and with a vigor and inventiveness unknown in Europe. Nevertheless, the subject of this book—American dancing *as a fine art*—scarcely existed until the late nineteenth century. Ballet, the classical dance of Europe, seemed more than an ocean away from an expansive, industrious nation with vast stretches of wilderness still to conquer and little time for unproductive pursuits. Stunted by the spiritual ascendancy of Puritanism, the Victorian denial of sensuality and the body, and a provincial feeling of inferiority in the face of European culture, nineteenth-century America failed to produce the enlightened urban elite and self-challenging artists needed to subsidize the development of a serious artistic dance. Surely there has never been an easy equation between artistic seriousness and artistic achievement: American entertainers in the commercial theater have danced at a high pitch of art for generations. Yet few Americans suspected, as recently as eighty or ninety years ago, that

Maria Calegari, Lourdes Lopez, and Merrill Ashley with the New York City Ballet in Balanchine's *Serenade*. (© 1984 Martha Swope)

dance—like painting, sculpture, music, or literature—could actually express something significant about their culture and their world.

The absence of an overwhelming native tradition proved to be the most important stimulus to the growth of a native artistic dance in this century. American dance became almost by default an art of the modern age—reinventing itself out of the materials at hand, exploring with enormous urgency the qualities of a medium ideally suited to the immediacy of modern expression. Drawn from the extraordinary confluence of cultures and peoples that comprise the

nation—"its vitality, its freshness, its exuberance, its overabundant youth and vigor, its contrasts of plenitude and barrenness," as choreographer Martha Graham has written—American dance has come to reflect the dynamics of a nation where people shape their own destinies through ingenuity and industry, with crossfertilization and synthesis, individual initiative and renewal, the major sources of its creativity.

Just over fifty years ago, on a spacious outdoor platform near White Plains, New York, a ballet called *Serenade* premiered as a kind of lesson or textbook for students at the recently founded School of American Ballet. Its founder was a Russian-trained former choreographer for the legendary Ballets Russes in Europe named George Balanchine, the summation of a classical tradition stretching back to the French court of Louis XIV, now beginning to create ballets along swift new American lines. Seventeen women had come to his class in stage technique on the March afternoon he set to work; the next day, nine; the day after, six; the structure of the finished ballet continued to reflect the scale of these rehearsal situations, so that when a dancer arrived late and searched for her place in formation, or another slipped accidentally and fell to the floor, the choreographer skillfully wove these incidents into the dance. Honoring the fables of his imperial Russian past with fragments of a romantic tale of love and fate, loss and transcendence, Balanchine drew his imagery from the great *ballets blancs* of the nineteenth century: ballets that insisted on a hierarchy of ballerina and cavalier, with an anonymous corps de ballet—literally "the body of the dance"—emerging in moonlight to dance behind soloists and stars. But Balanchine recast these images in a more *democratic* style inspired by the wholesome, unaffected behavior of the young Americans he saw before him. *Serenade*'s corps performed as an ensemble of individual soloists, rushing and leaping across the stage with a fierce, athletic abandon, shaping and reshaping a stream of familiar images with "a straightforward yet passionate clarity and freshness," noted Balanchine's American sponsor, Lincoln Kirstein, "suitable for the foundation of a non-European academy."

Generations of classical dancers and choreographers had evolved a supremely rational canon of steps and gestures that could serve many different imaginative visions; but *Serenade*'s truest subjects became the elation and darkness of Tchaikovsky's score and the dancers' candid engagement with the movement itself. Divesting ballet of the airs and pretenses of the Old World, drawing on a tradition of American vigor that needed no literary excuse to exercise itself, *Serenade* reflected Balanchine's extraordinary gifts for teaching Americans "how to look grand and no-ble," as the late critic Edwin Denby observed, "but not be embarrassed about it."

At the same time that ballet became an unmistakably American art, numerous artists believed that such rehearsals of foreign glamour could never fully respond to the conditions of American life. Ballet was European, a system of rules affirming the status quo; with an onrush of technological and cultural change shattering older forms of art and thought, a new generation of dance modernists began to approach their art through a consummately American idea—that America is a place to start over, to escape the past and give birth to entirely new ways of living. Proceeding with extreme self-consciousness about the nature of their craft, choreographers set about to explore fundamentally American attitudes about the body, space, time, and composition with an American sense of self-reliance and possibility.

Martha Graham's *Frontier—An American Perspective on the Plains,* created a year after Balanchine's *Serenade,* was a fully realized masterwork of this new, modern dance. A frontier woman stands with one foot planted on a pole fence, gazing out across a vast imaginative landscape. Poet Charles Olson once called SPACE, "writ large," the central fact to man born in America, and *Frontier* captures this moment of recognition with an enduring image from the American past. Renewing the freshness and optimism of the nation's pioneer heritage, *Frontier* focused attention on more urgent social questions as well. "All life today," Graham announced, "is concerned with space problems, even political life"—thinking pointedly of the German call for *Lebensraum* and America's continuing urbanization. *Frontier* confronts the plains, "the distances, the vistas," the choreographer remarked years later; in order to create a sense of infinite horizon, she had decided to use a set for the first time in her eight-year career. But instead of calling on a theater designer to contribute the conventional backdrop used in dance performances, she asked a young Japanese-American sculptor, Isamu Noguchi, to create a three-tiered pole fence as the focal point of V-

Martha Graham in *Frontier* (1935). (© 1980 Barbara Morgan)

shaped ropes stretching to the upper corners of the proscenium, wedding "the total void of theater space to form and action," Noguchi later recalled.

The choreographic structure of *Frontier* was adapted from a preclassical European dance form, the rondo, or ring, taught in dance composition courses at New York's Neighborhood Playhouse by Louis Horst, Graham's longtime musical director. Horst composed the musical score for *Frontier:* Incisive, dissonant trumpets and snare drums blared and beat the rhythms of conquest, as the barefoot solo dancer—Graham herself—defined the unbounded perimeter of her new territory with tiny, controlled steps and expansive, jubilant leaps. Kicking one leg high into the air, with an arm flung wide, she sprang repeatedly in all four directions, always returning to the pole fence to reassert her fresh dominion over the land. "Certainly no American settler ever danced like this, nor was there even a log cabin in sight," observed critic Walter Terry. But the *Americanness* of the dance was evident to audiences from its first performance at the Guild Theater in New York City in April 1935: In purely abstract terms, Terry noted, *Frontier* "rebuilt the American heritage of blood and bone upon the stage."

Over the last fifty years, dance in America has shifted the highest tradition of classicism from Russia to the New World, while modern choreographers have continued to risk the new, diving headlong into unexplored realms of experience to change the shapes of dance expression around the world. Suspended between the classical dance of Europe and the freedom of the New World imagination is Merce Cunningham, the third Promethean giant of American dance, for whom "the most revealing and absorbing moments of life are the ones which have no past or future—that are, as it were, without relevance—when the action, the actor, and the spectator are unidentified—when the mind, also, is caught in midair."

Cunningham's *RainForest* (1968) presents a race of human beings engaged in a singularly unpretentious activity. Dancing in a floating jungle of helium-filled silver Mylar pillows by

Ellen Cornfield in Merce Cunningham's *RainForest*. (© Herbert Migdoll)

Andy Warhol, kicking the pillows that drift across their paths, they careen through space in thoughtful, upright postures, or else engage in the obscure, comforting rites and gestures of primitive people. Watching their activity might be compared to observing an afternoon in a city park, where many disparate events might happen simultaneously, creating different impressions in different viewers—"as nature does," says the choreographer, "at any given moment." Cunningham's dances combine the footwork of the ballet with the active torso of modern dance —and even suggest that very ordinary movements can be drawn into the image of a dance: Riding a bicycle, crawling, fidgeting, animal imitation, even standing still might merge with an overall dance momentum that can occur anywhere—in gymnasiums, parks, and museums—

not just under a proscenium arch. Purged of symbolic and expressive content, Cunningham's dances offer only the contemplation of an arresting human drama, bound by physical possibility and the limits of the imagination.

Visual design played an equal role in the creation of the work: Minutes before *RainForest*'s premiere at the second Buffalo Festival of the Arts, Warhol wandered among the six dancers, snipping ragged holes in their beige leotards and tights to provide a textural contrast to the shiny high-tech pillows. Music is another equal partner: Influenced by the example of John Cage, the father of contemporary experimental music and Cunningham's longtime musical director, composer David Tudor's *RainForest*—with its electronic drones and hums, shrieks and birdcalls—sounds like a primeval torrent that has continued for a thousand years. Rather than depend on metrical pulse, which has dominated Western dance for centuries, Cunningham's dancers sustain their own rhythmic continuity and insistence, based on the integrity of individual momentum and gesture. "Dancing is for me," says Cunningham, "beyond a series of steps or the reproduction of a story or the expression of a mood or feeling or the visual display of music, an amplification of our energies in a way special to it."

And viewers, too, contribute to the experience. They are free to interpret its sights and sounds on their own terms, reflecting the need for individual resourcefulness in an age of information: At its New York premiere at the Brooklyn Academy of Music, *RainForest* seemed to signal the arrival of a whole new way of looking at the world.

Serenade, Frontier, and *RainForest*—a neoclassical ballet, a modern dance, and a movement event opening into a postmodern era—are all abstract, plotless works exploring the qualities of their medium in ways that characterize the modern enterprise in all the arts. Twentieth-century dance has been and is about dancing first and foremost—the realization that a dance can be its own end, rather than just an aspect of some larger event or a means for conveying a story.

Even our great narrative dances have concerned themselves primarily with the colors, textures, and native eloquence of movement itself.

And yet "abstract" dances must appeal to much more than the hunger of the naked eye for stimulation. Audiences must sense not only how dancers move but what *moves* them: Successful dances create universes that are at once real and imagined, expressing complex feelings and attitudes about beauty, health, and eroticism, mental and spiritual well-being, the relationship of the individual to society at large, the importance of order and continuity and the value of rebellion, the raw physicality of the playground, home, and workplace, and what it is we admire most in human motion. And if there is a hero in this, as Lincoln Kirstein once suggested, "it is the choreography." That is why this book focuses on the choreographers themselves: the romance of their self-invention and achievement, the historical forces that contributed to their work, and the institutions they have built to serve their gifts.

·   ·   ·

Like "water running through our fingers," as Merce Cunningham once remarked, a dance is a seamless flow of ephemeral moments, that vanish with an ineffability akin to an act of nature. Watching dances on a television screen must inevitably become a very different order of experience. Indeed, before WNET/Thirteen's *Dance in America*'s inception, in 1976, as the first continuing dance series in major network history, many people doubted that the masterpieces of American choreography could be committed to prime-time television at all.

Although dance has a long if sporadic history on America's most popular entertainment medium, the simple fact was that few directors and choreographers had figured out how to translate the immediacy and scope of live performance for the home screen. When a ballerina rises on pointe in full arabesque, framed by a complementary corps de ballet, a television close-up reveals only the soloist and a triangular-shaped expanse of floor behind her. A more distant view reduces the dancers to ants on the screen, exposing the pattern of the choreography and little else. To minimize the disturbances caused by shifting points of view, many directors interpret the choreographer's effects themselves, creating very different dances for television. Surely TV contributes certain advantages to dance presentation: unobstructed sight lines from all angles, intimate close-ups, fades and dissolves, superimpositions, slow motion, and shifts in focus that offer new insights and even modify ideas about established works. Nevertheless the critical triumphs of several experimental television series—"Omnibus," "The Seven Lively Arts," and especially CBS-TV's "Camera Three"—in the 1950s and 1960s failed to reassure major network executives that a national audience existed for a regular series dedicated to the nation's best dance companies. "Who would give up Marcus Welby for a two-inch dancer?" asked *The New York Times* as recently as 1971.

It took the emergence of public television in the 1960s and 1970s to change the future of all the performing arts on television. As early as 1959, public TV stations like WNET/Thirteen in New York began to commit themselves to the potential of quality arts programming in prime time. By the early 1970s, WNET studio presentations of American Ballet Theatre and Alvin Ailey had uncovered a dance audience of millions and prospects for even more comprehensive dance programming. In collaboration with executive producer Jac Venza and Joan Mack, head of development at WNET, Emile Ardolino, producer of over fifty documentaries for the Jerome Robbins Film Archive at Lincoln Center, urged the creation of a program that would reflect those elements of choreographic vision and style that are uniquely American, as well as backstage documentation of various aspects of the life and work of American companies and choreographers. Venza invited a twenty-two-year veteran of television, Merrill Brockway, the former executive producer of "Camera Three" and a director well known for his explorations of music, theater, and dance, to serve as series producer. Brockway in turn invited Judy Kinberg, a five-year associate at

"Camera Three," to complete the producing triumvirate.

On June 12, 1975, the National Endowment for the Arts, the Exxon Corporation, and the Corporation for Public Broadcasting announced that WNET's new series would receive an initial grant of $1.5 million for the first year of a projected series of sixteen or more one-hour specials. The decision had been made to serve and respect *choreography* above all else—to translate dances by major companies without massive changes or video effects or glitzy attempts at popularization. It seemed a conservative goal by some standards, but for prime-time television it was revolutionary. In order to achieve it, the producers knew that they would need the cooperation and trust of the choreographers themselves.

·   ·   ·

"Television needed these fresh voices," Emile Ardolino says. "We needed their opinions as much as we needed their dances. As producers, we had particular ideas about what would and wouldn't work. But for us the greatest pleasure was seeing choreographers we respected and admired doing what they really wanted to do."

The first collaborator from the world of ballet was Ardolino's friend Robert Joffrey, who had worked for NBC opera broadcasts in the 1950s and taken his own company on the "Ed Sullivan Show" in 1965; he understood TV's potential for building new audiences for live performance. Now, a decision was made to present mostly excerpts: a kind of sampler from the Joffrey repertory, emphasizing the strongest possible casts and the individual dances best suited to the television medium. These included the City Center Joffrey Ballet's signature work, Gerald Arpino's crowd-pleasing rock ballet *Trinity* (1970); a vigorous solo from Arpino's *Olympics* (1966), performed by dancer Russell Sultzbach; and a fragment from Joffrey's own romantic *Remembrances* (1973), danced to music by Richard Wagner. Historic aspects of American ballet's European past were excerpted as well: two scenes from Kurt Jooss's legendary antiwar ballet *The Green Table* and the Conjurer's solo from Léo-

On the *Dance in America* set for the Joffrey Ballet's reconstruction of *Petrouchka,* with (from left) Rudolf Nureyev, producer Judy Kinberg, director Emile Ardolino, and artistic director Robert Joffrey. (© Herbert Migdoll)

nide Massine's *Parade.* Both choreographers were flown from Europe to restage their dances and appear in on-camera interviews.

Working closely with director Jerome Schnur in an Austin, Texas, studio, Joffrey adapted the *Remembrances* pas de deux for the camera, and Arpino solved the problem of presenting *Trinity* without the use of theater wings. Careful preplanning for each shot reduced the amount of rehearsal time before the camera, sparing the dancers the worst tolls of fatigue, but Schnur was working with an old-fashioned camera crane from Hollywood, which meant that sometimes an entire day's shooting resulted in only four minutes of dancing. The show came in considerably over budget.

Nevertheless, the first *Dance in America* program, aired on January 1, 1976, successfully captured the vitality of a youthful ensemble company without having to feature a major star. Close to 5 million people watched the Emmy-nominated show during a year when only 11 million saw a live dance performance at all. But a survey taken during the spring 1976 Joffrey season in New York revealed an even more remarkable fact: Forty-five percent of the audience had seen the *Dance in America* program, and fifty-nine percent of those attending the Joffrey for the first time were doing so because they had enjoyed the company on television. The fear voiced by a few choreographers that television would satiate the hunger of paying audiences

Twyla Tharp's *Sue's Leg,* with (from left) Rose Marie Wright, Tom Rawe, Kenneth Rinker, and Twyla Tharp. (© Herbert Migdoll)

proved wildly unfounded; a television series born in response to the dance explosion of the 1970s would soon become "as responsible as any single institution," according to *The New York Times,* "for the national dance boom."

Although the Joffrey program opened *Dance in America*'s first season, the series had first taped Twyla Tharp and Dancers, in an attempt to introduce daring new work to national audiences who might never have seen such dance before. The director of the program was Merrill Brockway, sometimes called the father of *Dance in America* and the director of many of its programs until he left the series five years after it

began. Brockway had first worked with Twyla Tharp at "Camera Three"; their collaboration resumed in the den of the director's Upper West Side apartment, where they poured over work tapes of *Sue's Leg,* one of the choreographer's more accessible kinesthetic feats, until the director felt he knew every lunge and shimmy by heart. Work commenced in September 1975, in the old Twentieth Century-Fox studio on Eleventh Avenue in Manhattan, where *The Exorcist* was shot. The enormous amount of preparatory work on each camera angle made it possible to tape the dance in three-to-five-minute segments, occasionally using a hand-held camera. *Sue's Leg* made excellent use of Fox's thirty-foot cyclo-rama for crane shots, avoiding low angles that might point cameras into the lights; the dancers performed on a specially designed sixty-by-fifty-foot foam rubber and plywood dance floor commissioned by the series, to spare them the concrete floors in most television studios.

But Brockway needed access to every possible lighting effect, and the absence of a computerized lighting board meant that stage-hands were constantly scrambling up ladders to make changes by hand. "The only place in New York that met our requirements was Brooklyn NBC," says Brockway, "but two soaps were being shot there, and we weren't likely to displace *those*." After conducting a nationwide search, *Dance in America* settled on Opryland in Nashville, Tennessee, the site of America's largest televised country music events, which became the unlikely home for nearly all of *Dance in America*'s subsequent studio projects. "Once we found Nashville," Ardolino agrees, "things became very focused."

Brockway still harbors special feelings for *Dance in America*'s third program: "The first conversation I had with Martha Graham, she said"—and here Brockway assumes a regal tone—" 'I don't collaborate.' But she turned out to be one of the great collaborators."

Except for the "Dance of Vengeance" from *Cave of the Heart,* Graham insisted on showing only complete works rather than excerpts. The spatial arrangements between dancers were altered slightly for *Appalachian Spring* to clarify the relationship of the Pioneer Woman to the rest of the cast; Brockway and Graham both acknowledged that the most complex moments in *Diversion of Angels* could not be fully adapted for television, and they presented them as clearly as possible without changes. During the taping of *Frontier,* crew members were asked to leave the control booth and stage because "the dance was so personal to her that she felt exposed," says Ardolino, who stayed with soloist Janet Eilber on the floor. The final selection for the program was *Adorations,* a celebration of the Graham technique of the 1970s specially commissioned

by the series. Demonstrating a new mastery of camera movement and placement, and a new deftness in choreographic adaptation and editing, the first ninety-minute *Dance in America* program—and the first taped at the Nashville facilities—demonstrated the cumulative effects of everything learned during the first two programs. Commenting on the Graham program, *The New York Times* announced that *Dance in America* had "finally hit its stride."

The final program for the year—an hour-long special on the Pennsylvania Ballet—brought the first year's programming to a total of four and one-half hours, ninety minutes short of the original proposal. But the overwhelmingly positive critical response and the enthusiasm of viewers had established a profile for the young series as well as a presence on the airwaves for the best of American dance.

·   ·   ·

Dance in America's second season presented a balanced offering of two ballet companies, two contemporary troupes, and the historical "Trailblazers of Modern Dance." For the American Ballet Theatre program, the series hoped to tape Jerome Robbins's *Fancy Free* but settled instead for Eugene Loring's masterpiece, *Billy the Kid,* with guest host Paul Newman describing its story in detail. For the second half of the program, *Dance in America* wanted Antony Tudor's *Lilac Garden,* but Tudor would agree only if Gelsey Kirkland danced the leading role. When Kirkland became available, Tudor changed his mind, insisting that he must have Natalia Makarova instead. Then the choreographer changed his mind again, on grounds that Makarova was the wrong age. As a way out of this dilemma, critic Arlene Croce suggested substituting Sir Frederick Ashton's *Les Patineurs,* and Ashton agreed to the taping.

For the Merce Cunningham program, the series was dealing with a master of video/dance and left him alone. The Dance Theatre of Harlem program presented the company in the context of its social importance in its community, stressing the connections between ballet and other styles of black dance. And with Pilobolus, the

Pilobolus in their *Monkshood's Farewell*. (© 1977 Lois Greenfield)

series again asserted its interest in more adventurous American dance experiments.

Only six years earlier, at Dartmouth College, in Hanover, New Hampshire, in a modern dance class taught by a young UCLA graduate named Alison Chase, three undergraduates—Moses Pendleton, Jonathan Wolken, and Steve Johnson—had decided out of the blue to choreograph a dance together at the end of their first semester. They named the new work *Pilobolus,* after a very intelligent single-celled phototrophic fungus that flourishes in New England barnyards. Bodies interconnected at unlikely levels and angles, hinging and cantilevering in all directions in a kind of stream-of-consciousness sculptural graffiti. "Our athletic backgrounds let us be pretty free in our contact with each other," Pendleton recalls. "In the same way that a wrestler takes a competitive approach to physical contact, we simply took an aesthetic one. It couldn't have been less self-conscious in that sense."

During the summer, Pendleton, Wolken, and Johnson moved to the Pendleton family farm in Vermont to continue their collaborations; their work together began to resemble a previously unknown species of entertainment engulfing gymnastics, modern dance, pantomime and slapstick, Chaplin and Rabelais, pro wrestling and the collegiate follies. Joined by Lee Harris, a Dartmouth computer science major, and an art student, Robby Barnett, Pendleton and Wolken enjoyed an unexpected success at a Frank Zappa rock concert at Smith College, in Northampton, Massachusetts. In December a brief New York season arranged by Chase's former teacher, choreographer Murray Louis, garnered outstanding reviews, and a new company, Pilobolus, was figuratively and literally off the ground with a dance later seen on *Dance in America*. *Ocellus* researched "what it's like to be upside down or sideways rather than right side up," said Wolken. Pendleton compared it to programming a flight to the moon.

By 1973 a Juilliard-trained modern dancer from New York, Martha Clarke, had arrived in Hanover and begun working with Barnett and Chase. Soon the two women joined the company, and with a commission from the American Dance Festival, at Connecticut College, contributed to the creation of *Ciona* (1974), also shown on the series. The presence of women "was a testament to what we had been saying," Pendleton claimed. "Most of our things require balance and agility rather than just strength. A great deal of *Ciona* is multiplying single forms and movements, making them bigger and more complex. For instance, we took an ordinary

Alison Chase and Martha Clarke in the most popular work in Pilobolus's repertory, *Untitled* (1975). Nine-foot-tall Victorian women dance around the stage until two naked men appear from beneath their skirts. "It's about two women, their relationship with each other," says Moses Pendleton, "their repressed sexuality, their fantasies, and their realities." (© 1977 Jack Vartoogian)

cartwheel and attached another person, upside down. The motion itself was still there, but it was no longer a person doing a cartwheel; it was more like a coin oscillating on its edge. By joining together and confusing appendages, by making entities larger than the individual, you get a certain abstraction and at the same time an expansion of references. The ambiguity opens up a connotative range."

Borrowing a personal credit card from their new company manager, Pilobolus journeyed to Scotland's Edinburgh Festival, performing for

three weeks to sensational reviews; traveling to Holland, they set to work on their most ambitious assemblage to date, the macabre howler *Monkshood's Farewell*—a "medieval piece" reputedly based on James Thurber, Bruegel the Elder, Hieronymus Bosch, Sowerby's *English Wild Flowers*, Princess Margaret's unpublished memoirs, *The Canterbury Tales*, *Morte d'Arthur*, and a Craig Claiborne soup recipe. "Until *Monkshood's*, we tended to put things together from an abstract point of view," says Pendleton, "even though the works had always had a basic theatricality. But this was the first time that we began to organize the material with a dramatic logic." On *Dance in America,* all six Pilobolus members jousted—with a man for a horse, a male knight and a female lance—and later returned as a band of cretinous spastics from Bruegel or Bosch. In another section the women stood on the backs of the four crawling men, inching across the world like stone colossi.

In the 1980s, the core group of Barnett, Chase, Wolken, and Pendleton continues to choreograph, while second- and third-generation performers tour the work of the creators on the road. Martha Clarke formed her own company, Crow's Nest, and later directed the sensation of the 1984 off-off-Broadway theater season, *The Garden of Earthly Delights.* Moses Pendleton, who lives alone in a sparsely-furnished twenty-two-room Connecticut mansion, has choreographed his own version of Erik Satie's historic *Relâche* for the Joffrey Ballet; Robert Joffrey dubbed him "the Charlie Chaplin of the ballet world."

"Moses broke his toe two days before rehearsals began," Brockway recalls of the *Dance in America* taping, "and Jonathan Wolken strained his back on the set. Meanwhile, I've got a quarter-million dollars wrapped up in this project and they have no understudies! I said, 'I'm gonna call Tim Wengerd [then with the Graham Company].' Well," Brockway says with an amused chuckle, "they got well awfully fast."

· · ·

By the third season, 1977/78, the addition of works by George Balanchine and the New York City Ballet firmly established *Dance in America* as television's most important forum for America's major dance companies. Paul Taylor joined the series, and the San Francisco Ballet's *Romeo and Juliet* marked the program's first attempt to translate a full-evening ballet for home audiences, as well as the beginning of a fruitful association with Michael Smuin.

Responding to the growing understanding and awareness of viewers, the fourth season included two more Balanchine programs, the Eliot Feld Ballet, and a ninety-minute Greek drama, Martha Graham's *Clytemnestra.* The 1979/80 season brought the first *Dance in America* collaborations with both Peter Martins and Jerome Robbins of the New York City Ballet, along with more unconventional offerings: "Divine Drumbeats: Katherine Dunham and Her People" focused on the mother of black American dance; a second Pilobolus program was recorded live at the American Dance Festival, in North Carolina; and Brockway's "Beyond the Mainstream" program introduced experimental dance on prime-time television, which only five years earlier had worried about the eccentricities of Twyla Tharp.

In 1980/81, *Dance in America* presented its most ambitious projects to date: the Joffrey reconstructions of Diaghilev's Ballets Russes; the two-hour San Francisco Ballet production of Smuin's *The Tempest,* live from the War Memorial Opera House; and Balanchine's video spectacle *The Spellbound Child.* The 1981/82 season featured two live-on-tape Paul Taylor Dance Company performances from the American Dance Festival, and "Bournonville Dances" from the repertory of the Royal Danish Ballet, performed by the New York City Ballet. The following year the Joffrey's complete *The Green Table,* "Balanchine Celebrates Stravinsky," and Peter Martins's *The Magic Flute* were aired, along with *Dance in America*'s first acquisition, Twyla Tharp's *The Catherine Wheel,* directed by the choreographer herself. The 1983/84 season featured Smuin's *A Song for Dead Warriors,* "A Choreographer's Notebook: Stravinsky Piano Ballets, by Peter Martins," and a two-part documentary on the life and work of the late George Balanchine—a summation of one of the series' most revered and privileged relationships, featuring rare documentary footage of the choreographer and his dances during his early years in the United States.

Hailed as a major artistic and technical achievement and a historic American record, *Dance in America* has created a historic alliance between the live and electronic arts, remaining one of the most visible manifestations of the cultural surge of the 1970s and 1980s. Unquestionably, the series has increased the nation's appreciation of an art form, broadcasting to areas of the country where dance is rarely if ever seen and educating Americans about the nature of the art itself, through narratives written by some of America's finest dance writers, including Arlene Croce, Elizabeth Kendall, Dale Harris, Nancy Goldner, Tobi Tobias, and Holly Brubach. Subscribed to by some two hundred and fifty public television stations around the United States, the series has proved more popular than televised drama, more popular than even the *Masterpiece Theatre* series. Only opera has attracted larger audiences to public television.

Judy Kinberg, the last member of the original producing team still with the program, states the achievement of *Dance in America* in the simplest terms: "We have been privileged to live during one of the richest periods in dance history, and at the same time, in the same city, with George Balanchine and Martha Graham. When people talk about the age of Petipa or of Diaghilev, for example, we look at photographs and try to imagine how it must have been. Bal-

anchine used to say, 'Dancing is not about words. Teachers shouldn't talk—they have to show.' Well, thanks to Balanchine, Graham, and other choreographers who took a chance with us, now we have something to show."

American dance has explored a democratic impulse to see the world in a new light rather than to confirm familiar images of what already exists in the theater. The companies that have appeared on *Dance in America* represent a range of styles and approaches unequaled anywhere in the world—a body of work as much an expression of the American spirit as our literature, film, music, and visual arts. By driving toward the collective, the conspicuous, and the eventful, American dance has fashioned a moving image of a nation possessed, remembered, seen and felt, brooded over and imagined through the material of the body in space and time. Even before vast audiences realized it—and over 50 million Americans will witness a live dance event in 1985, with millions more watching on television—the shapes of that vision became a way of seeing ourselves.

THE BALLET
IN AMERICA

FROM THE OLD WORLD TO THE NEW

Five centuries ago a style of entertainment emerged in the courts of Renaissance Italy that consummated a new fascination with the affairs of man. Combining elements of medieval masques with myths drawn from classical Greek and Roman civilization, these early ballets—from the Italian *ballare* ("to dance")—bore little resemblance to ballet as we know it today. Interspersed with pageantry, song, recitation, and pantomime, dances were performed by courtiers with a vigorous gaiety and a stately, ceremonious grace barely distinguishable from the ballroom manners of the day. Italian dancing masters carried their new craft across the continent, with nearly every royal household inaugurating magnificent entertainments to glorify the civilized authority of their rule. By 1581 *Le Balet-Comique de la Royne Louise* fully unified all the elements of these spectacles, with ten thousand guests witnessing its six hours of performance in the Salle Bourbon of the Louvre. "I think that I may claim to have pleased, with a well-balanced production," declared its choreographer, the Italian Balthazar de Beaujoyeulx, "the eye, the ear, and the understanding."

The idea of the ballet as a consummate artistic expression, bridging antiquity and the "modern," gathering music, dance, design, and drama in a single event, gradually became inseparable from the ideal of royal civilization itself.

In seventeenth-century France graceful sarabands, pavannes, gavottes, and courantes deepened an image of nobility, regulated passions, and exalted spirituality suitable for the eyes of Louis XIV, the greatest monarch in Europe. In 1661 he founded an academy headed by composer and choreographer Jean-Baptiste Lully and dancing master Pierre Beauchamps "to reestablish the art of dancing in its perfection." The French school codified the five positions of the feet and a basic vocabulary of poses, movements, and gestures still described in French throughout most of the world—*plié,* to bend; *tendu,* to stretch; *battement,* to beat—instituting an authority and power unsurpassed by any other form of Western dance.

The *danse d'école* remained the province of dancing courtiers until the seventeenth century, when fully trained professionals began to appear in subsidized theaters throughout Western Europe. As new images of civilized pleasure, the *opéra-ballets* linked song and dance with romantic scenes from classical mythology, celebrating the vivacious charms of the first ballerinas. Now, the worldly-wise and beautiful Marie Camargo would lower her heels and shorten her skirts to expose her thrilling footwork and leaps, while her greatest rival, Marie Sallé, discarded burdensome wigs and panniered skirts to enhance the chaste, lyric expressiveness of her style.

The earliest ballets developed as new syntheses of decor, pantomime, music, dance, and spectacle. Here is the third intermezzo from *Apollo Slaying the Dragon,* presented in Florence in 1589. (Courtesy The Victoria and Albert Museum)

Ballet arrived in America in 1735, staged by an Englishman, Henry Holt, for the amusement of the Charleston, South Carolina, elite. From the very beginning, these cultivated delectations seemed at odds with the utilitarian, egalitarian spirit of the colonies. Throughout the rest of the century theatrical seasons of pantomimes, spectacles, and "French ballets" were commonplace in Charleston, New Orleans, Philadelphia, Baltimore, and New York, their sensuality regularly denounced by heirs of the Puritan conscience as a relic of Old World decadence. In 1785 the first American dancer to achieve widespread popular acclaim, John Durang (1768–1870), performed his famous hornpipe in patriotic "dramatic-pantomimes" based on American aspirations and ideals. Such provincialism would dominate the development of theatrical dance in America for decades; in Europe, meanwhile, the first *ballets d'action* were combining imaginative dance steps and pantomime in coherent, wordless dramas of the highest order.

In France Jean-Georges Noverre (1737–1810) emerged as "the Shakespeare of his art," dispensing with merely decorative choreography and broadening the expressive resources of dancers to serve the characters and situations they portrayed. After Noverre, a choreographer could actually hope to create "a living tableau of the emotions, customs, and manners of all the people in the world." With its new dramatic compass, the ballet moved beyond traditional plots drawn from classical antiquity: Jean Dauberval fashioned a sentimental domestic comedy, *La Fille Mal Gardée* (1784), with peasant dances and stock figures from the commedia dell'arte. Twelve years later, Charles Didelot's *Zephyr and Flore* dressed dancers in flesh-colored tights and body-revealing draperies and sent them literally flying through the air on wires; the theatrical rage of London, it also introduced the *pas de deux* as a kind of tender conversation between two lovers, with its ballerina rising for brief periods to dance on the very tips of her toes. By the early nineteenth century, ballet dancers were beginning to resemble the dancers we know today, presenting an extraordinary syllabus of poses, preparatory steps, turns, small and large jumps, beats of the leg, and flowing gestures of the arms, shaped and colored in almost infinite variety. Full turn-

MONS.ˣ VESTRIS Jun.ʳ in the favorite Ballet
(call'd) LES AMANS SURPRIS.

The measured virtuosity of the male soloist—especially Auguste Vestris, with his multiple pirouettes and leaps—dominated classical dancing by the late eighteenth century. (Courtesy Performing Arts · Research Center, The New York Public Library)

out of the legs at 180 degrees enabled dancers to move swiftly and with easy extension and elevation in any direction, projecting the body's full silhouette through the proscenium arch. Deeply implicated in Western ideals of morality and beauty, the ballet was beginning to transcend its aristocratic origins, becoming the expression of choreographers and dancers themselves—their individual temperaments, humors, inclinations, and dreams.

Despite ballet's increasingly populist dramatic sympathies, the new American democracy still lacked the artificial vistas of a theatrical horizon. In 1774 the first Continental Congress had urged the closing of all places of public entertainment, and an antitheater law had actually gone into effect in Philadelphia in the late 1780s. But by the 1830s the United States was prepared to share in the international sensation created by European ballet in its finest hour: Leaving behind an image of the classical world, a new, romantic ballet would appeal directly to audiences seeking some fantastic release from the toil and oppression of the Industrial Revolution. Presenting the conflicts and reconciliation of man and nature, elevating passion above reason in a manner calculated to seduce mass audiences uninterested in older, classical restraints, ballet became a kind of wish fulfillment—and for the first time seemed part of that breakthrough in consciousness that had led to the founding of the American democracy.

· · ·

The romantic ballet paralleled a decisive break with the past in all the European arts: German literature, the paintings of Delacroix and David, and the music of Beethoven and Berlioz were all reactions against the sovereign formalism of the eighteenth century. And suddenly, as Marie Taglioni wafted around the stage on the tips of her toes in the supernatural *La Sylphide* (1832), ballet came to symbolize all the unnameable longings of the human soul and its quest for the unattainable. A new feminine archetype was emerging throughout the Western world: Innocent, fragile, beyond sex, the ballerina became an object of worship, dancing in box-pointe slippers at "the final barrier to a doomed aspiration," as Rudolf Arnheim has noted.

At mid-century, *Giselle,* choreographed by Jean Corrali and Jules Perrot to music by Adolphe Adam, helped to sweep ballet to new heights of artistic achievement and popular acceptance. Blending the ordinary and the marvelous, the daylight world of man and nature with the dark, deliciously terrifying impulsiveness of the supernatural, *Giselle* told the story of an innocent peasant girl, danced by the violet-eyed Carlotta Grisi, deceived in love by Albrecht, a care-

Marie Taglioni, wafting through the air on impeccable pointes in *La Sylphide,* the ballet that established forever the mystique of the nineteenth-century ballerina.

ennese," Taglioni's greatest rival, Fanny Elssler. Well-wishers drew her carriage on foot through the streets of Baltimore, and the House of Representatives adjourned for lack of a quorum during her Washington, D.C., engagement. A few native ballerinas also managed to rise to prominence: The meek and virtuous Mary Ann Lee danced as the first American Giselle, and in 1838 her fellow Philadelphian Augusta Maywood achieved overnight fame in Paris at the age of fifteen, later choreographing a version of *Uncle Tom's Cabin* for her own company in Italy.

With her great beauty, her intelligence and charm, and a repertory of vigorous dances that contrasted sharply with the bloodless grace of many romantic ballerinas, the celebrated Fanny Ellsler (1810–1889) met with rapturous acclaim during her two years in North America. (Courtesy Performing Arts Research Center, The New York Public Library)

less young aristocrat. Giselle goes mad and dies but persists in loving him from beyond the grave, saving him from the Wilis—the spirits of maidens who died on their wedding night and now seek to capture any man who wanders into their glade and dance him to death. This picturesque struggle with the seducer, culminating in the redemptive tragedy of an innocent's death, haunted American popular fiction throughout the nineteenth century; *Giselle* was greeted with enormous acclaim in Boston, San Francisco, and other American cities only a few years after its Paris premiere.

Over the next few decades plagiarisms and adaptations of dances from Milan, Paris, Bordeaux, and Trieste arrived in America in a great flood, with major European artists making the arduous journey across the Atlantic for provincial fame and fortune. Enthusiasm reached its peak during the 1840/41 tour of the "Pagan Vi-

A rehearsal at the Metropolitan Opera House in New York, around 1900, a time when it was still impossible to fill a competent corps de ballet with American-born and -trained dancers. (The Byron Collection, courtesy the Museum of the City of New York)

American dance schools were founded to train corps de ballet dancers to support the visiting ballerinas—but, without official patronage or the cultural confidence to recast the art of Europe in American terms, the romantic era failed to produce an American company capable of conveying a tradition into the future. European academies continued to produce glorious dancers who often traveled to America, and ballet "spectacle-extravaganzas" appeared in theaters across the nation, but by the 1870s the old romantic ballet was little more than a memory. What remained was a metaphysical legacy that continues to shape the art of the twentieth century: Through the romantic purity of design, technique, and expression, the classical dancer was freed to express the highest emotions of the soul, to become an impersonal instrument for conveying the most refined ideals. Choreographers and audiences had recognized that "the true, the unique, the eternal subject of a ballet," according to Théophile Gautier, *Giselle*'s librettist and the first great critic of the dance, "is *dancing.*" After 1879 the center of classical ballet would shift from Paris to the relative calm of the self-contained Russian Empire, where the fundamental discoveries of the Romantic age would mature into a new classical era.

·　　·　　·

Various French, Austrian, and Italian ballet masters had contributed to the growth of Russian ballet since the seventeenth century, but it was only after Charles Didelot arrived in the early nineteenth century that the Russian academy was reorganized along the lines of the most recent innovations in Europe. Didelot is remembered as the father of Russian ballet, but the man responsible for its complete triumph was Marius Petipa (1818–1907), a former partner of Elssler and Grisi who had visited America briefly in the 1830s. Arriving in St. Petersburg as a young man with an appointment as "soloist of the czar," Petipa served for twenty-three years before finally becoming ballet master at the age of fifty-one—the beginning of a thirty-three-year career preserving and extending the highest principles of French classicism.

St. Petersburg was Russia's window on the

West, and the arrival during the 1880s of Swedish and Italian instructors, as well as of the virtuosic Italian ballerinas, helped to elevate the allegro facility and strength of the Russian dancer. Petipa merged these qualities with the simplicity and grace of the French school to create a unique synthesis fulfilling the heroic intensity of the Russian character—producing as well a brilliance in execution and expression never before seen in Western dance. In his lifetime Petipa was known as "master of the grand spectacle," refining the theatrical elements of romantic ballet into rich fantasies set in faraway times and places. Satisfying the whims and passions of a glittering elite, ballet became the social art par excellence in St. Petersburg, enveloped by an atmosphere of scandal and high romance; meanwhile Petipa examined the logic of movement and the dynamics of choreographic design with an acuity unmatched by any of his contemporaries, forging a new image of classicism's academic roots and a dance language of extraordinary dramatic power.

Following French tradition, he carefully ranked his dancers according to talent, technique, and body configuration, then cast them in roles appropriate to their gifts. The title *ballerina* was bestowed only on women of unusual brilliance and expressiveness, and *danseur noble,* even more rarely, on men with exceptionally well-proportioned bodies and elegant techniques. Beneath them, soloists in Petipa's ballets performed important roles, with demi-soloists dancing in small groups and occasionally appearing in brief solo passages. At the lowest level, the corps de ballet served a function similar to the chorus in Greek tragedy, creating an atmosphere or reacting to the narrative to help audiences interpret events. When a classical ballerina presents herself to her cavalier, framed by a uniform corps, the resulting image of harmony and order grows from a recognition of hierarchical excellence that Petipa refined beyond all previous limits. He would restage some seventeen different European ballets, including the version of *Giselle* best known today. But primarily it was his sixty original works—including *Don Quixote*

(1868), *La Bayadère* (1877), and *Raymonda* (1898), and especially his masterpieces set to Tchaikovsky's music, *The Sleeping Beauty* (1890) and *Swan Lake* (1893–95, with his assistant, Lev Ivanov)—that gave the Russian Imperial Ballet a technique and repertory that continues to dominate the image of ballet around the world.

By the beginning of the twentieth century, however, the success of the Russian ballet was beginning to stimulate its undoing: Marius Petipa was over eighty years old, his ceremonious art calcified by conservative demands for familiar spectacle. A group of young St. Petersburg aesthetes saw the need to reverse the tide of almost medieval decadence, hoping to transform their city into a kind of northen Paris. The leader of this group, and the man most responsible for Russian ballet's ultimate diaspora to the West, was Sergei Pavlovich Diaghilev, who would render ballet synonymous with Russia for the first half of the century and sweep the art of dance into the modern age.

· · · ·

Born in 1872 in Perm, a distant city in the Urals, Diaghilev was still a young man when he became editor of an influential art review, *Mir Iskusstva (The World of Art),* and assistant director of the state-controlled Maryinsky Theatre. Abruptly dismissed from the Maryinsky in 1907, his career in ballet was seemingly over. But in the spring of 1909 he invited to Paris an extraordinary generation of Russian dancers and artists who would bring with them an urgent new vision of ballet as a serious art form, freed from imperial patronage and controlled for the first time by the artists themselves. The Ballets Russes was an eruption of energy and ideas from the supposed barbaric darkness of the East that utterly transformed the dance-theater tradition of Western Europe.

Long associated with sedate opera house performances in belle époque Paris, ballet would never again undergo such complete revitalization through the overthrow of the past. The Ballets Russes introduced exotic one-act spectacles—three or four an evening, set in ancient Egypt, Hellenic Greece, Persia, India, Russia, and

Sergei Diaghilev with one of his discoveries, choreographer Léonide Massine. (Courtesy Performing Arts Research Center, The New York Public Library)

Versailles—that rocked the Théâtre du Châtelet. The fantastic Art Nouveau designs of Léon Bakst, with their opulent Oriental colors and swirling patterns, transformed Parisian haute couture overnight. But primarily it was the dancers themselves—Anna Pavlova, Adolph Bolm, Tamara Karsavina, and especially the seemingly superhuman Vaslav Nijinsky—who came to symbolize Russian ballet in its golden age. Male dancers had been all but exiled from European ballet stages, with their roles sometimes danced by women *en travesti,* but Nijinsky's androgyn-

ous grace and stupefying feats of virtuosity shattered forever the serene femininity of nineteenth-century ballet. Five feet four inches tall, with sloping shoulders, massive legs, and strange Tartar eyes, Nijinsky was not a classical dancer at all: He was a golden slave, a harlequin, a specter, a blue god, the embodiment of the violence and beauty of nature itself. Artists, intellectuals, and denizens of café society flocked by the thousands to greet Diaghilev's artistic revolution, as ballet suddenly became, in Richard Buckle's phrase, "the art form of the moment and a wonder of the world."

The choreographic architect of this renaissance was a twenty-nine-year-old dancer, Michel Fokine, who had discovered a range of expressive action previously unknown in classical dance. Significantly, a major influence on his developing work had been an American, Isadora Duncan, who had arrived in St. Petersburg in the winter of 1904/05 to dance barefoot in a flowing Greek tunic, celebrating the physical freedom of the modern era. Discarding the mechanical, gymnastic dance steps of the imperial divertissements, Fokine began to invent continuous, naturalistic dance sequences involving the movement of the entire body—even rejecting the pointe shoes, rigidly held torso, and canonical five positions of classicism in order to suit his dances to the quality of his music and his stories. As Noverre had dreamed as early as the eighteenth century, ballet once again aspired to expressiveness and beauty through the "imitation of life," integrating music, story, design, and movement into a single unified action.

Directly inspired by Duncan's work, Fokine's *Chopiniana* (1904)—reworked and rechristened *Les Sylphides* for the first Russian season in Paris—was an unabashed meditation on the romantic ballet, inviting the interpretative powers of dancers in a dreamlike atmosphere for winged sylphs. Unimpeded by pantomime or story, dance melted into dance with a previously unknown musical naturalness, merging ballerinas and the premier danseur with the corps de ballet for the first time. Surrendering a lofty aura of technical perfection, *Les Sylphides* distilled the

Danced by twenty-two sylphides and a young man, *Les Sylphides* became the most widely performed ballet of the twentieth century. (Courtesy Performing Arts Research Center, The New York Public Library)

classical divertissement into a modern image: an *abstract* ballet, sustaining its interest through the cumulative expressiveness of the human body, design, and music alone.

With *Les Sylphides,* Diaghilev embarked on his career as impresario and arbiter of international modern art, catalyzing some of the most astonishing dance-theater collaborations of the century. Under Diaghilev the ballet would become a new kind of total theater, incorporating music, design, and innovative scenarios as equally important elements of the event: Nearly the entire school of Paris—Braque, de Chirico, Derain, Ernst, Gris, Matisse, Miró, Picasso, Rouault, and Utrillo—contributed set designs and costumes, and composers Milhaud, Poulenc, Ravel, Richard Strauss, and Prokofiev received important commissions. Diaghilev's greatest musical discovery was an unknown twenty-eight-year-old Russian emigré soon to have an incalculable effect on the future of twentieth-century music. Igor Stravinsky composed the score for Fokine

and Léon Bakst's *The Firebird* (1910)—the first direct collaboration between composer, designer, and choreographer at the Ballets Russes.

But *Petrouchka* (1911) was the supreme achievement of the original *Mir Iskusstva* group and the greatest example of the collaborative trials and triumphs Diaghilev encouraged in the early years of the Ballets Russes. Stravinsky had composed a new concerto for piano and orchestra titled "Petrouchka's Cry," based on the fable of the murderous Russian Punch hauled off to hell by the devil himself. While an organ grinder reminds the puppet to be cautious, Petrouchka's only reply is a shrieking laugh, which Stravinsky suggested "with diabolic cascades of arpeggios." Diaghilev urged the composer to expand the music into a kind of ballet Grand Guignol set in the hurly-burly of the nineteenth-century Russian Butterweek Fair preceding Lent, when temporary wooden theaters and carousels crowded the square outside St. Petersburg's Winter Palace. The original leader of the *Mir Is-*

Rudolf Nureyev, Christian Holder, and Denise Jackson in the Joffrey Ballet's production of *Petrouchka*. (© 1985 Don Perdue)

kusstva aesthetes, Alexandre Benois, contributed sets and costume designs and constructed a scenario suited to Stravinsky's completed score.

The musicians laughed out loud during the first rehearsal, but Fokine was finally able to comprehend Stravinsky's rapid and furious clarity: Fokine's *Petrouchka* became the story of the pathetic and suffering Pierrot of French pantomime, hopelessly in love with a beautiful ballerina doll, Columbine, and jealous of her affection for the brutal, stupid Blackamoor. Diaghilev attempted to keep Nijinsky away from the role, fearing that his greatest star would be turned into a grotesque. But through Nijinsky's hard-won interpretation, Petrouchka became "a Hamlet among puppets," his tormented, spastic movements creating a wordless portrait of a human soul's rebellion against its condition. Stravinsky called Nijinsky as Petrouchka "the most exciting human being I have ever seen on stage"; Sarah Bernhardt announced that Nijinsky was "the greatest actor in the world."

Shaping the character of a passive straw puppet manipulated by an evil sideshow impresario, Fokine may unconsciously have drawn on the dancer's passive subservience to his mentor and protector as inspiration. But for Nijinsky the struggle to create *Petrouchka* actually helped to crystallize his desire to break away from Diaghilev's domination and to achieve his own identity as an artist. Already he had begun to fashion a new ballet to Debussy's shimmering, dreamlike tone poem, *Prélude à l'Après-midi d'un Faune,* composed two decades earlier as an expression of the new formal freedom of modern music. Isadora Duncan, Fokine, and Petipa had all looked to the ancient world for ideas and inspiration, but Nijinsky wanted to search beyond civilization for an unknown, archaic Greece—to discover what Lincoln Kirstein later called "an innocence of primordial impulse."

Immersing himself in a study of sixth-century B.C. Greek vases and stone reliefs, Nijinsky began to explore a similarly flat, two-dimensional style of movement bearing little resemblance to Fokine's sensual virtuosity. Working with his sister, Bronislava, he analyzed the shapes, weight, and rhythm of a tense, earthbound muscularity with entirely modern exactitude and restraint. When company rehearsals finally began in 1912, Russian dancers who had questioned Fokine's reforms did not know what to make of Nijinsky's static, angular precision. Tempers flared over the course of 120 rehearsals; the twelve-minute dance was not metrically linked to Debussy's music, and the choreographer was reduced to pounding out the counts on the rehearsal pianist's hands.

At the ballet's legendary premiere, *Afternoon of a Faun* (1912) opened on a vision of a wild creature, half man, half beast, resting on a rocky crag. A group of nymphs come to bathe

Vaslav Nijinsky as the Faun, with his sister, Bronislava Nijinska, as the Lead Nymph, in Nijinsky's *L'Après-midi d'un Faune*. (Courtesy Bibliothèque de l'Opéra, Paris)

along a stream, only to flee, frightened by the faun's appearance. Retrieving a fallen scarf, the faun returns to his perch and, in the ballet's final image, thrusts his body ecstatically upon it, as in an act of love. "Like a storm, the approval and disapproval broke loose, giving an incredible noise," young Hungarian dancer, Romola de Pulzsky, later recalled. It was unclear which side dominated the uproar, and Diaghilev ordered the work performed again—the first of many such impositions of his will on the public. *Afternoon of a Faun*'s lack of obvious virtuosity, its measured erotic elegance, and its mood of prehistoric stillness signaled the first break within the classical tradition in four centuries—the beginnings of an era of absolute freedom for the contemporary choreographer.

• • •

With World War I and the Russian Revolution denying the Ballets Russes access to new dancers from its native academies, Serge Diaghilev ceased his fight for the values of Russian art and took a capricious turn toward novelty that would define his company during its silver age. As early as 1917 Diaghilev's penchant for the exotic had reappeared in the guise of modernist chic—a cult of the contemporaneous anticipating some of the more radical multimedia experiments of American dance later in the century.

Parade (1917) was "Jean's ballet," named for the twenty-three-year-old writer and artist Jean Cocteau, who delighted in offering outrageous suggestions for new dances. *"Étonne-moi, Jean,"* said the impresario, and Cocteau obliged, persuading the dadaist boulevardier and composer Erik Satie to create a delightful musical collage incorporating elements of the American jazz and ragtime with realistic sound effects—prefiguring the *musique concrète* of the Italian futurists in the 1920s. Cocteau approached Picasso, who contributed a cubist cityscape as a backdrop, along with a series of unprecedented costumes for a dancing horse, two acrobats, a Chaplinesque American girl, and a Chinese prestidigitator danced by Diaghilev's latest protégé and choreographer, Léonide Massine. By far the most striking were the cubist-inspired carapaces worn by the French and American Managers—"whom Picasso visualized as animated billboards suggesting the vulgarity of certain types of show-business promoters," Massine later wrote. "For the American he devised a montage of a skyscraper with fragmentary faces and a gaudy sign reading PARADE, which was taken as the title."

Parade was less a ballet than a series of balletic music-hall and circus routines intended to capture the fragmentary, even random quality of contemporary living. With its boulevard hawkers' increasingly hysterical attempts to lure an audience into a theater event that does not quite exist, the dances arranged by Massine seemed strangely anecdotal. The author of this cubist burlesque merely hoped to "insult habit,"

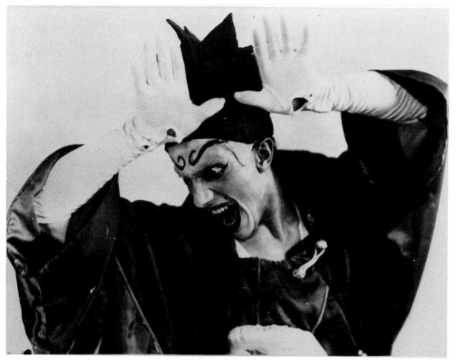

Léonide Massine, the choreographer of *Parade*, as the Chinese Conjurer. He envisaged the role as "a parody of the usual pseudo-oriental entertainer with endless tricks up his sleeve." (Courtesy Bibliothèque de l'Opéra, Paris)

as Stravinsky suggested, with "a machine to produce a poem," but the poet Guillaume Apollinaire invented a new term, *surrealism,* to describe *Parade*'s "manifestation of a new spirit" that would "modify the arts and the conduct of life from top to bottom." The ballet was greeted with wonderment and delight by some, but other members of the audience, recalling the recent deaths of 120,000 Frenchmen at the Battle of the Aisne, shouted *"sales boches"* ("dirty krauts") at the opening-night benefit for the war fund. Cocteau was delighted, Diaghilev pleased, and Satie's career as an avant-garde instigator made at a stroke. Nevertheless, *Parade* was performed only six or seven more times, becoming one of the most famous of the lost Ballets Russes works until Robert Joffrey and the Joffrey Ballet set about recovering it for modern audiences in the early 1970s.

Increasingly influenced by shifts in fashion and Diaghilev's compulsion to shock and amaze, the Ballets Russes in the 1920s often relied on spectacular sets and costumes from the Paris avant garde to form its principal attrac-

tions. When Massine, the company's new choreographer, left in 1923, he was replaced by Bronislava Nijinska, an inventive modernist still regarded as the greatest of all women ballet choreographers for her work on *Les Biches, Le Train Bleu,* and Stravinsky's *Les Noces.* The Ballets Russes's bequest to the future also included works by an escapee from starvation in postrevolutionary St. Petersburg, trained at the old Imperial Academy and the Maryinsky stage and permitted by the new Soviet government to take a repertory of experimental ballets to Europe in 1924. Viewing the dances of the young Georgi Melitonovitch Balanchivadze in Monte Carlo, Diaghilev hired him without fanfare as his chief choreographer, rechristening the newcomer George Balanchine. Within a few years Balanchine would create a modern burst of glory for the traditional dance of Europe.

After tossing off a number of fashionable avant-garde experiments for Diaghilev, Balanchine produced *Apollon Musagète (Apollo, Leader of the Muses),* to music by Stravinsky, in 1928. It was the turning point of Balanchine's life. In-

Pablo Picasso (in cap) with workmen, preparing the front curtain for *Parade* (1917), now preserved at the National Museum of Modern Art in Paris. (Courtesy The Stravinsky-Diaghilev Foundation)

spired in part by his study of Hellenistic sculpture, the paintings of Michelangelo, and the example of the composer's disciplined restraint, the choreographer had discovered a bold, effortless clarity of line, asserting that a modern ballet might find its starting point in the craftsmanlike realization of musical purpose. A celebration of the civilizing powers of art, *Apollo* reaffirmed the imperial style to which Balanchine was heir but recast it in a more contemporary image—acknowledging the canonical five positions but also

introducing turned-in legs, protruding hips, scuttling walks, and angled wrists and elbows that altered traditional technique in dynamic new directions. Diaghilev welcomed the dance with great pleasure, declaring, "It is pure classicism, such as we have not seen since Petipa."

Balanchine's creative range proved to be extraordinary: The following year he departed from his modern classicism, assimilating the movements of circus acrobats, an obscene orgy, and an erotic seduction, in *Le Fils Prodigue (The*

The New York City Ballet in Balanchine's *Apollo*, with Peter Martins and (left to right) Maria Calegari, Kyra Nichols, and Suzanne Farrell. (© 1983 Martha Swope)

Prodigal Son), choreographed during Diaghilev's final season, in 1929. Adapted not from the Gospel of St. Luke but from Pushkin's short story "The Station Master," *Prodigal* was divided into four scenes: a venerable father's farewell to his agitated son, the son's depraved conduct among debauched companions in a foreign land, the son's poverty and debasement, and his final return into his father's beckoning arms. Balanchine's brusque violations of the classical norm shocked many audiences, but for the choreographer of *Apollo* such roughhewn imagery was the story's ideal translation into ballet terms. "Once there was a man who had everything," he said, "then he had nothing, then he had everything again."

Even with a young genius to create its new works, it was unimaginable that the Ballets Russes would continue beyond Diaghilev's death in Venice in 1929. Of the sixty-eight ballets Diaghilev produced, only thirteen survive today, but the model and inspiration of the Ballets Russes would become the overwhelming stimulus for the formation of ballet companies around the world.

By the late 1970s and 1980s, historical interest in the ballet of Europe and Russia—from *La Fille Mal Gardée* to the masterpieces of Diaghilev and beyond—has reached unprecedented heights. More and more, American ballet has focused its energies on the preservation of older works and the recovery and reconstruction of dances previously shrouded in legend.

But all choreography, whether from another age and continent or our own, is born with a special blessing or curse: It exists only in the moment of performance, and then cannot prove itself an art. Beginning with Noverre's private system of dance notation in the eighteenth century, steps, patterns, and gestures have been recorded by a number of different transcriptions; today, film and videotape are important means of documentation. But the principal method for handing down a ballet has traditionally been direct transmission from artist to artist: A dance's qualities of shading and attack, amplitude and restraint, style and feeling survive best in the memory of those who have danced it before. And

Denise Jackson, Robert Joffrey, and Rudolf Nureyev at a rehearsal for the Joffrey Ballet's production of *Petrouchka*. (© 1979 Brownie Harris)

yet memory fails, and time alters memory; the task of reviving collaborations between artists whose work may survive only in sketches, written notes, or the fragmentary memories of early dancers and choreographers requires a conscientious judgment that Robert Joffrey has come to exemplify more thoroughly than anyone in American ballet.

For the past twenty-five years the Joffrey Ballet has maintained an image of youthful exuberance and athleticism, served by an essentially modern repertory. Arguably, however, the most significant premise of the company has been the revival of international masterworks of the twentieth century, including major ballets by Ashton, Balanchine, Cranko, De Mille, Massine, Robbins, Tudor, and the German Kurt Jooss.

But the collaborative works of the Ballets Russes provide the ultimate challenge for anyone attempting to reconstruct ballet's recent past. Robert Joffrey's special fascination with Russian ballet in the West culminated in 1979 with guest artist Rudolf Nureyev's performances on Broadway in *Homage to Diaghilev,* followed by

Dance in America's Emmy Award–winning "Nureyev and the Joffrey Ballet: In Tribute to Nijinsky" in 1981. Reconstructions of *Petrouchka, Le Spectre de la Rose, Afternoon of a Faun,* and *Parade* provided American audiences with firsthand looks at vital aspects of our ballet heritage.

. . .

"I've always been involved in the Diaghilev period because it was so *marvelously* a collaboration," exclaims the ebullient artistic director, seated behind his big desk in a twelfth-floor office at City Center in Midtown Manhattan. The hallways outside have grown quiet, with company rehearsals just concluded for the day, but Joffrey appears ready to talk dance, design, and music well into the evening.

"With *Petrouchka,* it was like playing Sherlock Holmes, trying to find all the sketches, putting them together, then seeing what fit," he recalls. "Part of our production we bought from an older production at La Scala, in Milan. I remember a wonderful Russian man who came—an art dealer who had a lot of Benois sketches—and we got photocopies from a collection in

Hartford. Many of these sketches were from later productions, and the Blackamoor's pants would go from gold to green, or one curtain would have a church, the other a monster sign. . . .

"I found a most unusual photo of Nijinsky from an English magazine," he continues proudly, "the only color photo I know of in existence of Nijinsky as Petrouchka. When Nureyev came to us, he had brown boots. And I said that, from all our research, Nijinsky always wore blue boots. So Rudolf changed and wore blue boots."

For the initial attempt in 1970, Joffrey engaged Léonide Massine, the first Petrouchka in America, who had danced the title role here in 1916, and an assistant, Yurek Lazowski, who had performed the lead and assisted Fokine in his last production in 1942. Diaghilev had boasted that he could make a choreographer "out of an ink-stand" and, indeed, in 1913 he had selected the seventeen-year-old Léonide Massine directly from drama school in Moscow, in short order transforming him into a major dancer and company choreographer.

"I thought, 'What a wonderful combination!' " Joffrey recalls. "But Massine—being a choreographer himself—decided to change things. We didn't know any different, because most of the dancers around who could advise us had danced Petrouchka in the thirties and forties, and Massine was talking about the versions of 1915, '16, '17, and I trusted him. He would say, 'Oh, Fokine was never pleased with the opening, so I will help Fokine. . . .' "

When the Joffrey's bid to return Petrouchka to America premiered in May 1970, critics attacked the work for its inaccuracies when compared with the 1925 Royal Danish version staged by Fokine—still in the active repertory in Copenhagen and a much more convincing piece of dance-drama. Joffrey and his dancers returned to work, with Lazowski in charge this time. "A lot of Russian dancers—Verninska, who danced one of the Nursemaids, and others here in America who had worked with Diaghilev—helped to remember things," Joffrey continues. " 'This is what happened here,' they'd say. 'Oh,

I remember, we bowed here and we took the ribbon and the sleigh came on'—that sort of thing. And so we began to fit the parts together."

This time it worked: Petrouchka was successfully returned to the Joffrey repertory a year after its initial failure. For the Dance in America version—the largest show the series ever produced—nearly 150 dancers and extras were called on to appear as aristocrats, drunken peasants, cadets, grooms, nursemaids, masked revelers, and carnival performers—even a dancing bear and the devil himself re-creating the buoyant Butter-week Fair at Shrovetide that the librettist Alexandre Benois remembered fondly from his youth.

For the Diaghilev season on Broadway in 1979, Rudolf Nureyev appeared the natural candidate to re-create the roles of the artist who had returned the male dancer to preeminence. The ascendance of the male dancer in America had proceeded gradually through the achievements of Jacques d'Amboise, André Eglevsky, Igor Youskevitch, and especially Edward Villella in the 1950s and 1960s, but the arrival of Nureyev in the West secured the ballet's manly new image as box-office magic. A brilliant virtuoso, always a flamboyant, temperamental artist, Nureyev danced with a masculine sensuality and power never before seen on American stages, personally reestablishing the wide theatrical popularity of the nineteenth-century classics and becoming the greatest sensation in ballet since Nijinsky himself.

Nureyev had first learned the role of Petrouchka in the early 1960s from Alexander Grant, who had danced a version with London's Sadler's Wells Ballet in the 1930s. But he chose to view the tragicomic puppet through the lens of Russian history and his own understanding of the need for personal freedom—a need that drove both Nijinsky and Nureyev to flee Russia for the West nearly a half century apart.

"This is not simply the story of a puppet," Nureyev told Ballet News in 1980. "It is the story of a human life when it is manipulated. Actually, it was a parable. It could have political overtones. If you are Russian you know of the

Rudolf Nureyev and Denise Jackson in Fokine's *Le Spectre de la Rose,* restaged by the Joffrey Ballet. (© Herbert Migdoll)

uprisings in 1905—I think of this when I look at the strong movements of the police in the marketplace. Petrouchka is also like a Gogol character, a little human being who cries, 'I exist! I exist! This little me!' " Petrouchka's longings and fears, his desperation and pathos, dominate Nureyev's performance. At the end of the ballet, battered by the crowds in Admiralty Square, the straw puppet is scattered to the winds, only to reappear above the proscenium arch, shouting his freedom to the sky. "When Petrouchka dies," says Nureyev, "he is still asking for justice. Only the human has a soul that cannot be suppressed."

·   ·   ·

Le Spectre de la Rose presented Robert Joffrey with a much simpler project: Bakst's 1911 designs for a young girl's bedchamber from the 1830s, preserved in London Festival Ballet's production, were reconstructed by Geoffrey Guy; Nicholas Beriosoff, who learned the choreography from Massine in the mid-1930s, was available to restage the ballet. But recapturing its fragile eroticism posed the greatest challenge: *Le Spectre* dramatizes the coming of age of a romantic young girl, symbolized by the visitation of the spirit of a rose given to her at her first ball.

Nureyev personally selected principal dancer Denise Jackson as his partner, although he had originally wanted Joffrey to choose. The director had politely declined. Jackson recalls, "I think he was afraid that if he selected the girl, Rudolf would be temperamental at the last moment and say, 'I won't dance with this one,' and they'd have a scene." Having performed as the ballerina doll in *Petrouchka,* she would now be preparing another famous role originally created by Tamara Karsavina, the most brilliant, stylish, and intelligent of Diaghilev's early ballerinas. Jackson learned the steps from Nureyev's partial memories of Margot Fonteyn's version—which proved remarkably accurate when filled in with Fonteyn's handwritten notes. "Rudi was very good in the coaching of it," says Jackson. "I remember him working with me on just how to take my coat off. He asked me to see a film of Pavlova, at the Lincoln Center dance library, doing a Christmas ballet in which she has a huge hoop skirt on, and a coat. She had a very still quality, and then suddenly she took off the coat with an impetuous, breathless quality—you know, the sensuality."

The Spirit of the Rose was Nijinsky's most famous role, one compared by Jean Cocteau to "the sad but imperious advance of a perfume." "In working on the ballet," reports Nijinsky biographer Richard Buckle, "the youthful dancer had instinctively sensed that for a *man* to be dressed in rose petals and to carry on in this giddy nonstop way, waltzing by himself, as he did at the beginning and end of the ballet, was absurd. That a sexless, inhuman creature should appear and dance thus was a different matter. Nijinsky abolished the classical correctness of the *port de bras* [arm movement], curling his arms around his face and holding them, when extended, with broken wrists and curled-up fingers, so that they became Art Nouveau tendrils. . . ." Fokine's choreography, with its constant leaps and fluttering beats, also imposed a tremendous hardship on the legs. On opening night, after his famous flight through the window at the end of the ballet, Nijinsky fell gasping for breath into Diaghilev's arms. "This leap," wrote Cocteau, "is so pathetic, so inclined, so high—it defies the laws of gravity—that now, whenever I sense the soaring perfume of a rose, I shall recall the indelible impression of that phantom."

Nureyev had always wanted to attempt the role but resisted until the Joffrey season on Broadway. "I've been coached by Papa Beriosoff," he told *Ballet News.* "He showed me certain steps. Well, I wasn't quite satisfied with all that version. Of course, he swears that he had been with Fokine for many years and he had it from the horse's mouth. Having seen a version in Paris, I remembered certain passages, so I retained those, which I think were better than what Papa showed me. Then when I was in New York, Baryshnikov showed me his version, which was rehearsed by Eglevsky. So I selected what would be the most natural thing, what would be the best by my standard, to my mind, and put them together." He found the secret in the movements of the torso and arms: "In contrast to the frequently static shape of the girl, if you don't have constant change of form and shape, you've lost it. The torso, for example, is fluid; it must move continuously. It is the stem of the rose."

·   ·   ·

With *Afternoon of a Faun,* Robert Joffrey was once again cast upon his own resourcefulness. Although the choreography had survived, the set design by Léon Bakst had not been re-created in years. Bakst's subtle layering of colors on a flat background proved very difficult to duplicate, and the sketches for the costumes differed from what was usually seen in performance.

"Very early on, Rouben Ter-Arutunian was doing the costumes for us, and he supervised a lot of the research," Joffrey continues. "We read descriptions by the ballet critic Cyril Beaumont about the colors. Later we did a version of our own and even refined some things with more information. For example: What is 'apple green?' We all think of a color, but is it really apple green? There is no sketch showing that green in the costume, but we know there was green because of Nijinsky's writings.

"With the choreography, we were lucky

The Joffrey's reconstruction of Vaslav Nijinsky's *L'Après-midi d'un Faune,* with Nureyev as the Faun and Charlene Gehm as the Lead Nymph. (© 1985 Don Perdue)

to get Elizabeth Schooling from the Royal Ballet in England. She had danced in the *Faun* very early on with Ballet Rambert, which knew it, of course, from the Diaghilev company, because Marie Rambert had been Nijinsky's assistant on some of his projects. Also William Chappell, a designer who had danced the Faun very early in the thirties, helped us with the Nijinsky role. When we were in San Francisco, I asked Nijinsky's daughter, Kyra Nijinska, to come and show me things. When we were in Seattle, Lara Obadyna, who had danced a Nymph in the Diaghilev company for years, cried when she saw our production. She said, 'In all the years I danced it, we never had a backdrop. We danced against black velvet curtains.' ''

Nureyev's performance as the Faun proved his most successful re-creation of a Nijinsky role. The sensual contemplation of Nureyev's sustained, staccato movements was "in keeping with my idea of the half-man, half-animal," he told *Ballet News.* "When he is aroused, he is aggressive, sharp, demanding. He is attacking. When I was in Egypt at Abu Simbel, I saw a series of hand positions—they were like frames in a film—and I thought that Nijinsky, in studying Greek art, must have discovered the same frames of movement. . . . But in the ballet these sharp movements frighten the Nymphs away, and the crux of the piece comes when he remembers the veil and substitutes it for her. . . . The act of passion is legato."

·   ·   ·

The re-creation of *Parade* had personal significance for Robert Joffrey. *Parade* is sometimes called the first multimedia ballet, and Joffrey's own multimedia *Astarte* had made the cover of *Time* magazine in 1968. In addition, the Joffrey Ballet had already re-created two of Picasso's most important sets for the theater: *Le Tricorne*—Massine's *Three-Cornered Hat,* revived in 1969—and Stravinsky's *Pulcinella,* with its Italian background of Naples. But *Parade* proved by far the most difficult of all to remount, principally because of the artist's notorious habits of improvisation. There were no drawings of the American Girl's costume, because Picasso had simply costumed the dancer in a department store. There were no sketches for the female acrobat, Massine had objected to Cocteau's scenario and changed the male acrobat's solo to a pas de deux, and Picasso had improvised a second design directly on the leotard and tights of ballerina Lydia Lopokova. Picasso's cubist cityscape was lost, but other elements survived, including the original curtain, which lighting designer Jennifer Tipton flew to France to study. For the costume of the Chinese Conjurer, Joffrey learned that an art dealer in Paris owned an original sketch, and "after a lot of correspondence—it was like getting to see the pope—we finally got to see the original to check the color," Joffrey explains.

"I think Massine remembered the dance well," he continues. "But choreographers always change [things]. He had a lot of notes, and there is a gut feeling of how a choreographer responds to the music; the steps and sequences may change slightly. But, after all, he did create the 1917 version. It's the same music and costumes, and I'm sure a lot of it came out the same." With additional help from Diaghilev's secretary, Boris Kochno, still living in Paris, as well as many former dancers, the Joffrey's *Parade* premiered in its complete form in 1973.

"You never really have a ballet," Joffrey says in conclusion. Outside City Center, the sky is black, and the sound of cars seems far away. "I always feel it's a lending library. You have a book and it's yours for a short period of time. How well you take care of the ballet . . . ." He pauses, as if listening for something; the halls of the Joffrey Ballet are empty.

"One should take very good care to know the beauty of a ballet," he says finally, with a gracious bow of the head.

THE
NEW YORK CITY BALLET

· A CONTINUOUS PRESENT ·

By the close of the century's first decade, the American flight from civilization to nature had found archetypal expression in movement, with Duncanesque homegrown "classical" dancing practiced by thousands of young girls across the nation. After nearly five decades of half-trained "fancy dancers" appearing in ballet "spectacle-extravaganzas" around the nation, Americans retained only the vaguest notions about the nature of dance as an art; the genteel fascination with Europe that had characterized the Gilded Age had led to the foundation of the Metropolitan Opera in New York and the first American symphony orchestras, but the modern American response to ballet awaited the phenomenal appearance of former imperial ballerina Anna Pavlova at the Met in 1910. With the arrival of Russian ballet in the United States, the American ballet of the twentieth century began.

Pavlova had almost immediately left the Ballets Russes and its modernist repertory to begin touring in a vast repertory of unadventurous romantic works, replete with graceful poses, leaps, and thrilling footwork calculated to dramatize the strong points of her technique. Nonetheless, she moved with "an intensity of spirit, a passionate compulsion, and a grace that made every movement significant," as the English ballerina Margot Fonteyn has written, that rekindled a mythic authority unknown in Ameri-

can ballet since the mid-nineteenth century. Virginal and bacchanalian at once, Pavlova's art held no threatening mystery: Like the Duncan "aesthetic" dancers, she too performed "Hindu" dances and impersonated flowers in her recitals, and Americans could safely view her work as an artistic form of entertainment. Pavlova became the ballet's first great twentieth-century popularizer, bringing Russian dance coast to coast in America between 1910 and 1924, and attracting thousands of young girls to ballet at a time when few schools existed to train them. When her abridged version of *The Sleeping Beauty* (1916) appeared amid a series of circus acts, drill teams, and an ice show at New York's vaudeville Hippodrome, the dance of the Old World became a little less a symbol of foreign culture and more a curious wonder.

Brief ballet vignettes soon became popular in vaudeville revues and follies nationwide; Gertrude Hoffman's ersatz Russian ballet company proved a major success on national tours, while a dancer named Gloria Gilbert made a small career turning twenty pirouettes from a single preparation with a ball bearing hidden in her slipper. Producer Otto Kahn even managed to arrange a season for the original Ballets Russes at the Met in 1916, but the New York engagement and the company's later tours baffled and offended nearly as many audiences as they pro-

Anna Pavlova in *The Dragonfly* (1911). With her sincere stage personality and scintillating virtuosity—Fokine thought she flew rather than leaped—Pavlova inspired young Americans like Agnes De Mille and Doris Humphrey to pursue careers in dance. (Herbert Mishkin, courtesy International Museum of Photography at George Eastman House)

foundly stirred. In many cities the repertory's exotic scenarios and lush eroticism aroused the guardians of public morality; in the South, dancers portraying the black eunuchs in Fokine's *Schéhérazade* were told to wear tan pants over their bluish-gray skin during the orgy with the all-white harem. Few American critics could comprehend the discipline that lay behind the spectacle. Nijinsky was described by a San Francisco newspaper as "probably an All-American halfback—gone wrong." The Ballets Russes did little to displace Anna Pavlova's newly ethereal image of the ballet's soul; Diaghilev was not far

off the mark when he suggested that "Americans still think of the ballet as light entertainment, to be enjoyed after a hard day at the office."

It was nearly fifteen years before large-scale ballet returned to the United States with the first tour of the new Ballet Russe de Monte Carlo in 1933. Picking up the pieces of Diaghilev's shattered enterprise at the beginning of a thirty-year history of divided troupes, intrigue, and dissension, the various Ballet Russe companies forged a durable image of the art as a kind of stylized dance-theater where "people fall in love with nymphs and birds and have to suffer for it," as Bernard Taper has noted; old standards and effervescent new entertainments assembled by some of the world's greatest choreographers, danced by glamorous stars with fiery temperaments and Russian names—prima ballerina Alexandra Danilova, the "baby ballerinas" Toumanova, Baranova, and Riabouchinskaya—lured growing numbers of Americans to ballet, despite the Great Depression. Many of the finest Russian choreographers, dancers, and teachers had remained in America in the wake of Pavlova and the Ballets Russes tours, establishing schools and contributing dances to some of the earliest American ballet troupes then in formation—in Atlanta, San Francisco, Philadelphia, Dayton, Chicago, and New York City. With the presence of Russians embodying the wisdom of the past and present, and a new willingness on the part of patrons and philanthropists to support the establishment of ballet as an institution, the time had arrived for Americans to struggle toward establishing a tradition of their own.

Sergei Denham's Ballet Russe de Monte Carlo even became a kind of *American* Russian ballet, with American dancers in the corps sometimes choosing to "Russianize" their names in order to appear legitimate on a playbill. This kind of "spectral blackmail" raised the hackles of a wealthy young Harvard-educated critic, poet, and dance historian, who never doubted that ballet was an art with a future in America. While still a teen-ager, Lincoln Kirstein had acquired a passion for Nijinsky and the Ballets Russes, and later traveled to Europe to see the company firsthand. In 1933, viewing the work of George Balanchine in Paris, he intuitively recognized an approach to ballet that held enormous promise for transplantation to a nation still discovering its own relationship to the past. After Diaghilev's death, Balanchine had also choreographed sophisticated musical revues in London, embracing the commercial need to make ballet entertaining. Diaghilev had liked to call him "my American choreographer." But Kirstein's admiration was more fundamental: "I knew that what Balanchine made meant ballet to me," he later wrote, "because ballet was about dancing to music, not about painting or pantomime."

Kirstein invited Balanchine to establish an American ballet company concerned only with progressive creations rather than past masterpieces from the Diaghilev and Maryinsky repertories. Balanchine pondered the offer, finally declaring himself only too pleased to come to the country that had produced Ginger Rogers. Arriving at Ellis Island late in 1933, Balanchine informed the press in broken English that it was "swell" to be here, and proceeded through immigration straight to the Barbizon Plaza. A company would come in time. "But first," he insisted, with Kirstein's assent, "a school." It was a move of enormous significance for the future of American ballet.

Reaching into his own small fortune from his father's Boston-based department store, as well as funds provided by the family of a friend, Edward W. W. Warburg, Kirstein opened the doors of the School of American Ballet on January 2, 1934, in the former studio of Isadora Duncan on the corner of Fifty-ninth Street and Madison Avenue in Manhattan. Six months later, with a cast of unknown American-born dancers and students, *Serenade* premiered at the Warburg estate in upstate New York. In its opening tableau, seventeen women posed in a natural stance, each with one hand raised against a brightening light. Was this Balanchine's lingering farewell to the Old World, or simply his dancers's stunned realization of the exquisite shape of their own arms? As their gazes shifted slowly downward, feet and legs suddenly flashed open into first position, as if to announce the arrival of classical dancing in a new land.

From the beginning Balanchine saw American ballet as a living art, not an attempt to voice a distant past or present. Nevertheless, the 1930s proved an inopportune decade to attempt the establishment of an elite performing-arts institution in America. During the Depression artists were expected to address the conditions of American life directly, and Kirstein and Balanchine's newly founded American Ballet found itself condemned for its "Riviera aesthetics." By 1938, after a few years at the Metropolitan Opera in New York, Balanchine was without a company of his own and at work elsewhere—everywhere from the Ballet Russe de Monte Carlo to Hollywood and Broadway, where *Variety* praised his "ace job on the Terp angle." His sublime muse became the glamour of American music and entertainment in the 1930s and 1940s—the urbane romanticism epitomized by George Gershwin, Irving Berlin, and the man the choreographer considered the greatest of all American dancers, Fred Astaire. Kirstein would later remark that "Rodgers and Hart and Samuel Goldwyn was the direction that established Balanchine in America." According to Ray Bolger, a song-and-dance man in the 1936 Rodgers and Hart musical *On Your Toes,* working with Balanchine was "like spinning from Juilliard to the Louvre to the Royal Academy of Dramatic Arts to Stillman's Gymnasium."

But the transformation of "Russian" ballet into an American idiom required a more dramatic response to the American situation, its myths, its everyday shapes and rhythms. Even the Ballet Russe—with Massine's *Union Pacific* (1935) and several other works—had glanced beyond conventional images of ballet's Franco-Russian past. In the summer of 1936, Kirstein formed a new company, Ballet Caravan, to present *American* dancers in ballets choreographed by *Americans* for *American* purposes. Dispensing with Russian glamour, the company asserted ballet's "superhuman released essential energy" as a legitimate reflection of democracy: "There

Clark Tippett as Alias in American Ballet Theatre's production of Eugene Loring's *Billy the Kid* for *Dance in America*. (© 1976 Martha Swope)

were no ballerina roles," Kirstein later wrote, "no parts at all except through continual experimentation with stray hybrids, classical ballet infused with Martha Graham movement or with Broadway revue."

In Eugene Loring, who choreographed *Billy the Kid* for Ballet Caravan, Kirstein found a choreographer equally convinced that ballet could affect Americans in specifically American terms. Born LeRoy Kerpestein in Milwaukee, Wisconsin, Loring had begun dancing in high school and worked as a bank messenger, secretary, telephone operator, and tropical fish salesman before finally appearing on Kirstein's doorstep with a letter of introduction in 1936; Kirstein followed a suggestion from his friend James Cagney and presented Loring with a libretto based on the legend of William Bonney, the punk outlaw who had terrorized the American Southwest in the 1880s. *Billy the Kid*'s slow-motion fisticuffs, its poker games, gun duels, and mimed horseback riding blended easily with Loring's rough, workmanlike classicism. But it was not an image of civilization American audiences were universally disposed to accept, at least not in place of the grand Russian repertory: Ballet Caravan's Milwaukee sponsors rejected their native son's offering as an unfit subject for a ballet, and by

1941 Ballet Caravan was disbanded. Nevertheless, the larger success of *Billy the Kid* helped legitimize later ballets on American themes, including Agnes de Mille's *Rodeo: The Courting at Burnt Ranch* (also choreographed to music by Aaron Copland) for the Ballet Russe de Monte Carlo in 1942. *Rodeo* led directly to De Mille's work the following year on the musical *Oklahoma!*, in which her use of balletic choreography as a colorful means for advancing the story line—an approach to show-dancing pioneered by George Balanchine in *On Your Toes*—would change the course of the American musical theater forever.

With the founding of Ballet Theatre (later American Ballet Theatre) in 1940—a "dance gallery" presenting a repertory of work from all eras and countries—ballet in America came of age. Surviving the war without reliance on visiting European companies, looking instead to major stars of their own such as Alicia Alonso, Nora Kaye, and Igor Youskevitch, American audiences grew increasingly comfortable with classicism. Small but informed audiences in several major cities were more and more able to measure new productions against the standards of the past and to view ballet with intelligence and taste. Ballet Americana began to resemble a modest folk art better left to musical theater and film, and works from the Franco-Russian past grew increasingly popular; in San Francisco, the Christensen brothers actually introduced home-grown versions of the full-evening Russian repertory. But by the late 1940s the major force in the American ballet ascension had shifted to the still-controversial genius of George Balanchine, who was responding to the American situation with a different approach to ballet as an art.

Running against the current of American dance-theater in the 1940s, Balanchine had ceased to view dance as an inclusive art, capable of approaching the world on the world's own terms; instead he was creating great lyric dramas through the movement of classical bodies to music alone. "The ballet must speak for and about itself," he wrote—a sentence that meant little to American audiences accustomed to storytelling, lavish scenery, and extravagant costumes at the ballet; "The curtain should just go up, and if the spectators understand what's going on, it's good—if not, not." Balanchine's enemies portrayed him as a man who cared about classical style as an end in itself; but, as the choreographer continued to assemble ballets to classical music, old and new, drawn from a variety of French, Italian, German, and American sources, he "more and more clarified the dancer's momentum in motion," Edwin Denby noted. "You watch with pleasure, as if she were doing what she spontaneously likes to do."

Balanchine's first plotless neoclassical ballet, *Concerto Barocco*, was assembled for a Latin American tour in 1941. It "has no subject matter," the choreographer wrote, "beyond the score to which it is danced and the particular dancers who execute it." The Palladian grandeur of its carefully sculpted, interweaving images appears as a visual equivalent to the passionate decorum of Bach's Concerto in D-minor for Two Violins. "As the two violins take up their parts in the music," Balanchine has written, "two soloists enter. . . . They support each other as the music of one violin entwines the other; they depict and develop dance themes that recur with the repetition and development of themes in the orchestra." The second movement captures the tender nobility of the ballerina as she is partnered through slow lifts and soaring arcs, moving against the shifting backdrop of the corps; the third, allegro movement for the entire corps, fulfills the structural sublimity of the Bach score. Like *Ballet Imperial,* created that same year, *Concerto Barocco* exemplified the American dancer's growing lack of self-consciousness: No longer needing to appear as cowboys, filling-station attendants, gold rush forty-niners, or imaginary swans and sylphs, American dancers were at last able simply to be themselves.

In 1946 Lincoln Kirstein returned from wartime service in Europe to establish a new company, Ballet Society, primarily as a vehicle for George Balanchine's creations. With no one to satisfy but himself, the choreographer chose to challenge the new maturity of dancers trained

The "Phlegmatic Variation" in George Balanchine's *The Four Temperaments*, led by Adam Lüders. (© 1977 Costas)

at his thirteen-year-old School of American Ballet: To a score personally commissioned from Paul Hindemith six years earlier, Balanchine created *The Four Temperaments* (1946), the first of many ballets to streamline, distort, heighten, and intensify the fundamental possibilities of the classically trained body dancing to music. By directing classicism towards the extremes of modernist abstraction, Balanchine would transform the tradition that Nijinsky had attempted to shatter into a fountainhead of contemporary renewal.

Danced today in practice clothes—leotards and tights for the women, T-shirts and tights for the men—*The Four Temperaments* used the idea of the four medieval humors—Melancholic, Sanguinic, Phlegmatic, Choleric—to define its major sections. But Balanchine discovered in the heart of classicism an entirely modern speed, a stark intensity and weighted distortion: Feet flex muscularly, hips thrust forward in propulsive syncopation, arms bend at abrupt angles, and bodies slump forward, dancing half-bent-over to the floor. Classical gestures "are courtly," Kirstein has written, "yet respond in accent, celerity and syncopation to the colloquial cadence of the day." Like Petipa, Balanchine was adapting a centuries-old academic vocabulary to his own era, channeling the American dancer's "angelic unconcern with emotion" into an entirely new landscape of lyrical expression. Investigating the materials of his art as radically as postwar visual artists and composers were examining their own, Balanchine would erect a modernist repertory based on music by Stravinsky, Webern, Ives, Bartók, and Schönberg that remains among the shining achievements of contemporary art.

In 1948 the City of New York offered Balanchine and Kirstein the use of City Center, a former Masonic temple in Midtown Manhattan; in accepting Kirstein promised, "I will give you in three years the finest ballet company in America." Balanchine and Kirstein's New York City Ballet became the principal workshop of the Mozart of choreographers, who would continue his radical break with the past and simultaneous avowal of the deepest traditions of classicism until a year before his death in April 1983. Enshrined in the New York State Theater at Lincoln Center since 1964, and currently under the direction of Jerome Robbins and Balanchine's leading protégé, Peter Martins, City Ballet sustains an academy, a style, and a repertory that constitute, arguably, the finest institution of dance in the world, directly affecting the establishment and growth of companies in Atlanta, Boston, Chicago, Kansas City, Los Angeles, Milwaukee, Pittsburgh, Philadelphia, Salt Lake City, and San Francisco.

Every corner of contemporary dance has learned from Balanchine's understanding of the American dancer and the pleasure and instruction his work affords. New York City Ballet dancers have created an image of American civilization through the lyrical mechanics of classicism, epitomizing "in their quirky legginess, linear accentuation, and athleticism a consciously thrown-away, improvisational style," Kirstein has written, "that can be read as populist, vulgar, heartless, overacrobatic, unmannered, and insolent. . . . It is a style of living which may be interpreted as having small respect for its forebears—its elders and, naturally, betters." The spread of Balanchine's training and

Choreographers at the New York City Ballet in 1951 (from left): Jerome Robbins, George Balanchine, Ruthanna Boris, Antony Tudor, and Todd Bolender. (© 1951 Philippe Halsman, courtesy Hastings Galleries Collection)

repertory has taught American audiences how to look at classical dancing unselfconsciously, without reference to an Old World past or to their own native mythologies.

· · ·

Nearly thirty-five years after its founding, in 1982 the New York City Ballet had temporarily moved its rehearsals a few hundred yards north, from the basement of the State Theater to the School of American Ballet on Sixty-sixth Street, where some twenty dancers were preparing to assemble a new ballet. Tugging at their leg warmers, a trio of long-legged young girls from the corps de ballet prodded the resin box in the corner of the studio, etching the tips of their pointe shoes in the dust to secure their grips on the floor, chattering nervously, ignoring the gaze of on-lookers seated near the piano. More dancers poured through the wide studio door, exchanging greetings, splaying themselves along the broad gray floor, surveying their bodies suspiciously in the floor-length mirrors. Most were sore from the day before, and a few from last week; a careful warm-up is important, because the choreographer tends to be on time.

A pianist began churning out great swaths of music at a baby grand, but no one appeared to notice. A quartet of dancers moved across the floor in ragged canon, their passage glimpsed in snatches by students from the school, who watch unobtrusively from behind the swinging door. Above the mirrors, narrow strips of glass open on the panoramic skyline around Lincoln Center, a neat visual contrast to the scale and energy of the work in progress. The past, present, and future of the New York City Ballet share this beautiful hothouse, this ghetto—its members studying, working, and teaching within a few square blocks on Manhattan's Upper West Side. The finest *dancing* ballet company in the world, it is the reflection of one man who, even as a young choreographer in St. Petersburg, seemed to go about his business by divine authority.

"It's like the pope represents Christ," Balanchine remarked in one of his more celebrated half-serious pronunciamentos. "I represent Terpsichore, goddess of the dance." The thrust and fertility of Balanchine's inventiveness over the course of his sixty-year career seemed less the achievement of a demiurge than of a master craftsman at work with the tools of his trade. Balanchine insisted that he merely "assembled" ballets in a universe God created, serving the needs of the institution, the nature of the music, and the gifts of the dancers he saw before him. To observe Balanchine work the year before his death was to have the special pleasure, as his biographer Bernard Taper once noted, of seeing someone "completely attuned to his world."

Mr. B entered the studio alone, a gray-haired, medium-built man in his late seventies,

his hawklike face bearing an expression of casual yet imperturbable dignity. "I am an Oriental," his expression seemed to say, "from Georgia, in the Caucasus—and a Russian." The dancers smiled as the ballet master greeted them cordially. Then he sniffed dryly and moved toward the piano.

His preparations for the work at hand were all but invisible. He had absorbed the music well in advance, analyzing the written score to anticipate the overall structure of the ballet, the number of dancers it needed, the atmosphere, the quality of motion. The rest waited until this rehearsal; no steps were conceived in advance, and there were no notes—Balanchine rarely put pen to paper. Now, after consulting with the pianist, he clapped his hands and, without preliminary discussion of his intentions, arranged the dancers in a pleasing formation, continuing where they left off in a previous session. Then he asked the pianist for a few bars of music. As the dancers waited, Balanchine appeared to be dreaming with his eyes open.

"You do this," he said shortly to one dancer. "Maybe you do this." What he demonstrated was a distillation of what had passed through his mind's eye: an angled shoulder, perhaps, or simply a description of a classroom step. After open-heart surgery in the spring of 1980, Balanchine no longer walked through his dances, but he could still suggest a panorama of movement without really moving at all—"dancing with his hands," as one company member put it, and partnering his ballerinas with peerless insight and attention.

The dancer worked with these minimal suggestions, attempting to capture the dynamics and musicality of the phrasing with the full elasticity and grace of a classical line. Watching the pattern of the steps on the floor with cool, realistic scrutiny, Balanchine corrected for details, rarely saying anything was wrong, only warning, "Maybe you shouldn't." When the dancer mastered the phrase, the choreographer added more bars of music.

"He'll choreograph a section," marveled ballerina Merrill Ashley, "and maybe it's Stra-

Originally created for the Paris Opéra, *Symphony in C* reflects the scale and architecture of one of Europe's most magnificent theaters. (© 1983 Paul Kolnik)

vinsky—and we're all thinking of very complicated counts, and it's not in your body at all, and you're making mistakes and losing your place and picking it up later, and so on. But he can tell whether it's right or wrong." "He makes suggestions," said principal dancer Adam Lüders. "He doesn't ever impose anything on you. He gives you something, then sees what you'll do with it. He's not afraid you're going to ruin his work, because he doesn't visualize the work is going to be a certain way. Whatever happens, happens."

Balanchine never saw himself as the kind of choreographer who could create in the abstract, in some quiet room at home. He needed living bodies to look at; watching how one dancer could turn or another could jump, he said, he began to get a few ideas. His struggles were with the music, the mood of the dance, and the imagery it had to sustain. "The choreography is in the structure," says Suzanne Farrell, Balanchine's greatest ballerina during the last two decades of his career. "The steps just show it. The steps can be anything."

Such grand traditional ballets as Bizet's *Symphony in C* and Tchaikovsky's *Piano Concerto No. 2* are plotless tributes to Balanchine's French and Russian heritage, respectively; it is their overall architecture, shape, and energy, rather than any strict adherence to what French or Russian decorum "ought" to be, that create their bond to the classicism of the past. Mozart's *Divertimento No. 15* (1956) bathes in the limpid rationality of the eighteenth century; *Ballo della Regina* (1978), choreographed to the underwater ballet from Verdi's opera *Don Carlos,* is "transparently a mid-nineteenth-century seascape," Arlene Croce has written, "with bravura waves and naiads surging through the foam or glowing like pearls in the deep." Three different works gathered together in *Jewels* (1967) are musical evocations of national period styles: Fauré's *Em-*

Agon with Heather Watts and Mel Tomlinson. Balanchine called *Agon* "a machine that thought"—an episode of "diabolical craftsmanship." (© 1981 Paul Kolnik)

eralds, a romantic artifact from chivalric France; Stravinsky's *Rubies,* pulsing with the rhythmic vitality of twentieth-century America; and Tchaikovsky's *Diamonds,* with its sumptuous finale danced at a scale and intensity recalling the glories of the Maryinsky Theatre, where the ballet master began.

Pursuing ineffable moods over the course of 150 American ballets, Balanchine transformed the folk dances of Russia, the British Isles, Spain, and Bali, American modern dance, square dance and Cajun steps, and Broadway show dancing into material for classical ballet. In Stravinsky's *Agon* (1957), a transformation of seventeenth-century French dances to music composed in part on a pink piano in a Venice nightclub, the choreographer assembled his archetypal American achievement, exploding the traditional symmetry of classicism through angular tension and plasticity, his dancers rivaling one another in feats of wit and courage in an absolute arena of the present. And yet Balanchine also regularly tossed off amusing novelty dances and showy divertissements of "calculated vulgarity"; he also restaged a number of staples from the nineteenth-century story-ballet repertory, including Tchaikovsky's *Nutcracker,* which regularly sells out seven weeks at Lincoln Center each Christmas.

Balanchine's understanding of classicism was the source of his astonishing fecundity, but the choreographer reserved his most profound allegiance for the composer: Music is the ground his dancers walk on—their reason to move. "A choreographer can't invent rhythms," Balanchine once explained. "He can only reflect them in movement. The body is his medium, and, unaided, the body can improvise for a short breath. But the organizing of rhythms on a grand scale is a sustained process. It is a function of the musical mind."

The son of a well-known Georgian composer, Balanchine studied for three years in St. Petersburg's music conservatory before deciding to move people to music instead; a superb musician, sometimes making his own two-hand piano reductions of orchestral scores, he has often been called a musician who happened to be a choreographer. The sixty-four-member New York City Ballet Orchestra, under the direction of Robert Irving since 1958, became a remarkably sensitive instrument of the ballet master's musical judgment. Although his choreography never slavishly followed a score note by note or strictly interpreted all its musical effects, the result was nearly always "a joint progression," music critic B. H. Haggin has written, "in which music and movement enlarged and heightened each other's significance and effect." Careful never to select scores that might overwhelm the dancing, Balanchine choreographed surprisingly little to Bach, Mozart, and Beethoven, but his ballets to Delibes, Glinka, Drigo, Glazunov, Minkus, and other nineteenth-century dance composers are the present era's major link to the Age of Petipa; his new works to Tchaikovsky—especially *Serenade, Ballet Imperial,* and *Suite No. 2* (1960)—have vastly expanded the repertory of the greatest of all nineteenth-century ballet composers, honored by his own Festival at City Ballet in 1981.

Balanchine's commitment to distant musical eras never precluded his involvement with works by composers from the first six decades of the twentieth century—the raw material for City Ballet's unprecedented modernist repertory. The atonal, twelve-tone, and serial music created by such mid-century classical composers as Hindemith, Webern, and Schönberg is difficult in every way—for musicians, dancers, and audiences—but Balanchine explored their brash, unconventional sonorities with relentless inventiveness. Ravel was honored in a 1976 festival of ballets, but Balanchine devoted unique attention to the modern composer closest to him in spirit—a man who came to stand as a kind of paternal conscience to the company. Kirstein acknowledged this debt in a 1951 letter to Igor Stravinsky: "Balanchine, Robbins, and myself consider you our father and our future."

Balanchine's first work with a Stravinsky score was *Song of the Nightingale,* assembled for Diaghilev in 1925; he later declared that, as "an organizer of rhythms," Stravinsky was the

Balanchine and Stravinsky rehearsing Diana Adams and Arthur Mitchell in the original production of *Agon,* in the old City Ballet studios on 82nd Street and Broadway. (© 1957 Martha Swope)

greatest composer who ever lived. Stravinsky's constant invention under pressure, his range of styles, his sovereign professionalism, his bewitching pulse and constant rhythmic variety all inspired Balanchine to deal directly with the materials of dance through music—Stravinsky's "common order between man and time." Believing that every note of Stravinsky could be danced, Balanchine assembled thirty-nine Stravinsky ballets, some to scores never intended for choreography. Twenty-two years Balanchine's senior, the composer worked closely if sporadically with the company until his death in 1971,

attending rehearsals, offering suggestions, recommending other advanced composers, even conducting from the pit on occasion. "To see Balanchine's ballets," Stravinsky said, "is to hear the music with one's eyes."

"Music like Stravinsky's cannot be illustrated," the choreographer wrote in homage. "One must try to find a visual equivalent that is a complement rather than an illustration. . . . Just as the cabinetmaker must select his woods for the job at hand—palisander, angelique, rosewood, briar, or pine—so a ballet carpenter must find the dominant quality of a gesture, a strain

Stravinsky Violin Concerto—a sharply accented, relentless, and dazzling succession of dances, responding to nearly every note of Stravinsky's staccato score. (© 1977 Costas)

or palette of consistent movement, an active scale of flowing patterns which reveal to the eye what Stravinsky tells the sensitized ear."

The *summa* of the Stravinsky-Balanchine association came a year after the composer's death, with the first Stravinsky Festival of the New York City Ballet and then a second, centennial celebration a decade later. Thirty-one works were performed in a single week in 1972, including twenty-two new ballets by six different choreographers. Balanchine personally assembled seven new works, most notably *Symphony in Three Movements, Duo Concertant,* and *Violin Concerto*—the latter ballet donning "the full armor of visible music," as one Soviet critic noted. Balanchine often spoke of his "conversations" with composers of every era and sensed their presence during rehearsals and performances. Standing before the golden curtain at the New York State Theater on opening night in 1972, he announced, "Today is Stravinsky's ninetieth birthday, and he is here. Actually he took a leave of absence. He called me on the phone and said, 'George, it's all yours. Do what you want.' "

"The curtain wasn't raised," one critic later recalled. "It was ripped away."

·   ·   ·

For almost a half century, Balanchine was an American "maker and teacher," creating "a patrimony of ballets," Kirstein has written, destined to be "tended as carefully as the collection of six-hundred-year-old bonsai in Tokyo's Imperial Palace conservatory." And yet the ballet master always denied that the future of his work was his concern. He rarely troubled himself to remember his ballets, at best recalling the style, the shape, the thrust—seldom the steps. *Divertimento No. 15* was assembled four years after *Caracole,* but to the same piece of music, because he couldn't remember the earlier work; he often altered steps in his older ballets to suit different dancers, knowing that the musical structure of the dance could bear the changes. "Don't worry," he told one dancer struggling to master a part. "I change my mind all the time. If I didn't I'd still be doing the same things people did one hundred years ago."

"In forty years, ballet will all be different," Balanchine told Edwin Denby—but with his death other ballet masters control these changes, as well as important casting and production decisions. Balanchine's company began to alter within a year of his death in 1983: Over a dozen dancers left and a number of younger performers debuted in the company's older repertory. Peter Martins, the principal preserver of Balanchine's work, has begun to trust his own instincts, knowing that the only way recognized masterpieces can survive is if dancers look good doing them.

But in addition to Martins's discretion and taste, the survival of Balanchine's work beyond his own lifetime is largely dependent on the arrival of new dancers trained at the School of American Ballet—the cornerstone of the New York City Ballet and the fountainhead of its style. Even before arriving in this country, Balanchine had insisted that any plan to create an American company must include an academy providing fundamental instruction in the style he himself embodied—the style of the academy of pre- and postrevolutionary St. Petersburg, surviving from the early eighteenth century through the time of Pavlova and Nijinsky to Balanchine himself. The school grew steadily, with the choreographer calling upon advanced students for his various projects, until the founding of the New York City Ballet in 1948 provided a seamless transition from training ground to professional performance. Balanchine often said that he simply taught what he had learned as a child, but adapted to the bodies he saw before him: the style of the imperial academy but "with the cholesterol taken out."

Since 1969, SAB has been situated on the fourth floor of the Juilliard School at Lincoln Center, where four studios are in almost constant use for ten hours each day, September through June, training 400 to 450 students, ages eight to eighteen; the current enrollment includes dancers from some forty states and twelve foreign countries. The faculty features former dancers from Kiev, Moscow, Copenhagen, Berlin, Paris, and the old Imperial Theater in St. Petersburg, as well as past and present members of City Ballet well acquainted with the demands of the repertory. As a vocational school, SAB has been an unparalleled success: Graduates from the classes of 1979 through 1982 alone have become members of twenty-seven different ballet companies on three continents. Lip service is paid to the ideal of serving as a national dance academy, but the real purpose of the school is to provide dancers for the New York City Ballet, and the ambition of most serious students is to join the company one day. Lincoln Kirstein, president of the school, refers to it with a military analogy as "the West Point of the Dance." It is a meritocracy of the body offering young dancers the most complete challenge anywhere in American dance, providing a model for academies established in San Francisco, Philadelphia, Boston, and numerous other American cities. At the School of American Ballet, students dedicate themselves with a kind of moral elation rare in American institutions, transcending apparent limits of nature and individual temperament to become instruments of an American classical ballet.

·　　·　　·

Only one current member of the New York City Ballet attended the School of American Ballet from the earliest possible admission age. As a nine-year-old, Miriam Mahdaviani danced as an angel and a soldier in Balanchine's *Nutcracker,* and twelve years later she appeared on *Dance in America* in the peasant rondo from *L'Enfant et les Sortilèges,* dancing as the mild young shepherdess who beckons the others to come stroke the

Lincoln Kirstein—an "Imperial American"—at the School of American Ballet. Kirstein has waged a lifelong battle for the fulfillment of cultural possibility, promulgating the "angelic order" that Balanchine embodied. (© 1982 Paul Kolnik)

woolly lambs. Long-legged and coltish even by City Ballet standards, Miriam is filled with the unexaminable desire and compliant selflessness that is the soul of any great ballet company—one of the hundreds of girls who have streamed through the school during the dance explosion of the 1970s.

Miriam's formal dance studies began at the age of eight, with classes at a neighborhood ballet school in Forest Hills, Queens. But when her best friend needed a traveling companion for the long subway trip to SAB, Miriam agreed to audition. At the general call held annually after Labor Day, 100 to 150 children from the Greater New York area apply to the lower divisions; every Wednesday throughout the year, 5 to 10 more children audition, and approximately 30 in all are taken into the youngest division. No one can predict whether or not a young child will have the will and the talent to dance professionally, but a process is set in motion that will transform the lives of at least a few. "Are ballerinas born or made?" Balanchine once asked. "Well, first they must be born."

Very young dancers at the barre. What is a Balanchine dancer? "Someone who can do what Balanchine wants," answers Violette Verdy, now director of the Boston Ballet. (© 1979 Brownie Harris)

"They herd all the little kids into a room," Miriam explains cheerfully. "They don't really care if you've had ballet or not. They want to see long legs and relatively straight posture. They ask you to point your feet to see what your arch is like. They ask you to jump—any old jump. And they lift your leg to see what kind of flexibility you have. And that's it. They don't ask you to move at this stage. I suppose at age eight they expect you can be trained."

Almost as soon as they enroll, students find themselves performing in one of the great theaters in the world. "All the second-division children are invited to *The Nutcracker*," Miriam con-

tinues. "But I loved dancing in *A Midsummer Night's Dream* in the spring. It's not really classical, but I love to travel, to move, and that gave you the opportunity. And *Harlequinade* actually put the girls in white tutus; you have to point your feet and turn out."

While the children's division provides young dancers for Balanchine's theatrical spectacles, the preparatory division accepts new boys and girls ages ten to twelve or thirteen, with slightly older boys sometimes permitted to enroll. Within three years the steady, grinding work begins to produce results: a basic ballet technique is acquired along with the discipline that

Boys in class at the School of American Ballet. Male enrollment at the school has tripled to some eighty dancers over the past five years, reflecting a loosening of prejudices against male participation in what was once considered almost exclusively a feminine domain. (© 1982 Paul Kolnik)

must carry dancers through a lifetime of work. The classroom becomes the dancer's second home, the ballet barre a daily rediscovery of the actual possibilities of ligaments, muscles, and bones—what the poet Paul Valéry called "the soul's assent to exquisite restraints."

After completing the fifth year of the children's division and the first or second year of the preparatory division, thirteen-year-old students merge into the intermediate division. Now the boys are ready to enter separate classes, developing their own special qualities of strength, elevation, and acrobancy. To achieve the full subtlety, suppleness, and coordination required of classical dancers, a long period of progressive improvement is essential, one avoiding the headlong rush to master tricks that has marred the achievement of American men in the past.

Already young teen-agers are dancing with the lifted, energetic look of real dancers; the girls, meanwhile, are enduring the anticipated pain of learning to dance on the tips of their toes. "What a violin is to a violinist, a piano to a pianist, ballet shoes are to a female dancer—the most crucial equipment," says Balanchine's second wife, Vera Zorina.

With its strong backing and blocked, balsawood toe, the toe slipper binds the toes and arch of the foot together so that the body's entire weight can be borne by the top half-inch of the big toe's knuckle; the other four toes act as support. Beaten against walls, slammed in doors until the block is neither too soft nor too hard for dancing, the shoe is laced to the ankle with ribbons and fitted as snugly as possible. Because pointe shoes offer an elongated, graceful line to the leg, visibly increasing the dancer's speed, range, and quality of motion, the future ballerina learns to work with her pointes as a carpenter learns to wield a hammer and saw.

The immediate reward for these new accomplishments is one-hour variation classes in the standard Russian repertory. The girls are taught by Alexandra Danilova, one of Diaghilev's last ballerinas and the greatest star in American ballet during the 1930s and 1940s with the Ballet Russe de Monte Carlo. "She's the only one who speaks to the old classical rules of dance," says Miriam, "and knows all the old variations from *The Sleeping Beauty*, *Giselle*, and *Coppélia*, which are dances we don't have in our repertory." Danilova embodies ballet's high style—which she likes to call "deportment." The value of such instruction cannot be automatic; it resides in the gifts of teachers and the ability of dancers to surrender intelligently to the instructor's demands.

Performing the great variations of the Imperial Theater in classrooms, students begin to be more closely assessed in the first of many competitions on the road to the New York City Ballet. "A lot of people leave on their own," Miriam recalls. "They don't like the school because they find the training too rigid; their par-

ents don't like it; they decide they just don't want to dance anymore; or they see no connection between what they've been studying and what they used to call 'dancing.' " Teen-agers are asked to make momentous life decisions that might preclude other futures, including a normal academic education. After surviving competition stiffer than admission to Harvard, many dancers receive scholarships worth up to $10,000 a year covering living expenses, transportation, class tuition, and an academic education; entire families have been known to relocate to New York City in order to see a son or daughter through Balanchine's academy. With the prospect of a career enticingly near, SAB students, concerned with little else besides their need to improve as dancers, eke out their schoolwork at the nearby Professional Children's School between the busy, ordained rhythms of dance classes. Fourteen- and fifteen-year-olds live and board with families of local students, and older teen-agers share apartments or take rooms in residential hotels. From the age of twelve, Miriam was riding the subway from Queens alone.

In the first advanced division, at age sixteen or so, students begin at ten in the morning six days a week, with additional adagio, pointe, and variation classes five days a week for the girls and variation and gymnastics classes for the boys. Gearing themselves to the standards of the New York City Ballet, spending most of their waking hours in dance studios, locker rooms, and in travel to and from school, advanced students at SAB are unmistakable on the sidewalks around Lincoln Center, with their svelte figures, tightly bunned hairdos, and sprung walks, most appearing too self-conscious to be truly beautiful. Miriam fit the androgynous City Ballet mold with relative ease, but for others the struggle to remain slim assumes fanatical dimensions. "They would go to someone and say, 'You need to lose ten pounds,' and she might go and lose twenty," Miriam recalls. "There was one girl who lived on two bites of cottage cheese and an apple a day, with lots of coffee. She lost an incredible amount of weight, and today she's in the company. She must weigh about ninety pounds." Fifteen percent of all students in major ballet academies across America suffer from anorexia, according to author Suzanne Gordon. Even the healthiest students at SAB can acquire a neurotic obsession with weight, and gossip about food is a constant of life around the school. The ruthless demands of classical style—the need always to be more disciplined, more beautiful—have turned many into what Balanchine called "monsters of perfection." "We don't eat," dancer Toni Bentley has written. "We eat music."

In the advanced division workshops, and in tandem with the variation classes, students may spend six months learning repertory works or new ballets choreographed by faculty members or current City Ballet dancers. During her years at SAB, Miriam performed in Balanchine's *Symphony in C, Divertimento No. 15, Donizetti Variations,* and *Raymonda Variations,* and in Danilova's stagings of *Prince Igor* and *The Four Seasons.* Of the thirty students who will complete the most advanced class at the school, approximately ten will be received into City Ballet. Politics, changing aesthetics, and luck as well as talent play roles in filling these empty spots at City Ballet. But nearly every student who manages to complete the course of study is ready to perform professionally somewhere in the world; many City Ballet corps dancers would be soloists in other companies.

When Miriam was passed over by City Ballet following her year in the school's most advanced class, she was forced to consider the prospect of entering another sphere of competition, where one can be rejected by strangers after performing a casual walk across a studio floor. Although Robert Joffrey contends that there are jobs for every exceptional dancer in America, nearly a thousand dancers auditioned nationally in early 1982 for a half dozen openings in the corps of the Boston Ballet. Many less well-established companies come and go with the seasonal work; only twelve of two hundred professional regional ballets in America offer anything close to a year-round salary. Miriam

had given herself a certain distance from these tenuous prospects: She was the only SAB student simultaneously attending college full-time, living in a dormitory at Barnard College.

"I finally auditioned for the Pacific Northwest Ballet in Seattle," says Miriam. "I didn't really plan on going if I got taken, and Suki Schorer, my favorite teacher in the school, knew it. She told whoever was running the audition that I wasn't going to take it anyway. They would have used me, I was later told. . . . I also thought of going to Zurich, which has a company run by Patricia Neary"—a former Balanchine principal whom he liked to call his European representative. "I figured . . . well, I'd be in Europe and have the mountains and all that beauty. But then I decided I'd give it a second year in D class, because I wasn't really prepared to leave New York."

Miriam's persistence would be rewarded. In December 1979, Balanchine came to the school and took six or seven apprentices—"but not me," Miriam recalls. "That particular class had been so crowded that the teachers and students all felt that he really hadn't had a chance to see everyone. And so we asked him back to another variation class. We danced two at a time, so that he couldn't help but see. And at that point he took me and my best friend, Julie Kirsten."

Apprenticeship with the New York City Ballet does not constitute a dramatic break from the routine of school. Apprentices appear in only two ballets a season, without regular salaries or touring. Doggedly mastering corps parts in ten ballets, Miriam continued to attend Barnard part-time by switching her major from pre-med to English, avoiding a four-hour afternoon biology lab. She began attending company classes, usually held in the big rehearsal studio at the New York State Theater, where up to eighty dancers can work at a time. Balanchine was ill and rarely seen.

After spending the summer of 1980 dancing on Broadway in the company of ballerina Natalia Makarova, Miriam was finally accepted into the corps of the New York City Ballet in

December. She had one year of college left and quit without regrets. At the age of twenty, Miriam became one of seventy-eight other "boys" and "girls"—as most corps dancers will be known throughout their careers—who willingly gave up their potential in other areas of life to dance from eleven in the morning until eleven-thirty at night during the New York State Theater seasons, sacrificing all illusions of independence to the needs of a collective identity. Nothing they experienced in school prepared them for the emotional and physical demands of the New York City Ballet—the endless round of classes, rehearsals and performances in as many as fifteen to twenty-five dances a year for some, with a company maintaining an active repertory of some forty to fifty ballets. Few are able to rise to become soloists and principals—a painful realization for many. "Once in the company—and you usually enter as a corps member—you worry about whether you are going to be cast," writes Peter Martins, "and then when you *are* cast you wonder if your talents have been misunderstood and if this role is really right for you, or if you are capable of doing it and whether you will ever get any more roles. And you are always fighting the sense that no one is watching you or caring about you, in class and on stage. You worry about whether you can hold on to the roles you do have and when you should just give the whole thing up . . . because you've accomplished everything that you can accomplish and it's just going to be downhill from now on." Philip Roth once described the life of a City Ballet dancer as a cross between that of a boxer and of a nun.

By the time dancers enter their late twenties and early thirties, the purely physical peak is past, and chronic injuries from years of overwork have begun to take a toll. Most dancers survive in this seraglio of art and show business for fewer than five years, leaving to pursue other careers, to marry, or simply out of a realization that dance is no longer *enough*. For everyone but the internationally celebrated star, performing careers will end by the mid-thirties, and dancers must begin the sometimes traumatic readjustment to outside life. Some remain in the dance world as teachers, coaches, choreographers, or administrators, but without substantial pensions as in Denmark and Russia. Many former dancers must retrain for new employment.

For many reasons, as Mikhail Baryshnikov has said, the dancer's life is "a beautiful tragedy." But for most members of the New York City Ballet it does not seem a sacrifice to appear before 750,000 people a year at the summit of a lifetime of effort, dancing as subjects of a vision representing what author Irving Howe calls "the best, if not the only, reason for living in New York."

.   .   .

Refractions of music, celebrants in the drama of classicism, dancers with the New York City Ballet are entertainers—"performers in a circus," Balanchine once said. His skepticism about artistic and emotional self-indulgence is legendary. "I run my company tough. The dancers work hard and they like it. The school, too." Balanchine believed that ballet had to be like that so that dancers could discover their unrealized potential through dancing itself; he taught them how to move in ways they never imagined themselves capable of doing. "The choreography, the steps—these don't mean a thing," Balanchine remarked two decades before his death. "It's the person dancing the steps—that's the choreography."

Balanchine created numerous ballets with great male roles: *Agon, The Four Temperaments, The Prodigal Son,* to name only a few. He developed the greatest of all American-born male ballet dancers, Edward Villella, and drew on a number of superb Danish male classicists, including Martins, Adam Lüders, and Ib Andersen. He choreographed for male superstars such as André Eglevsky in the 1950s and Mikhail Baryshnikov in the 1970s. But the Balanchine ballerina represented the summation of his achievement, shaped by his belief in the feminine principle as "an unbelievable force, an unbelievable perfection"—the agent, source, and muse of culture itself. Ballet, as the choreographer asserted many times, is a woman. "Everything a man does," he once said, "he does for his Ideal Woman. You live only one life and you believe something, and I believe that." Important ballerinas of City Ballet's past, their images enshrined in the ballets they helped to assemble, include Diana Adams, Melissa Hayden, Kay Mazzo, Violette Verdy, and Patricia Wilde. Suzanne Farrell, Patricia McBride, Allegra Kent, Karin von Aroldingen, Merrill Ashley, Heather Watts, Sara Leland, Kyra Nichols, Maria Calegari, and Darci Kistler inspired Balanchine's invention until the time of his death. Although by all accounts never a Don Juan, Balanchine married four of his ballerinas: Tamara Geva, Vera Zorina, Maria Tallchief, and Tanaquil LeClercq. "He marries his materials," said Alexandra Danilova.

As corollary to his notion of women's essentially receptive role in an imaginary world "having nothing to do with life," Balanchine did unconscionably little to encourage aspiring female choreographers: Only Ruthanna Boris in the early 1950s; Martha Graham, working with just one City Ballet dancer during a shared program in 1959; and Alexandra Danilova with her 1978 costaging of *Chopiniana,* worked with dancers at the New York City Ballet during Balanchine's tenure. "Women are everything," critic Marvin Mudrick imagined the ballet master saying, "adding *sotto voce,* 'Except in charge.' "

Against this kind of benevolent paternalism, City Ballet offers an experience of dancing in "a world pervaded by a modern consciousness," Arlene Croce has argued—embodying a moral beauty, a dignified independence and expressiveness incomparable among the creations of living male artists in any discipline. Whatever qualities Nature and Nurture bestowed on his dancers, Balanchine carried them a step further, providing what could be best and most meaningfully mastered. He often assembled new works simply to celebrate a dancer's gifts: Merrill Ashley, Kirstein's "mistress of allegro," worked with Balanchine on the ravishing complexities of *Ballo della Regina,* summoning a speed and aplomb that few ballerinas can manage. "I've heard it said that Balanchine told certain people, 'I gave it to her,

but she just did it, so . . .' " Ashley recalls. "Sometimes he'd sit there in the studio—he usually doesn't have much expression on his face when he's watching, so sometimes you think he's not—and he'd have his arms folded, but you could tell he was enjoying it somehow." Suzanne Farrell—Balanchine's "Stradivarius"—immeasurably deepened his neoromantic perspective over the last two decades of his life. In Ravel's *Tzigane* (1976), Farrell mirrors the inflated gypsy passion of the violin, her loose-limbed flamboyance and effortless musicality suggesting innocence and regal seduction at every turn. Farrell felt great stress during its making. "What is it?" she kept asking herself, but her trust in Balanchine resulted in a personal tour de force inseparable from her impact as a performer. In *Chaconne* (1976), performed to the divertissement from Gluck's opera *Orpheus and Eurydice,* Farrell's haunting adagio, stilletolike pointe work, and angled artillery of beats, matched by Peter Martins's contained authority, appear as archetypal forces beyond the realm of individual personality. From their first tentative meeting to their final comprehension of a shared universe of values, the scale of the music and the choreography absorbs all their attention, transforming them into gods on an Elysian field. Explaining Farrell's incomparable range to ballerina Diana Adams, Balanchine simply said, "Well, you see, dear, Suzanne never *resisted.*"

Balanchine consistently urged his dancers not to concern themselves with ideas about "art" and self-expression but simply to feel the music and perform the choreography. "Art exists when people use their technique to create," he once declared. "Technique is the skill, and then you are free to show your personality and form." When the curtain rises at the New York State Theater, dancers perform with bold, unselfconscious directness as an ideal: "First comes the sweat," Balanchine said, "then comes the beauty—if you're *very* lucky and have said your prayers." Without elaborate sets and costumes, the New York City Ballet dedicates itself to the temperament of the music, the grace and beauty of the classically trained body, and the poetry of

Tzigane, the first ballet created for Suzanne Farrell upon her return from six years with Maurice Béjart's Ballet of the Twentieth Century in Brussels. (© 1977 Costas)

movement and gesture. This universe is held together by a spiritual force that is finally the most interesting thing about a Balanchine ballet, as Edwin Denby once suggested; Balanchine's most perceptive critic went on to note his nearly Shakespearean sense of destiny, involving romantic meetings and troubled partings, noble confusions, frustrated alliances, blind struggles, and tragic errors, with an instinct for order imposed on a capricious fate that never allows lovers to pair for long. The grand master of plotless ballet created dances rich with human complication and feeling, joys, daydreams and ecstasies; as steps vanish into music, human gestures emerge, coalescing into poetic images that reverberate in the imagination. "The secrets of emotion Balanchine reveals," Denby concluded, "are like those of Mozart, tender, joyous and true. He leaves the audience with a civilized happiness. His art is peaceful and exciting, as classical art has always been."

For the choreographer, such speculations

One of the quintessential ballet partnerships in the world, Suzanne Farrell and Peter Martins, dancing Balanchine's *Chaconne*. (© 1978 Martha Swope)

about the nature of his work were all "too fancy"; he often claimed his ballets existed in a realm beyond words, vanishing at the close of rehearsal, or with the descent of the curtain. What most interested Balanchine was now. "Do it now," he told his dancers over and over. "What are you waiting for?" Within a few weeks of assembling a work, he would sit easily on the sidelines, urging the dancers through the steps to higher and higher levels of clarity and attack; at the premiere he would be everywhere backstage, adjusting a ribbon on a costume, making last-minute changes. At times he would throw barely completed works on stage, to be groped through in front of paying audiences as he watched from the wings; he seldom missed a performance.

· · ·

Perhaps it should not be surprising that a man critic Robert Garis called "the greatest creative mind of our time" became fascinated by the possibilities of television. As early as 1934 Balanchine expressed an interest in the camera, and more of his work has been filmed or televised than any other major choreographer's. But by the early 1960s he had come to distrust the medium. In making ballet "televisionesque," as he called it, most productions ended up as a kind of reportage, with as little fidelity to the enchantment of the stage as a newspaper account of a murder bears to the terrifying act itself. In the early 1970s twelve of his dances were "destroyed" by German filmmakers who lopped off limbs and obscured steps with bad editing and camera moves—"in order to win awards for themselves," he said later.

Still, his noncommercial television ventures had been successful, especially WNET/New York's production of *Agon* in 1966, as had his work with the Canadian Broadcasting Corporation through the 1960s and 1970s. That history gave *Dance in America* hope that he might consider another collaboration. After Emile Ardolino and executive producer Jac Venza made overtures through Lincoln Kirstein, series producer Merrill Brockway wrote Balanchine, and the choreographer consented to a meeting.

"He started out by saying, 'You don't want me, you want *stories*, you want Tudor,'" Brockway recounted in a 1983 interview. "But I said, 'You do stories too—the stories of tonality.' I talked about the sonata principle of statement, development, and resolution, and the antagonism between two notes." With a degree in musicology and experience as a classical pianist and accompanist, Brockway knew what he was talking about. Balanchine listened. "Then he began to ask very specific questions, which he knew from his work in Hollywood—questions about correct lenses, camera angles, and so forth," Brockway continued. "I talked heights, widths of shots. He talked Astaire. He kept saying he wanted to trust the dancing, and our willingness to do this seemed to impress him. And finally he left things totally open—which was one of his tricks. He said, 'Why don't you come to season, make proposal, then we see.'" On Balanchine's terms, naturally, after eighteen months of wooing, a relationship began.

The first and second Balanchine programs were taped together in *Dance in America*'s Nashville studio, which Balanchine preferred to the stage at the State Theater. Part I included *Tzigane*'s "Gypsy party" for Suzanne Farrell and Peter Martins; the andante movement from *Divertimento No. 15,* with its intricate classical architecture; and his modernist masterpiece, *The Four Temperaments,* which proved to be a major *Dance in America* success as well—the beginnings of new solutions for transferring large-scale dances to the home screen.

One of the first problems Brockway faced with *The Four Temperaments* was its speed, which necessitated not just following the action but anticipating it. Brockway preferred his camera work tight and tidy, and Balanchine concurred, believing that the structure of a ballet must appear compact—"like the structure of a building," he once said. Brockway's cameras usually followed the soloist through the dance, with selective cuts to a few corps dancers performing the primary steps, and then long shots of the ensemble work. In explaining the organization of the dance, the choreographer said that its three thematic sections did not always occur at predictable intervals. "I said, 'Shouldn't the audience know this is important?'" Brockway recalls. "And that was when we thought of using a different color scheme in the lighting for each theme." The director finally decided that he could make everything work except the finale, when the company forms two lines upstage and partnered women soar between them in a series of high lifts. The dancers seem too small for the screen. Balanchine disagreed, saying simply, "They don't stay too long." Brockway laughs, recalling the incident. "Of course he was right."

Part II featured excerpts from *Jewels* and the complete *Stravinsky Violin Concerto,* an abstract modernist work more difficult to capture on a television screen. With typical candor Brockway admitted that its big group movements were preserved more as a record tape of the ballet than anything else: "I know it's not *television.*"

Nevertheless the collaboration had come into full stride, and a second taping session in September 1978—"Choreography by Balanchine: Part III"—captured one of the most extraordinary moments in the dance of the 1970s: the first encounter between Balanchine and Mikhail Baryshnikov, dancing the title role in

Prodigal Son. "Some of us on the set had a bet that first day as to who would speak Russian first," Brockway recalls. "It was Baryshnikov. You could see the whole formal arrangement of generations in an instant. Baryshnikov appeared nervous, but Balanchine was clearly elated at the prospect of working with a dancer he admired in one of the most intensely dramatic roles he had ever created. Profusely welcoming Baryshnikov to the role, Balanchine offered careful advice on the quality each movement must capture. And, although in his late seventies, he demonstrated what he wanted.

"He was taking tremendous physical risks," says producer Emile Ardolino. "He was climbing on tables, people were helping him down; at times even Misha looked afraid." At the end of the ballet, when the Prodigal drags himself along the ground with a stick toward his father's beckoning arms, Balanchine said, "No, not like that."

"Misha had kneepads," says Ardolino, "but Mr. B took the stick and crawled across the floor to show him how he wanted it done"—an extraordinary moment captured on camera and later shown on *Dance in America*'s Balanchine documentary. "There was a tremendous feeling in the room," Ardolino continued. "Then Balanchine replaced the father. If Misha actually crawled into his arms, I can't remember."

Baryshnikov's performance proved his greatest triumph in the repertory of the New York City Ballet, and perhaps the finest dramatic role of his career. With his furious leap in the ballet's first scene, one leg thrust in the direction of the wilderness in which he will lose himself, he revealed a passionate daring unseen since Edward Villella danced the role in the 1950s and 1960s. His twining, sensuous pas de deux with Karin von Aroldingen as the Siren—that "goddess of whores"—and his mockery at the hands of the bare-skulled revelers seemed ideally suited to the dancer's gifts as an actor—suggesting the truth of his own exile from the mother country.

"Choreography by Balanchine: Part III," which also featured the quintessential partner-ship of Farrell and Martins in *Chaconne,* won Brockway a 1978 Directors' Guild of America Award. "Part IV" was shot during the same ten-day period, with Emile Ardolino as director. "It was done for the dancers," Ardolino remembers: Karin von Aroldingen in the romantic *Elegie*; Patricia McBride and Baryshnikov in the virtuosic *Tchaikovsky Pas de Deux* and the fairy-tale valentine *The Steadfast Tin Soldier;* Merrill Ashley in her tour de force, *Ballo della Regina;* and Farrell and Martins in that concentrated essay on classical vocabulary, *Allegro Brillante.* Ardolino was surprised that Balanchine wanted such a potpourri, but the choreographer was enthusiastic. "Public will like," he said. And the public liked: "Choreography by Balanchine: Part IV" won *Dance in America* an Emmy Award for Outstanding Classical Program in the Performing Arts.

Balanchine had his most ambitious endeavor still in mind: a full-scale television collaboration on Maurice Ravel's masterpiece, the opera *L'Enfant et les Sortilèges,* or *The Spellbound Child.* Based on a libretto by Colette, it is the story of a rebellious boy who refuses to do his homework and is sent to his room by his mother, where he rips up his schoolbooks in a rage, shatters the tea service, tears the wallpaper, and teases the cat unmercifully—only to have them all come to life and torment him in return. The boy is finally led by the cat into a garden where moths and bats and dragonflies assail him as well; when he binds the wound of a squirrel hurt in the scuffling, the animals forgive him, and he returns to the care of his mother, having learned a lesson in compassion.

"It was a bolder experiment than a lot of people thought," says director Emile Ardolino, who would win his own award from the Directors' Guild of America for the program. Balanchine had become familiar enough with video technology to go with the full range of special effects—simulzooms, ultra-mattes, DVEs, string- and hand-puppet animations—all kinds of things that required the presence of special experts. The uncontrollable fantasy world of *The Spellbound Child* was conceived with the award-winning

Balanchine rehearsing Mikhail Baryshnikov in *The Prodigal Son*. (© 1983 Martha Swope)

designers David Mitchell and Kermit Love, who built an extraordinary array of costumes for the singing and dancing clock and chair, the cat, the tea service, the frogs, insects, and squirrels, a dancing flame, and the shepherds and shepherd-esses who come alive from the wallpaper.

Balanchine's relationship with *Dance in America* had deepened into one of trust. During his final illness he acted as consultant on "Bal-anchine Celebrates Stravinsky" but finally al-lowed Ardolino to go it alone. Ardolino, Brock-way, and producer Judy Kinberg were perpetually astonished by such generosity.

"I would get an idea and Mr. B would slap his forehead and say, 'Why didn't I think of that?'" Ardolino recalls, both flattered and amazed. "He never seemed to suffer—he'd just go into a room and start working. There was finally no measuring what he was capable of doing." "A topic would come up, he would talk in essays," says Brockway. "But the most im-portant thing he taught *us* . . . was how to make television dance."

What survives beyond Balanchine's death is the finest existing record of his ballets as he himself wanted them to be seen on the home screen.

·   ·   ·

As City Ballet enters a new era under ballet mas-ters Jerome Robbins and Peter Martins, the Bal-anchine repertory will continue to be the van-tage point for an evolving portrait of the dancers themselves. City Ballet has always been the only major ballet institution in the world to develop virtually all its own ballets, one of the largest and most prestigious repertories in the world; it will continue to be dominated by the work of its founder and guiding light, with three-quarters of its dances by Balanchine, the remainder the work of company choreographers, including Robbins and Martins, former ballet master John Taras, dancers Jacques d'Amboise, Joseph and Daniel Duell, Bart Cook, and several other company associates. The ability to fashion long, coherent passages of movement to music, incor-porating natural drama and emotion into the structure and imagery of a dance, is something

that cannot entirely be taught—but, naturally enough, there is a choreographic aesthetic in what Arlene Croce calls "the House of Balanchine." Today the continuing creative life of City Ballet depends on these and other choreographers' ability to explore new directions, test limits, and respond to changing conditions within the com-pany and the world at large.

The two most important figures in the continuing life of City Ballet present sharp con-trasts in style, experience, and personality that are already defining the company in the post-Balanchine era. Charged with directing the day-to-day business of the company, Peter Martins served a seven-year apprenticeship to Balan-chine that proved to be of major significance not only to Martins as an individual craftsman but to the future of the institution as well. Robbins, on the other hand—for many years the only choreographer of international repute working in a company dominated by another artist. The former "New York play-school referee, the maestro of the slum kindergarten, the Peter Pan of Arts and Crafts," as Arlene Croce once de-scribed him, Robbins is perhaps better known in the entertainment world as a winner of Os-cars, Tonies, and Emmies, and as director-cho-reographer of such legendary Broadway musi-cals as *West Side Story, Fiddler on the Roof,* and *Gypsy*. Although he has developed no definitive ballet style, his works are identified with con-temporary American dance around the world for their showmanship, emotional intensity, and musical intelligence; he is often remembered as the choreographer who introduced a new kind of existential drama and the uninhibited energy of modern youth into ballet for the first time. Indeed, more than any other choreographer of his generation, Robbins inherited the tensions and anxieties of American life at mid-decade—but in the course of his long journey to the New York City Ballet he made a separate peace with this inheritance and accepted another, to change our way of thinking about ballet in America.

·   ·   ·

With the smash success of Jerome Robbins's first important work, *Fancy Free,* at Ballet Theatre over four decades ago, and the musical *On the Town* the following year, the former Broadway chorus dancer stood poised between the worlds of high art and American show business with a naturalness no choreographer has managed before or since. The second child of Russian and Polish Jews who had fled the pogroms in Eastern Europe, raised across the river from New York City in Weehawken, New Jersey, twenty-seven-year-old Jerry Robbins was "the boy next door," wrote George Amberg in the late 1940s, ". . . the neighbor in the chorus line, the hero of one of those wonderful success stories which nourish the hopes and aspirations of every struggling youngster in the theater world."

Robbins followed his initial triumph with the jazz suite *Interplay* (1945), originally created for a Broadway show, then transferred to the Ballet Theatre repertory. *Interplay*'s dancers had the boisterous high spirits of kids in a Broadway chorus line, performing playful games with an athletic naturalness that showed Robbins didn't need a plot to hold his steps together. After the success of *Interplay,* he set out to show he was more than "the great American 'yak' choreographer"; the following year he produced *Facsimile,* a troubled and troubling indictment of the American mood, exploring the boredom of erotic obsession with a crackling understated tension reminiscent of the work of Antony Tudor. Robbins had announced his intention to become the first American-born choreographer of ballets to address painfully serious issues in contemporary America—just as a novelist or playwright or scenarist was free to do. And in between ballets came new Broadway successes: *Billion Dollar Baby, High Button Shoes*—a Mack Sennett–style beach ballet that won him the first of many Tony awards for choreography—and the autobiographical *Look Ma, I'm Dancing,* about life in a ballet company. By the late 1940s Jerome Robbins was the hottest choreographer in America, cruising around Manhattan in a cream-colored Dodge convertible and living in a comfortable Park Avenue apartment.

In 1949 he surprised the dance world by joining the fledgling New York City Ballet as associate director. From the beginning Robbins saw himself as something more than a commercial genie churning out ballets and kicklines to the prescription of some producer's checkbook, whether at Ballet Theatre or on Broadway. He was an *artist* first, and City Ballet seemed his natural home. And yet, oddly, his first ballet for Balanchine's company, *The Guests* (1949), portrayed a group of outsiders who arrive at a fashionable uptown party to find themselves the victims of snobbery and smug intolerance. Robbins had yet to expunge his identification with the *arriviste*, the outsider; although he had fulfilled "the often frustrated attempt [of the Jew] to possess the American imagination and to enter the American cultural scene," as Leslie Fiedler has written of novelist Saul Bellow, he had yet to resolve "the need to make clear his relationship to that country in terms of belonging or protest." A current of social awareness and disaffection persisted in his work throughout the 1950s and into the early 1960s, emerging in bitter attempts to plumb the fate of modern man, searching for some new faith in a world out of balance. In 1950 Robbins created *The Age of Anxiety,* which sought to evoke "the basic emotions of a whole generation that has not yet outlived the horrors of a world war," Lincoln Kirstein wrote, "insecure about the conditions of an uneasy peace and the radical changes in a civilization that had heretofore appeared safe and enduring." At the potentially explosive meeting point between this destructive world and the controllable environment of the ballet studio, Robbins's acute powers of social observation and the inevitable tribal dynamism he knew how to set loose on stage gradually became a kind of compensation for the repressed anger and anxiety of the decade. Absorbed into the mandarin routine of the New York City Ballet, composing the movements of dancers into a total world, Robbins would discover what he considered the most enduring values, a harmony and a mitigation the outside world was lacking.

Robbins also danced for Balanchine, appearing in the American premiere of *The Prodigal Son* and earning *The New York Times*'s ap-

Jerome Robbins rehearses Mikhail Baryshnikov and Natalia Makarova in *Other Dances*. (© 1985 Brownie Harris)

probation as "the finest dramatic dancer of our ballet." But by 1952 he was asking himself, "What am I doing cavorting around on stage at age thirty-four?" Robbins spent the rest of an enormously creative decade as a choreographer and director, careening between the rock of high culture and the hard place of commercial entertainment. Sir Frederick Ashton had choreographed for musical comedy; Balanchine had personally insisted on the hitherto unknown expression "Choreography by . . ." instead of the more familiar "Dances arranged by . . ." on Broadway programs in the late thirties. But for these two choreographers the commercial theater was nothing more than an interesting and financially rewarding sideline to their real endeavors. For Robbins, success with *The King and I, Funny Girl, Pajama Game, Peter Pan,* and *A Funny Thing Happened to Me on the Way to the Forum* was manna from heaven—his real assimilation into the mainstream of American life.

Robbins's protective view of himself as an artist first—removed from the pressures of the marketplace and the coercive social passions of the age—compelled him to retreat periodically into the self-enclosed innocence of the ballet's world. Capable of deep loyalty to friends and causes, at times a fierce exposer of social evils, Robbins nevertheless loathed the idea that anyone or anything might hold a lien on his conscience. Called before the House Un-American Activities Committee on May 5, 1953, Robbins testified, "I feel I'm doing the right thing as an American," and admitted to having been a member of a Communist political association from Christmas 1943 until the spring of 1947. Although he had admired the party's stand against fascism and anti-Semitism, he had finally left because of its various attempts to influence his work and its attacks on the kind of "bourgeois formalism" that they believed Balanchine represented. Robbins gave the names of eight individuals involved in party activities, including Jerome Chodorow, whose award-winning musical *Wonderful Town* had been a major hit on Broadway that season; Robbins had actually served as its "play doctor" in Boston. Ironically, ten days after his testimony, the New York City Ballet premiered a Robbins masterpiece, *Afternoon of a Faun,* to Debussy's score, a tender study of ballet narcissism seen through the eyes of man and woman gazing into a studio mirror, with none of the troubled eroticism of Nijinsky's faun aroused at a glade.

·   ·   ·

"Chief problem," Leonard Bernstein wrote in his 1956 journal: "To tread the fine line between opera and Broadway, between realism and poetry, ballet and 'just dancing,' abstract and representational." With *West Side Story* (1958), Robbins and Bernstein discovered the perfect American subculture through which to theatricalize the alienation of the decade, bringing together show business and art, innocence and tragedy, angry hooliganism and social commentary in nearly perfect equilibrium. Conceived, choreographed, and directed by Jerome Robbins, *West Side Story* shifted Shakespeare's *Romeo and Juliet* from Verona to New York's Hell's Kitchen and the gang struggles between the Sharks and the Jets—the Puerto Rican and "white" juvenile delinquents of sentimental liberalism. At age forty and at the height of his career, he left City Ballet to choreograph and direct the ultimate Broadway musical, *Gypsy,* and launch a new sixteen-member ballet company of his own, Ballets U.S.A., at the Festival of the Two Worlds in Spoleto, Italy. Cool and restless American teen-agers in *N.Y. Export: Opus Jazz*

(1959) created the greatest sensation of any American ballet to visit Europe until the Dance Theatre of Harlem nearly a decade later. A seminal study in relationships and psychological alienation, *Moves,* assembled that same year, was danced in a silence broken only by "the skid and thud of dancers, the rustle and cough of audiences, and the quite dangerous obligato of thought," Clive Barnes noted after City Ballet's 1984 revival of the work.

But within only a few years the social climate that gave Robbins's jazz ballets their moral and aesthetic power—"the bravado that he discovered in youth," as Marcia Siegel has written, "the fear of involvement and the desperate need for conformity, the surplus energy that finds its outlet in skittish sexual attractions and athletic displays"—began to wear slightly thin. By 1961 the inauguration of John F. Kennedy and the emergence of a confident youth culture signaled the end of the defiant, nerve-racked 1950s underground. A Ballets U.S.A. season on Broadway flopped—"show biz," scoffed *The New York Times*—and a subsequent tour of the company collapsed in Pittsburgh. But success continued to shadow the choreographer. He won an Oscar for "brilliant achievements in the art of choreography on film" for *West Side Story,* and in 1964 he paid nostalgic tribute to his Russian-Jewish heritage in *Fiddler on the Roof* on Broadway. In 1965 Robbins returned to Ballet Theatre to choreograph a triumphant *Les Noces* to Stravinsky's score, pitting the barbarism of a primitive wedding against the needs of the individual for privacy and personal freedom.

At the same time, however, a number of major theater projects failed to get off the ground. Once again Robbins grew restless, weary of the cutthroat commercial world, money hassles, and fights with producers over rehearsal time. "He was at a point in his career," one associate claims, "in which he needed a new direction." In 1966 Robbins obtained a $300,000 grant from the National Endowment for the Arts to create the American Theater Laboratory, a resident company devoted to the development of collaborative theater in a nurturing environment. Moving

Allegra Kent and Peter Martins in Jerome Robbins's *Afternoon of a Faun*. (© 1983 Martha Swope)

his base of operations downtown to West Nineteenth Street, Robbins spent the next eighteen months working with young actors who could sing, dance, write, and play musical instruments—on everything from Shakespeare to the Japanese tea ceremony to the Kennedy assassination performed as Noh drama. Under Robbins's total control the projects saw a constant stream of new personnel, who would sometimes find their work dropped without explanation. Although Robbins claimed he was working harder than at any time in his life, the problems at ATL—according to several people who worked there—stemmed largely from the director's lack of sensitivity or feeling for collaboration. Not a single public performance resulted.

Then, one day in 1968, Robbins dropped by the offices of the New York City Ballet, where he was casually invited to contribute a new ballet for a coming gala. Robbins set to work on a pas de deux for Patricia McBride and Edward Villella, choreographed to piano music by Chopin. He soon added another couple, then made a pas de six; tours interrupted the rehearsal process, and then there were ten dancers in all. Urged on by Balanchine, who told him to make it "like eating peanuts," Robbins persisted for months on a chain of loosely connected dances that became *Dances at a Gathering* (1969), his first work for the New York City Ballet in thirteen years, and the true discovery of his new direction.

Danced against a broad sky, as if on some quiet meadow, *Dances at a Gathering* captured a uniquely American kind of romantic naturalism, blending classical ballet and character dancing in conscious revolt against what he now considered the faddism of current experimentation. "Why does everything have to be so alienated?" the fifty-year-old former wunderkind asked one interviewer at the time. Robbins's old acuity of characterization and dramatic interaction remained but mixed with a guileless fundamentalism that Edwin Denby described as all part of "the fabric of the music's time. . . . The variety and freshness of invention, the range of feeling, and the irresistibly beautiful music which the dance lets you hear distinctly [is] its mystery too." Robbins had finally learned a secret capable of dissolving the immanent conflicts and anxieties of the real world within the larger purity of the realm of art: "The dancers are themselves," he said simply, "dancing with each other to that music in that space." Robbins would return to the music of Chopin for a second ballet, *In the Night,* and later for *Other Dances,* an eighteen-minute ballet now in the repertories of the New York City Ballet, American Ballet Theatre, and other major companies.

Aired on *Dance in America* in 1980, this small masterpiece was specially crafted for the talent, temperament, and rapport of its original dancers, Mikhail Baryshnikov and Natalia Makarova. Robbins worked very quickly in assembling the dance, drawing on imagery from nineteenth-century photographs, from Isadora Duncan, and from Russian character dancing, mazurkas, and waltzes—even making a small joke about the Kirov Ballet's unspotted turns, with Baryshnikov staggering as if dizzy for a moment. But principally the dancing ebbs and flows through its music, revealing two human beings emotionally unshadowed, and reaffirming the bond between the theater and life. Makarova considers *Other Dances* her most successful work with Baryshnikov, and Robbins the most romantic of all neoclassical choreographers: "In *Other Dances,* the body seems to be weaving a shawl of Valenciennes lace," she has written; "the choreographic design is the fabric of the lace, and the space between the threads is filled with the pauses, the hesitations, the subtle nuances, that fine understatement of movement that for me is the most precious feature of the romantic—and, for that matter, of any ballet."

The values that Robbins celebrates in *Other Dances* reflect a laying aside of the turbulence and extremities of youth for an inspired musical craftsmanship. His numerous neoclassical works have been called "the warm side" of the City Ballet repertory, encompassing a world larger and richer than any American choreographer's in the ballet field. Robbins's maturity has become the expression of values that draw upon special qualities of American life but are finally removed from them—distillations of the civility and grace and purpose reserved for the highest reaches of cultural endeavor. He has often spoken of returning to Broadway with an original work, but the right project has not come along since 1966. The New York City Ballet has proved work enough to stir the kind of theater blood that only America could have produced, and a ballet master Robbins will, in all likelihood, remain.

"During this period," he once remarked, "people have constantly asked me when I was going to work in the theater again. I always find this curious, because there, I feel, is where I have always been working."

·   ·   ·

The most talented younger choreographer to emerge from inside the company in its first thirty-five years, Peter Martins has become the central figure in City Ballet's present and future life. As co-ballet master in chief, he oversees the company on a daily basis; as preserver of Balanchine's ballets, he keeps the current repertory fresh and helps with the restaging of older works; and as choreographer, he explores the company's

Natalia Makarova in *Other Dances* (© 1979 Martha Swope)

range of styles and musical preferences, demonstrating genuine choreographic inspiration—perhaps the rarest gift in all the performing arts. Yet Peter Martins's rise to preeminence, beginning in a century-old European tradition, proceeded through years of struggle and reeducation before culminating in a legacy that must sustain City Ballet in its post-Balanchine years.

Martins's career began with the Royal Danish Ballet in Copenhagen, where a distinct national style evolved through the work of Auguste Bournonville, who took over the shambles of the national company from his own father during the mid-nineteenth century. Influenced by the great French dancer Auguste Vestris, Bournonville's technique was exceptionally light, warm, and pure, requiring unusual elevation and strength to master its sailing leaps, supple beats of the leg, and flashing footwork. Embodying the Arcadian blitheness of the Danish people themselves, the Royal Danish Ballet today keeps alive a dozen full-evening ballets and portions of numerous other Bournonville works as the only

substantial repertory of dances with roots directly in the romantic era.

Balanchine always expressed great sympathy with the Danish style, admiring Bournonville's ability to "entertain with steps"—the love of speed, the fierce lyricism and prodigal range. As a young dancer with the Royal Danish, Martins had created a sensation in Balanchine's *Apollo,* dancing with an aristocratic elegance ideally suited to the title role. In August 1967, with City Ballet in Europe, Balanchine needed a quick replacement for the injured Jacques d'Amboise, and Martins flew to Edinburgh, slightly miffed at having to audition for what is still considered his greatest role. His reception there was the first of many rude awakenings: Suzanne Farrell reportedly took one look at her new partner, turned to Balanchine, and said, "Well, at least he's tall"; later the ballet master told him he was doing the dance all wrong. With coaching, Martins's debut with the company proved successful, and a few months later he was in New York City, appearing as a guest artist for a few seasons before

Dance in America's "Bournonville Dances," performed by the New York City Ballet in 1983, offered a series of divertissements—long stretches of pure dance entertainment—from a number of full-evening Bournonville masterpieces, including the Italian *Napoli* (1842), and pas de deux from *The Kermesse in Bruges* (1851) and *Flower Festival at Genzano* (1858). (© 1983 Don Perdue)

joining the company in 1970. His masculine bearing and exceptional clarity of style proved an ideal counterweight to Farrell's majestic, unpredictable daring—but unfortunately the ballerina left the company soon after his arrival to join Maurice Béjart in London, not to return until 1975. Although his immediate reason for being in New York had vanished, Martins still had every reason to expect a bright future with the company. His confidence and cool self-possession was soon interpreted—perhaps not incorrectly—as arrogance.

Over the next few years, Martins appeared in a number of established classical and neoclassical roles, performing with a cool, almost glacial reserve that seemed out of place in a company emphasizing energy and quickness of attack. Rehearsing a revival of *Theme and Variations*, Balanchine asked Martins to do little more than kneel and run around the stage—the first time in his career that anyone had asked him not to perform dance steps; after devoting the second day of rehearsals "to ridiculing my stiffness, formality, lack of expression, and general clumsiness," Martins has written in his biography, *Far from Denmark,* the ballet master removed him from the dance. Robbins continued to welcome him into new works, but Balanchine declined—especially after Martins began regularly skipping company class. "It's not a preparation for you to go onstage," Martins had said, explaining his early dislike. "If you go in expecting a class that will spoon-feed each muscle what it needs, like a massage, so that you are ready after a forty-five-minute barre to do the perfect double *tour,* landing in absolute fifth position—well, that's not what his classes are about. But that is what a dancer needs, right? And that is how I was brought up and became better and better, through classes like that. . . . [But] Balanchine was there to experiment, to break all those goddamn rules." Unwilling to surrender a conventional idea of correctness, Martins had yet to realize that dancing could be approached as a creative act, rather than simply an exercise in classical perfection.

With his career going nowhere, Martins found himself sitting in a restaurant booth one afternoon, pen in hand, gazing down at a contract with American Ballet Theatre, where stars of his magnitude were appreciated. But something made him hesitate at the final moment, and he impulsively declined to sign. Not long afterward, in a private meeting that proved to be the turning point of his career, Martins learned that Balanchine had assumed he was uninterested in the work of the company. No, Martins protested, he was very interested; and so the choreographer cast him in the new *Tchaikovsky Suite No. 3,* with Karin von Aroldingen. In rehearsal Martins was told to perform a certain run that made him look ridiculous. Everyone laughed, Martins was mortified, and the next day Balanchine dropped him from the ballet. Fed up, Martins approached Kirstein, who advised him to be patient—Balanchine had great plans ahead. Within a month, preparing the first Stravinsky Festival in 1972, the ballet master choreographed two of his most difficult modernist works, *Stravinsky Violin Concerto* and *Duo Concertant,* especially for his unhappy *danseur noble.* In his first collaboration with Balanchine, Martins proved his willingness to be remade in the City Ballet mold.

"When he choreographed *Violin Concerto,*" Martins has written, "I still had the tendency to make everything look 'beautiful.' Mr. B would deliberately make everything look 'ugly.' He would make me turn in. When he would do a crazy movement, I would be a little embarrassed and laugh. But Mr. B would say, 'That's it! *Do that!*' " With his compulsion only to be beautiful dispelled, Peter Martins would develop into the quintessential Balanchine male dancer, appearing in some fifty-eight different roles throughout the repertory over the next fifteen years, lending his measured intelligence and antiromantic attitude to Balanchine's invention in an extraordinary range of work. Indeed, Martins would create a new image of the male classicist in America, dancing with a clear, down-to-earth elegance neither overwhelmingly athletic nor narcissistic—enlivening the unforced naturalness of the Danish style with a willingness to experiment that seemed quintessentially American.

Martins might never have begun to choreograph except for an unfortunate problem that unexpectedly developed during a New York City Ballet Orchestra strike in 1976. A friend was unable to complete a new ballet in time for the Brooklyn performances of a small chamber group Martins had organized; there was only a week or ten days to arrange a dance to what Martins later described as "ugly and fascinating and quirky and funny" songs by the American composer Charles Ives, and he would have to do it himself. He was almost unable to move on his first day alone in the studio; but finally a few steps began to come. Continuing to develop the piece with dancer Daniel Duell, *Calcium Light Night*—named after the lamp placed on an empty stage after the close of an evening's performance—premiered successfully in Brooklyn; work later resumed with the addition of ballerina Heather Watts.

A superbly rational man who had once considered becoming an architect, Martins found himself becoming obsessed with the developing structure of the ballet—how it might begin, then proceed *rationally.* Drawing on his musical train-

Peter Martins at work on his first ballet, *Calcium Light Night,* with Heather Watts and Daniel Duell. (© 1978 Lois Greenfield)

ing at the Royal Danish Academy, Martins displayed an unmistakable feel for the Ives score, tracing its disjointed dreamy fragments with deft, laconic wit. Heather Watts's bizarre, angular, flexing march around the undressed stage, lit from above in performance by a square of neon tubing, and her scribbling pas de deux with Duell (and later Ib Andersen, a fellow Dane who performed the dance for television) seemed reminiscent of Balanchine in his modernist vein, yet smuggled in something that felt like Martins's own budding particularities. *Calcium* suggested the instinctive grasp of a future choreographer.

"I hear you did something, dear," Balanchine had said after the Brooklyn experiment. "Can I see?"

After what Martins described as "a fit of mild terror," Duell and Watts performed the dance for Balanchine in a studio at the State Theater. "You know, wonderful," Balanchine said, and *Calcium Light Night*—Martins's "statement of my perception of American manners and

American character"—entered the repertory of the New York City Ballet.

Martins followed with a pas de deux to Rossini ("as far away from the dissonance and oddities of Ives as I could get"), with Balanchine contributing its final passages; he next collaborated with the ballet master on a *pas de basque* for the ill-fated *Tricolore,* one of City Ballet's few unmitigated disasters. Then, in June 1979, Balanchine hinted that Martins might "listen to Scarlatti." Begun as a kind of intellectual exercise to challenge his range, *Sonate di Scarlatti* ended as a sunny, exuberant divertissement unfairly dismissed by some critics as "imitation Balanchine." Nevertheless Martins had exhibited a remarkably mature sense of procedure and an inventive command over the combination of steps that clearly marked him as the best young choreographer in Balanchine's stable.

Martins had never been entirely happy as a performer and was soon ready to stop dancing altogether, but Balanchine discouraged him, saying that performing would help his work. Along with advice, the ballet master offered musical scores and suggestions for eleven new works in all, then left him alone to proceed with methodical fluency through a range of styles. Martins choreographed Carl Nielsen's fifteen-minute *Lille Suite* in only ten days, finishing in time for the company's visit to his homeland in 1980. His first ballet to Stravinsky, *Eight Easy Pieces,* ought to be danced *en travesti* by three boys, Balanchine told him, but Martins resisted, assembling a dance for three young girls instead, later aired on an all-Martins program for *Dance in America* in 1983. Working with Stravinsky's much more difficult *Histoire du Soldat,* Martins handled the music's extreme rhythmic variety and compression with growing assurance. Nevertheless, Balanchine suggested that he think about making his ballets simpler, and Martins responded with two new works for the Tchaikovsky Festival in June 1981: In *Symphony No. 1,* he demonstrated an unsentimental yet convincing romantic sensibility, re-creating the composer's "Winter Dreams" as a vision of "vastness, sharp clean air." Cool, even cerebral, reminiscent of Balanchine, Bournonville, and Robbins in their formal virtues, displaying a deepening trust in the classical vocabulary, Martins's ballets were beginning to draw on the strengths of their dancers, mirroring the structure of the music in what the choreographer considers an act of blind faith: "I come to think that good ballet is made up of ninety percent music and ten percent dancing."

By the early 1980s it had become clear that "the apprenticeship Balanchine was conducting," critic Robert Garis argues, "wasn't really in choreography as an end in itself; it was in choreography essential to another role, that of ballet master and coordinator of a ballet company." In 1981 the master asked Martins to assemble a story ballet, *The Magic Flute,* to music by Riccardo Drigo, for advanced students at SAB. It was a work Balanchine had danced as a young man and long hoped to rechoreograph himself. The request was nothing less than an invitation for Martins to share in his Imperial Ballet past.

Heather Watts and Ib Andersen in Martins's *Calcium Light Night.* "The music is cracked, and so is the choreography and the world this dance describes," the choreographer has written. "It is some place full of lunacy, an acrobatic lunacy." (© 1985 Don Perdue)

"I had the score played," Martins recalls. "It didn't mean much. The plot was outlined in the score, but it was up to me to decide who the characters were, what they looked like. I could see that this ballet was supposed to be funny. And I began to have doubts. I went back to Mr. B. . . . And he said, 'Oh, dear, just *do.* If you do this, you can do anything.' " With its skillful use of character, plot, mime, and storytelling, buoyed by Balanchine's numerous suggestions and its own lighthearted comedy, Martins's joyous *Magic Flute* entered the repertory of City Ballet, with the choreographer's name appearing for the first time on the program's list of ballet masters.

Katrina Killian in Peter Martins's *The Magic Flute*. (© 1982 Martha Swope)

For the 1982 Stravinsky Festival, Martins was ready to traverse the distance Balanchine himself had covered in his journey from the Imperial Ballet. In addition to Stravinsky's "very American" *Piano Rag Music*—which Martins transformed into "a little Las Vegas number, with four boys and a girl"—Balanchine handed him a major score, *Concerto for Two Solo Pianos,* that he had always meant to do himself but had never had time for. "At first I was intimidated by the music," Martins later told *Dance in America* audiences. "This was no *Eight Easy Pieces,* that much was clear—this is a very complex score. Stravinsky called it 'symphonic' in its volume and scale. . . . Eventually I fell in love with this music. What I heard in it was passion, which I thought was unusual for Stravinsky." Working with

Balanchine's guidance for the last time, Peter Martins created his finest work for the stage.

On March 3, 1983, with Balanchine gravely ill at Roosevelt Hospital in Manhattan, Robbins and Martins were named co–ballet masters in chief of the New York City Ballet. By November, with ten works in the company's permanent repertory, Martins announced "with some sadness" his retirement from the stage, dancing in the company's one-thousandth performance of *The Nutcracker* on December 6, with Farrell as the Sugar Plum Fairy and Jerome Robbins as the mysterious toy maker, Drosselmeyer. "I'm too vain to dance badly," he explained, "too professional to direct poorly. One or the other would have to suffer for it. . . . I feel my performing career is not as important as the New York City Ballet."

. . .

Embodying an institutional vision of continuity within change previously unknown in the American arts, the New York City Ballet has established a system of human relations that survived the passage of its creator. "In our case there will be no 'replacement,' " Lincoln Kirstein has written; yet City Ballet dancers have continued beyond Balanchine's death to transcend the apparent limits of nature and individual temperament as instruments of a choreographer's craft. The greatest pleasure City Ballet affords is this pageant of change from evening to evening and season to season, as dancers usher repertory into the present and future, offering a range of expressive beauty unequaled, arguably, by any theater in the world.

It is "a mandarin illusion," as Kirstein once admitted, "But for the duration of the performance . . . a glimpse of an earthly paradise."

AMERICAN BALLET THEATRE

· THE MOONLIT ATMOSPHERE OF ·
LOVE AND DEATH

Ballet dancing first infiltrated the popular theater in the mid-nineteenth century, but ballet itself remained apart for decades, sustaining an aura of highbrow culture and snobbery that continued either to repulse or to magnetize the American public. One early beneficiary of impresario Sol Hurok's assertion that "Americans want their champagne French and their ballets Russian" was the ebullient and often difficult Mikhail Mordkin, a former premier danseur and ballet master with the Bolshoi in Moscow and partner of Pavlova at her Met debut. Mordkin had moved to America for good in 1924, establishing the "All-American" Mordkin Ballet thirteen years later, with financial assistance from one of his students, the dancer and New England heiress Lucia Chase. As the ambitions of his patron grew, he was gradually shunted aside and his company used as the basis for an entirely new approach to ballet as an American art. From its very first season in 1940, the new company demonstrated that Americans could indeed create "grand" ballet, and on a scale bolder than anywhere else in the world.

Unlike the future New York City Ballet, or for that matter the old imperial companies in Russia, the young Ballet Theatre grew like Topsy, with no single artist to guide her progress: Eliminating the role of company choreographer for the first time, Ballet Theatre announced its in-tention to present "the best that is traditional, the best that is contemporary, and, inevitably, the best that is controversial." Like the Ballets Russes in its later years, Ballet Theatre did not impart a unified style of dancing but rather hired the best dancers and brightest stars it could find—including a number of celebrated Russian and English artists—to fill its varied repertory. Eleven choreographers staged work independently, in separate wings created for classical, Russian, English, Spanish, American, and "Negro" dancing. Agnes de Mille's experimental *Black Ritual* would feature an all-black cast and Massine, Nijinska, Fokine, and Adolph Bolm would mount old and new ballets, as the idea of a dance gallery offering three or four separate works an evening seemed congenial to the development of an American tradition appealing to all tastes.

Thirty-two choreographers contributed seventy-eight works to the repertory of what swiftly became the dominant American company of the 1940s. Unburdened by the memory of a single native tradition, choreographers responded to the influences of the past and present in unique ways, absorbing ideas from Russia, France, Hollywood, Broadway, and modern dance companies; such eclecticism seemed inseparable from the company's attempt to take the measure of an American classicism. Scaled-down versions of the standard Russian classics

Martine van Hamel and Patrick Bissell in Petipa's *Paquita,* danced by American Ballet Theatre. (© 1984 Martha Swope)

necessarily played a major role: For commercial reasons alone, Hurok was obliged to bill the company as THE GREATEST IN RUSSIAN BALLET, satisfying the hunger of American audiences for the glories of the czar and the marvels of Diaghilev. When Michel Fokine restaged *Les Sylphides* for Ballet Theatre's first season, his experience suggested that American dancers clearly meant to leave their own mark on the romantic-classical tradition. Walter Terry recounts the story of a young Ballet Theatre soloist who insisted on leaping too high for the music.

"You're a sylph," Fokine pleaded. "You must be light."

Growing more and more exasperated, Karen Conrad finally placed both hands on her hips and announced, "I'm sorry, Mr. Fokine, but this is the way Philadelphia sylphs jump." Conrad's soaring *grand jetés* drew gasps from the opening night audience, and *Les Sylphides*—with its corps as "unified as the Rockettes"—received twenty-five curtain calls.

Ballet Theatre became one of the major American showcases for the world's ballet stars of the 1940s—among them ballerinas Alicia Alonso, Alicia Markova, Nora Kaye, and Nana Gollner, and the male *danseurs* Igor Youskevitch, Anton Dolin, and André Eglevsky. But even as Ballet Theatre shed new light on the romantic

Terry Orr in American Ballet Theatre's 1976 production of *Billy the Kid,* for *Dance in America*. (© 1984 Martha Swope)

past, something else in the American character shrank before the evocation of a fantastic landscape of fairies and sylphs. Many audiences were uncomfortable with the decorativeness, the implausibility, and the sometimes spurious pathos of the romantic-classical tradition. Ballet Theatre soon became the stronghold of a new kind of dance-theater realism, inspired in part by experiments in modern dance, by the naturalism of the American theater, and by an unabashed engagement with the historical experience of the nation.

Eugene Loring's *Billy the Kid,* the best-known work created especially for Lincoln Kirstein's Ballet Caravan, was revived by Ballet Theatre in its second season as the archetypal triumph of early American ballet. Through the use of dance montage, dreamy flashbacks, and sudden shifts in scene, *Billy* suggested the cinematic energy of quick-cutting action Westerns: In the ballet's opening sequence dancers appear to be trudging across an open prairie, cracking whips, pulling at horses' reins, and scanning the horizon in an image of Western expansion. A

The original cast of *Pillar of Fire* at Ballet Theatre (right to left): Hugh Laing, Nora Kaye, Lucia Chase, Antony Tudor, and Annabelle Lyons. Classicism achieved a more profound psychological expression through Tudor's insistence that dance could be a medium of modern drama. (Courtesy Performing Arts Research Center, The New York Public Library)

brawl erupts in a dusty border town, leading to the accidental death of Billy's mother. The six-year-old future desperado kills the assassin in turn, and for the rest of his short life sees the face of the murderer—originally named "Nemesis" and now known as "Alias"—in each of his enemies and victims. Spurred on by this spectral figure, Billy becomes killer and victim, antihero and hero gunned down in a finish echoing both the myth of the movie Western and Lincoln Kirstein's view of the civilizing power of ballet as an art: the

triumph of law and order over the chaotic brutality of the frontier.

Although Ballet Theatre presented original works by a number of American choreographers, the pioneering ballets of an Englishman, Antony Tudor, most firmly established the company's emerging dramatic character. Agnes de Mille once called him the first choreographer to dress his dancers like his own father and mother: Tudor assembled dances in a psychological landscape never before imagined for the ballet stage, creating full-blooded characters with vivid motivations and complex inner lives. Transforming Fokine's notion of ballet as "an imitation of life" into a tool for interpreting the human psyche, Tudor would contribute eight essential works to Ballet Theatre in the 1940s, fashioning the most deeply imagined dance-theater repertory in American ballet.

Arguably Tudor's greatest dance and his first in America, *Pillar of Fire* (1942) tells the story of a passionate young woman named Hagar, unable to compete with her pretty younger sister, frightened and on the verge of spinsterhood. Surrendering herself in desperation to a debauched young man, Hagar is cast out by family and community, only to be redeemed by the selfless love of a man known as the Friend. *Pillar* is set in the year 1900, but with no specific locale; nevertheless, for American audiences, the Puritanical darkness of provincial New England is almost palpable. With an expressionist urgency more often associated with modern dance, Tudor was able to define unique movement qualities for each individual character; choreographed to Arnold Schönberg's tempestuous *Verklärte Nacht, Pillar* moves through an academic vocabulary of steps in a seamless choreographic design—and yet the formal, understated movement seems to spring almost unbidden from the vivid inner reality of Hagar herself. In showing how psychological need can disrupt and distort the natural flow of academic ballet without sacrificing its intrinsic musicality and line, Tudor discovered a new landscape of expressive classicism for future American ballet choreographers from Jerome Robbins to Eliot Feld and beyond.

Ballet Theatre had become a place for serious artistic exploration—and yet many of its dancers were not that far away from the Broadway chorus line. With the general shortage of dancers and choreographers throughout the American theater, the commercial stage often raided the ballet world and vice versa; many of the best choreographers learned to exploit the frank, spontaneous affability and untroubled ease of dancers in the popular theater. The major American-born talent that Ballet Theatre would nurture during its early years was a street-smart twenty-six-year-old soloist and former chorus boy who began putting movement together with a few friends at a Borscht Belt summer camp in the Poconos, outside New York City, in 1943. Jerome Robbins had been longing to dance something *American,* and eight months later Ballet Theatre had a staggering hit on its hands. Sol Hurok dropped his Russophilia to run *Fancy Free* every night for two weeks of an extended Metropolitan Opera House season.

The story of three innocent sailors on a hot summer night's shore leave gathering in a bar to pick up girls, *Fancy Free* had an immediate impact that Americans had never before associated with the ballet: Sailors and soldiers by the thousands were leaving New York City for the war in Europe, and Robbins had studied their movements in bars from Fire Island to Times Square. "The Russians used their folk dancing," he shrugged. "I used ours." With a nervous, syncopated jazz score by the young Leonard Bernstein, Robbins successfully captured a genuinely American jazz-based swagger and displayed a sixth sense for characterization with the breezy energy and verve of a Broadway musical. Agnes de Mille called *Fancy Free* the first ballet to get not just laughs, but *belly* laughs; just as important, its popular success meant that ballet at last established itself as a medium through which an American choreographer might say something directly about the contemporary world.

The company's early identification with dance-dramas by Tudor, Robbins, Agnes de Mille, and others left no area of American ballet entirely slighted. A choreographer who had turned down an invitation to join the company at its inception, George Balanchine assembled his great *Theme and Variations* (known today as *Tchaikovsky Suite No. 3*) especially for Ballet Theatre in 1947. Ballet Theatre welcomed works from other emerging neoclassical traditions as well: As a kind of souvenir from its first European engagement at Covent Garden in 1947, the company acquired *Les Patineurs (The Skaters),* Sir Frederick Ashton's celebration of the recently

The hilarious dance competition from Jerome Robbins's *Fancy Free,* featuring Jean-Pierre Frolich, with Mikhail Baryshnikov and Peter Martins seated behind. Emerging from an essentially balletic idiom, its stylized rumbas and "boogies" flow with extraordinary naturalness from the rhythmic complications of Leonard Bernstein's symphonic jazz score. (© 1979 Paul Kolnik)

discovered elegance, wit, and good manners of a British-style classicism. Presented by ABT on *Dance in America* along with *Billy the Kid, Les Patineurs* creates a radically different impression with its suave classical figures and gracious waltzes composed by Giacomo Meyerbeer; the ballet represents Ashton's successful attempt to nurture the virtuosity and élan of British dancers new to classical style. Four couples glide on stage as the ballet opens—the men in nineteenth-century top hats and tails, the women in long red dresses—moving in and out of deep arabesques as if traveling across imaginary ice. "Slippery ice/is paradise/for dancers, if their feet

Karena Block and Fernando Bujones in *Dance in America*'s presentation of *Les Patineurs* by Sir Frederick Ashton. (© 1984 Martha Swope) are wise," wrote Nietzsche, and, in this study of human variety colored from a provincial English palette, Ashton made brilliant use of a simple metaphor—reportedly assembling the ballet around ice-skating figures without ever having observed the sport himself.

In the forty-five years since its founding, American Ballet Theatre—renamed for a 1957 State Department tour—has continued to explore across continents and centuries, presenting works by choreographers ranging from Dauberval, born in France in 1742, to Twyla Tharp, born in Portland, Indiana three centuries later. In recent years modern ballets by Alvin Ailey, John Butler, Lar Lubovitch, and especially Glenn Tetley have extended the company's traditional eclecticism to embrace the brash, kinetic spirit of the contemporary age. ABT does not present a coherent style, like the New York City Ballet; rather its diversity suggests a different direction for the future of American ballet: its continued growth as an international forum, expanding across a number of styles and traditions. Historically Ballet Theatre has shown Americans dramatic images of themselves as a nation and reflected on the world at large; a portion of the company has sought a psychological truthfulness seldom associated with ballet, while the rest emphasized the grandeur of the nineteenth century and a range of modern, neoclassical styles from both sides of the Atlantic. Producing repertory on a scale comparable to the nation's most prestigious opera and theater groups, ABT has become the great American ballet company, reflecting the entire spectrum of ballet in the West.

Nevertheless, for many Americans, classical ballet has remained something beyond America—simply because its most fervent artistry continues to emanate from the Old World. The full-evening Russian-style classics have come to dominate most American repertories that can afford them, bringing together glorious orchestral music, lavish costumes, and decor, and virtuosic dancing in major theatrical events. With spectacle "the dominant mode of American cultural expression," as Christopher Lasch has suggested, American Ballet Theatre has become an expression of empire—as ballet was during the age of Louis XIV and the time of the Russian czars.

·   ·   ·

Downtown Boston. The Metropolitan Center, a dark rococo music hall recently enlarged for opera, theater, and dance, and nearly completed for the cultural preferment of the city. Unfinished construction everywhere behind the basilica: a vast wall of bricks rising across a sea of mud, rubble, and pulverized sidewalks where police barricades check the advance of unwanted strangers from the Tenderloin. Inside the Metropolitan Center, on the cavernous main stage, a huge cast is racing through a rehearsal of Kenneth MacMillan's *Concerto,* a grueling neoclassical exercise danced to a thunderous Shostakovich score. *Concerto's* intricate pattern building requires clarity and correctness, a firm sense of pacing, and an even mind. Shadowed upstage by dancers from the second and third casts, the soloists are angry, petulant, pumping adrenaline to force themselves through to the finish. *Concerto* takes *guts.* Young Susan Jaffe, still learning the most bravura solo, careens around the edge of the stage like a jet-propelled zephyr, with great circular spins and air-splitting leaps, her eyelids fluttering, as if some magnificent force has taken hold of her body and refuses to set her down. Shouts from the wings: "Go, Susan!" She finishes, embarrassed, staggering slightly against one of the flats. The other dancers applaud.

In addition to *Concerto,* the company's weeklong Boston appearance will include divertissements from Marius Petipa's *Raymonda* and *Le Corsaire,* an Auguste Bournonville pas de trois and a pas de deux from his *Flower Festival at Genzano,* Ashton's *Les Rendezvous, Fancy Free, Billy the Kid, Configurations*—a neoclassical work by the Washington-based choreographer Choo San Goh—and *Airs* by modern dance choreographer Paul Taylor.

But for its opening night gala, ABT has chosen to present a nineteenth-century Russian masterwork that continues to haunt the imagination of Americans: *Swan Lake* is quintessential

Company class at American Ballet Theatre. "I have no idea how the spirit of the company is, I'm usually too busy to notice," says Susan Jaffe, one of Baryshnikov's leading ballerinas. (© 1982 Jack Vartoogian)

ballet, bathing audiences in a moonlit atmosphere of love and death, weaving together the rational and the irrational, the earthly and the ethereal, into a myth greater than any single performance of the work can ever be. At least a portion of its four acts is performed by virtually every major classical troupe in the world; its vi-sion of innocence, betrayal, and reality transformed has become an essential element of the ballet's imagination of itself—almost a celebration of its purest memories. Even Balanchine restaged its second act in 1951, more "as a treasured experience of style," Edwin Denby noted, "than a question of steps," restructuring the choreography to locate the essence of the ballet in Tchaikovsky's music.

From its founding Ballet Theatre nurtured its own tradition of performances, presenting a one-act version of *Swan Lake* based on Anton Dolin's restaging of his earlier version for Diaghilev. Twenty-five years later, the popular success of a complete restaging of this second act, based on the Royal Ballet's version, prompted artistic codirector Lucia Chase to decide that the time had arrived for ABT to enter the ranks of the world's great ballet companies with its first full-evening classical production. Leningrad's Kirov Ballet—the Soviet descendant of the old imperial company in St. Petersburg—and the Bolshoi from Moscow had recently toured the West, presenting full-evening versions of *Swan Lake* that stimulated a host of new interpretations throughout Europe. Rudolf Nureyev's dark and troubled adaptation received an unprecedented *seventy-eight* curtain calls at its Vienna premiere. In England, the Royal Ballet continued to present a version originally staged in the mid-1930s by one Nicolai Sergeyev, a former regisseur in charge of maintaining ballets during the last years of Petipa's tenure and until the time of the Revolution. Sergeyev had fled Russia with thirty manuscripts documenting works of the Imperial Ballet in Stepanov notation, including the steps and floor plans for twenty-three separate dances within *Swan Lake,* without a parallel musical score or notation for the upper body. Sergeyev's restaging of *Swan Lake* premiered in London on November 20, 1934, later touring to the United States in the late 1950s—as close to an original full-evening Russian ballet as anyone had ever seen in the United States. ABT would turn to this version as its model.

Progressive American choreographers had always looked to the past as a source of renewal, but now Lucia Chase insisted that a classical full-evening work could be transformed into an image of Russian classicism with an American stamp. Over intense in-house objections that led to the resignations of Agnes de Mille and Jerome Robbins from the company's artistic advisory committee—de Mille suggesting that the money

be spent on three new works of "artistic" interest instead—ABT's full-evening *Swan Lake* premiered in Chicago in February 1966, staged by David Blair of the Royal Ballet. When this production opened at the New York State Theater three months later, audiences and critics were ecstatic and ABT's artistic future clear: Although contemporary ballets continued to join the repertory, they were usually outshone by glittering new one-act French, Russian, and Danish dances, as well as full-evening versions of *Giselle, Raymonda,* and *The Sleeping Beauty.* With the great American ballet company raising masterworks from the crypt of the nineteenth century, the age of the ballet superspectacle was born, greeted by unsophisticated audiences, especially, with deep-throated bravos and roses flung to the stage. Ballet Theatre enjoyed a surge in popular recognition corresponding to the American dance explosion itself.

Almost immediately ABT faced the daunting prospect of transforming itself into an institution capable of satisfying a growing public's hunger for prestige ballet. As recently as 1964, ABT had performed its entire repertory with fewer than fifty dancers. *Swan Lake* required a cast of sixty—the Kirov drew its dancers from a roster four times as large. *Swan Lake* also introduced a range of styles new to the company—character dances and classical pantomime—and deepened the challenge posed by the vast lyrical panorama of enchanted swans. The unity of tone, the perfection of detail, the self-evident naturalness of a pure classical style traditionally requires a deep academic preparation. The Bolshoi Ballet in Moscow is the apex of a system of over twenty state-supported schools sharing a unified pedagogy, each drawing students from community centers and schools in their respective regions; the Vaganova School of the Leningrad Kirov has survived since the early eighteenth century. ABT, by contrast, continued to attract the vast majority of its soloists and corps from schools and academies across America, with a broad range of standards and aesthetic goals. These new ballets also seemed to require a cavalcade of great ballerinas and dan-

An all-star spectacle of the 1970s: Rudolf Nureyev, Cynthia Gregory, and Erik Bruhn in the classic *Raymonda*. (© 1975 Martha Swope)

seurs from abroad, either as guest artists or as principal company members, throughout the decade of the 1970s. The enchantment of the star capable of illuminating an entire opera house stage has always been an indispensable part of the romantic-classical tradition: International dancers of the past were already irretrievably part of Ballet Theatre's legend. But during the 1970s, ABT became the American home of virtually every available ballet star in the world: Erik Bruhn of Denmark, Anthony Dowell of Great Britain, Ivan

Nagy of Hungary, the Italian Carla Fracci, Yoko Morishita of Japan, and Marcia Haydée of Germany brought a kind of transcendent glamour and artistry essential to the new repertory. For the better part of the decade, with the company buying stars as if it were the New York Yankees, the principal question during a Ballet Theatre season was not what dances were to be performed, but what international celebrities were dancing them.

The company roster soon included Fernando Bujones, the finest American-trained male classicist, a product of the School of American Ballet; Martine van Hamel, a prodigiously gifted dancer trained on three continents; and the nation's finest native-born ballerina, Cynthia Gregory, originally from the San Francisco Ballet. And most significantly, the Russian defectors appeared: guest artist Rudolf Nureyev and principal dancers Mikhail Baryshnikov and Natalia Makarova, dancing not only the classical roles they knew from the Soviet Union but also in works from ABT's modern repertory. Ideally, such changes in style and content renew a dancer emotionally and technically, nurturing different aspects of a performer in a way that the New York City Ballet has never attempted to do. But the "new" American Ballet Theatre failed to provide its stars with much in the way of important new choreography to sustain their growth as artists. Even as ABT became the most glamorous dance company in the world, younger company choreographers such as Michael Smuin, Bruce Marks, and Dennis Nahat left to direct their own companies in San Francisco, Salt Lake City, and Cleveland, respectively. Eliot Feld, the most important new choreographer to emerge at Ballet Theatre in three decades, left within a year of his first success, reportedly declaring that he no longer wanted to play second fiddle to ballets like *Swan Lake*. Such defections only deepened ABT's commitments to the classics: The appearance of stars—preferably Russian—actually came to dominate artistic planning. For all the glamour and popularity of ABT in the 1970s, more than a few critics began to argue that America's exemplary ballet company had surrendered itself to the cultural imagination of Europe and the charisma of foreigners.

Within the company itself, these changes were unleashing dangerous forces as well: Resentment against the invasion of foreign stars grew to indignation as the decade progressed. The return of the nineteen-year-old Bujones from his gold medal–winning performance at the International Ballet Festival in Varna, Bulgaria, was eclipsed by Baryshnikov's first performances with the company in 1974; a year later, Cynthia

Fernando Bujones in *Paquita*. (© 1980 Lois Greenfield)

Gregory resigned briefly in protest after the announcement of *nine* guest stars for the coming season. The presence of outsiders limited the possibilities for company dancers to move into more prominent roles: when *Swan Lake* was presented on WNET/New York's *Great Performances* series, Natalia Makarova and Ivan Nagy danced the leading roles. More significantly, however, the mastodonic expense of the new classical ballets was slowly pushing the company to the brink of financial disaster. ABT ended years of homelessness by establishing an annual presence at the Met in 1977. With thirty-eight hundred seats to fill and a potential box office of $4 million a season, more grand ballets seemed the only suitable response. Nevertheless, a successful restaging of Petipa's full-evening *La Bayadère* contributed to a staggering $900,000 deficit that first season.

With the company in increasing disarray, Donald M. Kendall, chairman of Pepsico Corporation, came on as chairman of ABT's board of directors. Kendall invited Herman Krawitz, a former assistant manager of the Metropolitan Opera, to become the board's executive director. "A blunt man with a quick temper and a sturdy ego," according to Walter Terry, Krawitz put the company in the black in twelve months through an aggressive fund-raising campaign. With his new authority and dollar signs to back him up, Krawitz insisted that Lucia Chase and Oliver Smith, company codirectors for over three decades, make way for new blood. The man he hoped would replace them was the greatest dancer of them all, Mikhail Baryshnikov.

· · ·

Baryshnikov's Western adventure had begun during a 1974 North American tour of the Kirov Ballet, with a sprint past the KGB down a Toronto alleyway and into a waiting car. Like Rudolf Nureyev sixteen years before him, he had left family and friends behind in Russia to pursue new creative opportunities in the West; the Kirov had become "a realm of frozen beauty," its repertory limited and dancers typecast, restricted in their opportunities to perform at all. Only a relative handful of Westerners had seen Baryshnikov during his six years with the Leningrad company, but their reports scarcely prepared audiences for a dancer of unequaled purity and correctness, capable not only of staggering feats of virtuosity but also of investing familiar academic steps with fresh musicality and excitement. The highest product of a centuries-old academy, Baryshnikov was trained by the late Alexander Pushkin, the teacher of Nureyev and others, who had worked unswervingly in a tradition stretching back to the original thirteen instructors at the Royal Academy in Paris in 1671. But in America, as Arlene Croce observed, Baryshnikov became a "one-man revolution": Over the next five years, he performed great classical roles with American Ballet Theatre and contemporary ballets by Alvin Ailey, John Butler, Paul Taylor, and Twyla Tharp, among others, merging brilliant acting and unheard-of virtuosity within the larger choreographic textures of nearly every dance he attempted.

From his pinnacle of celebrity in the West, Baryshnikov suddenly stunned the dance public and thrilled balletomanes in 1978 by leaving ABT and lucrative guest appearances with other companies to dance for the New York City Ballet. There he would be just another principal dancer in an unfamiliar, quintessentially American repertory. "Dancers have to be mad and hungry," he explained. His early months at City Ballet proved difficult, but as he grew more comfortable with the speed and complexity of City Ballet's style, his respect for what Balanchine had done with the academic tradition in America deepened. "I think he deflated certain of my fantasies about myself," Baryshnikov would say. But due to injuries more than anything else, he was ready to move on.

When the offer came from ABT, he considered it coldly. At age thirty-one, he had at least another decade of performing ahead of him. He had no experience as an administrator, nor was he a choreographer who could use the company for his own creative purposes. He was, however, known for his successful ABT restagings of Ivanov's *Nutcracker* and Petipa's *Don Quixote (Kitri's Wedding),* the latter aired on *Dance in America* in 1984. With its classical ballets and eclectic repertory, Ballet Theatre had always seemed his natural home. Living in a palatial white mansion on the west bank of the Hudson with film actress Jessica Lange, who would soon give birth to their daughter, Alexandra, Baryshnikov was beginning to wish for a new kind of permanence—weary of living "from departure to departure," as his friend, the poet Joseph Brodsky, suggests. "He despises himself for being a dancer," Brodsky argues. "He considers his body a machine, something apart from himself." Baryshnikov needed another vehicle for expression.

Donald Kendall and Baryshnikov met over dinner. "I brought vodka I had flavored with peppers from my own garden," Kendall told *The New York Times,* "and we had smoked salmon from Georgia and Armenia, which Misha hadn't seen since he'd left Russia, and by three o'clock in the morning, everything was settled." Bar-

Leading by example, Baryshnikov attends and occasionally teaches the men's class at American Ballet Theatre. (© 1980 Jack Vartoogian)

yshnikov would have complete artistic control over the company, within financial guidelines determined by the board of directors. In October 1979, he resigned from City Ballet and announced that he would assume direction of American Ballet Theatre within a year's time. "I would say that Baryshnikov knows how to dance," said Balanchine. "He is intelligent and he has skill. He came and he learned. That is what he wanted."

The outcry that followed Baryshnikov's ascension to ABT's directorship cast the Russian dancer as Rasputin, contemplating his own training and repertory as the basis for transforming America's exemplary company into a second-rate version of the Kirov. His recent experience of Balanchine's brand of neoclassicism was reason enough to suspect that ABT's traditional dramatic values would be swept aside for the sake of sheer dance power. What would become of the traditional American versions of the nineteenth-century classics if they were to be brought into line with Soviet practices in the early 1970s, when Baryshnikov left Russia? And how could archetypally American ballets like *Fancy Free,* which Baryshnikov had danced a few times at City Ballet, survive without the dramatic spontaneity and daring that had characterized the company in the past? The crisis within the company worsened in ensuing months: Twenty-four weeks of bitter contract disputes over salaries, unemployment benefits, and tour per diems erupted in an October lockout that lasted two months, with dancers taking the unprecedented action of picketing outside their own studios. The issue of foreigners had taken on new heat when the most recent of the Soviet defectors, Alexander Godunov, signed a contract reportedly worth $150,000 a year—while the corps de ballet suffered on breadline wages as low as $150 a week. Although Godunov resigned in sympathy, the lockout resulted in the cancellation of a season at the Kennedy Center in Washington, D.C. The general aftermath of the settlement, which doubled salaries for some corps members, proved an uneasy one. Nevertheless, when Baryshnikov rejoined Ballet Theatre as artistic director in September 1980, he placed the memory of the strike behind him and began laying out a strategy for the company's renewal.

Cancelling the fall season, he set to work in new studios, moving from the Upper West Side of Manhattan to downtown, just above Union Square, where administrative offices and dancers shared the same complex for the first time in the company's history. Acknowledging a certain absurdity in the star system—and a dislike for demands "that smell like blackmail"—he announced that no guest artists would appear with American Ballet Theatre at all. Closing the company school, he made plans to reopen it to select scholarship students who might conceivably join the company one day and urged younger members of the corps to take dance classes together in house, rather than study with different private teachers around Manhattan, as most had done for years. Trimming the active repertory from fifty works to a more manageable thirty-two, he added no new ballets at first, choosing instead to restage portions of *Swan Lake, Giselle,* and the company's celebrated forty-year-old *Les Sylphides,* originally staged by Fokine himself. Baryshnikov wanted these dances closer to the versions he knew from the Kirov. "Since I'm running the company," he announced, "I'd like to see the dancers doing the ballets the way I think they should be done. That's why I'm here." He also instituted character dance classes to improve the mazurkas and czardas that are the traditional pride of the Kirov and important to effective productions of the full-evening classics.

Then he continued the trend toward classical and neoclassical acquisitions, gathering three new one-act fragments from the Kirov's Petipa, a pas de trois by Bournonville, Sir Frederick Ashton's *Les Rendezvous,* and two dramatic works by Balanchine, *Prodigal Son* and *La Sonnambula*—half-suggested by the choreographer himself, bringing the number of his works in the repertory to five. At the same time, Baryshnikov confirmed his interest in contemporary work, adding Paul Taylor's baroque *Airs,* reviving Twyla Tharp's *Push Comes to Shove,* and making a serious effort to gear the company toward the needs of the choreographers who worked there. By his second year, Baryshnikov had established a young choreographer's workshop, choosing six promising newcomers to work with ABT's second company, Ballet Repertory, newly upgraded from a local touring group to a kind of in-house apprenticeship program.

Baryshnikov's most controversial move, however, was in the direction of youth.

·   ·   ·

A little more than a year into Baryshnikov's tenure, over half the corps de ballet of fifty-seven dancers had joined the company within the last two years. As the first generation of Americans to grow up knowing they could perform classical ballet for a living, their average age was just eighteen; many had never danced professionally before. Trained in academies across America, drawn to work in one of the world's most varied repertories and an atmosphere of international glamour, most have discovered the ballet's ceremonies of innocence in classrooms and studios, where Baryshnikov immediately raised their level of performance through his example alone. Within months of his arrival as artistic director, the corps moved to a higher and purer technical level, and within a year seemed entirely transformed. "When they dance *Sleeping Beauty,*" he admitted, "it's like seeing Shakespeare in Russian. But the style will come."

Heralded babies like Melissa Allen and Deirdre Carberry began five months of annual touring at the age of fourteen. Brooklyn-born Nancy Raffa, Tenniel-faced, braces still on her teeth, was a gold-medal winner at the prestigious Lausanne Festival in Switzerland at the age of seventeen. Susan Jaffe, a spectacularly composed beauty, originally trained in Maryland with the mother of another brilliant ABT juvenile, Peter Fonseca. Cheryl Yeager, for four years a corps member until elevated to soloist, danced Pavlova's role in *Les Sylphides* during the company's first performances under its new director. Robert La Fosse, Christine Spizzo, and Lise Houlton also emerged from the corps, just as ABT's Nora Kaye, Jerome Robbins, John Kriza, and others rose in the 1940s. Cynthia Harvey, the first of the young ballerinas to receive a full-evening classical lead, read her name on the bulletin board as the replacement in *Swan Lake* for

Cheryl Yeager in *Les Sylphides*. (© 1981 Martha Swope)

an injured Natalia Makarova during the spring 1981 Metropolitan season. In her dressing room, she found a bouquet from the corps along with a note, "You are our hope!"

The slow development of classical dancers is preferable to thrusting kids into a vacuum, but in his haste to leave his mark on the company, Baryshnikov swiftly created an ensemble troupe with no room for vanity or temperament. With new dancers achieving prominence every season, and futures depending on the nature of the roles they receive, a feeling took hold among the younger dancers that hard work would get them ahead. The "new" American Ballet Theatre had youthful quickness, strength, and virtuosic daring rather than subtlety and dramatic depth; several of the company's new acquisitions—including Choo San Goh's *Configurations* and Lynn Taylor-Corbett's *Great Galloping Gottschalk*—seemed designed to display the restless, slightly hollow virtuosity of the young. "One-half of the repertory is in the arms, legs and bodies of very young dancers," Baryshnikov insisted. "They're taking roles next to leading dancers. Each year somebody else will be coming up."

Baryshnikov's children's crusade was met with passionate attacks from long-standing audiences and critics who did not appreciate watching America's most glamorous company transform itself into a vehicle for youthful ensembles and twenty-year-old ballerinas. The new emphasis on youth left many of the company's more experienced dancers disheartened, performing as seldom as once or twice a week during a season, just as in the era of guest stars. "I'm not happy," Cynthia Gregory declared. "I feel left out." Bitter anger flared among the seasoned, middle-level soloists the company so desperately lacked in the mid-1970s; more than half the soloists are now new to the company during Baryshnikov's tenure, and he has rewarded those who do as they are told. Rebellion and stylistic inconsistencies were dealt with firmly: Twelve dancers were not rehired during Baryshnikov's first year, most of them in their late twenties and early thirties; a number of others elected not to return for a second season under the new artistic director. In the studios and classrooms, the dominant influences became the new, Soviet-trained ballet master and mistresses, who pushed the company toward the grandeur and bravura of Russian-style dancing; at times it seemed a vitality encompassed entirely by its effects. "The Soviet style is definitely there, especially in the molding of the arms and head," Cynthia Gregory told the late Walter Terry. "At first I fought it, but I'm getting used to it. I think it is very good for the corps—but there is a danger of turning them into robots." Choreographer emeritus Antony Tudor, a survivor from a previous era, suggested that Ballet Theatre used to have people who happened to be dancers, but now seemed to have dancers who only happened to be people.

Exploiting its youth, denying guest artists seasonal work, American Ballet Theatre was dangerously thin at the top for several seasons, with the departure of no less than ten principal dancers in the late 1970s and early 1980s, and the addition of only four new ones: Kevin McKenzie, from the Washington Ballet; Danilo Radojevic, from Australia; Alexander Godunov, who returned for a year after the contract settlement; and Magali Messac, a French ballerina previously with the Pennsylvania Ballet. Budding superstar Patrick Bissell, a principal since the spring of 1979, and Baryshnikov's first partner in America, Gelsey Kirkland—once on the cover of *Time* magazine as America's ballet supernova—were fired the day before a performance in Washington, D.C., for being "chron-

ically late and chronically absent" from rehearsals; Bissell soon returned, as did Kirkland, temporarily, a few years later. By the spring of 1984, Baryshnikov filled the top ranks again with five young dancers who had risen through the company: Victor Barbee, Cynthia Harvey, Susan Jaffe, Robert La Fosse, and Ross Stretton.

Baryshnikov's company has remained something quite unlike a Kirov Ballet West. He has maintained Ballet Theatre's traditional quest for an American "dream" repertory, opening the studios to Jerome Robbins, Merce Cunningham, Paul Taylor, Jiri Kylian of the Netherlands Dance Theatre, and Kenneth MacMillan of the Royal Ballet whenever they choose to participate, and even revived such ABT signature works as *Pillar of Fire* and *Fancy Free*. While a search continues for a permanent company choreographer, Baryshnikov appears ready to hand over the part of the company once given to 1940s Americana to Twyla Tharp. But the fact remains that the full-evening Russian classics have become inseparable from ABT's public image and its self-image as well. Baryshnikov wants them to be the pride of the repertory—"more glamorous and classy," he says.

When he first arrived as artistic director, the fate of *Swan Lake* seemed the most problematic of all the major classics: Baryshnikov rarely danced a four-act Siegfried himself because, as he put it, he wasn't "tall enough, not attractive enough." For a while there was talk of a radical break with tradition, but the new artistic director ended up tinkering here and there with details of choreography, drama, and mood, while keeping the outline of the ballet significantly the same. When his *Swan Lake* was tested in performance on March 27, 1981, at the Kennedy Center in Washington, with Martine van Hamel and Kevin McKenzie in the leading roles, a few critics cried out that Baryshnikov had crushed the beating heart of the ballet. His response was curt. "Critics live in a very narrow world," he replied, turning the tables. "They are angry because I change things, but classics are always changing."

Since its premiere on January 15, 1895, Petipa and Lev Ivanov's *Swan Lake* has been in almost continual production somewhere in the world, troubled by the issue of authenticity even at the Kirov and Bolshoi. It has undergone vulgarization, assault, and transcendent reinterpretation; it has been staged as an abstract tone poem, a projection of lambent mood, a lyrical ode with tragic overtones, a melodramatic tragedy, an allegory of sexual power, and much more. But as an enduring work of art, the best-known ballet of the nineteenth century has remained an important means for demonstrating what Americans have made of their cultural inheritance. If *Swan Lake* remains a cultural given—even a symbol of the status quo—then it is also less an enemy of all that is honest and uncontrived than a challenge to the future.

"Like so many others," Arlene Croce has written, "I go to *Swan Lake* not to re-see a ballet but hoping to see the ballet beyond the ballet. The performance is only the occasion for meditating on what might have been. Tchaikovsky's unrealizable vision is large enough to have made what one can see of it the most fascinating ballet in the world."

·   ·   ·

Backstage fifteen minutes before curtain time, stagehands are still jostling heavy scenery back and forth across the cavernous Metropolitan Center stage, while an anonymous gaggle of swans, sweatsuits drooping beneath bristling classical tutus, paw at a dusty rosin box near the edge of the dimly lit space. More swans work silently at portable barres set up on a wooden platform above the concrete floor offstage, performing slow warm-ups that are in effect brief classes, preparing every muscle for performance. Tonight's Siegfried stands in the wings, nearly wrapped in the plush folds of a curtain, wearing an end-of-the-world look as he balances in relevé, circling his left foot slowly in the air. Baryshnikov is small—only five-seven—and powerfully built, with small features and a handsome shock of blond hair. Like all the Russians, he seems to brood through his warm-up, but perhaps he has special reason for concern: Halfway through *Swan Lake* in Minneapolis, he

injured his ankle on stage and was unable to finish. "Some days I'm not all together," he admitted. "I'm tired as they are. I'm sore. I have my physical problems. I'm one of them."

Across the Metropolitan Center stage from her Prince, ballerina Cynthia Harvey holds meditative balances on pointe, facing the closed curtain. A few days before her sixteenth birthday, in 1974, Harvey joined Ballet Theatre as an apprentice and has steadfastly studied Odette/Odile from the wings ever since. Few roles in the performing arts make greater technical and artistic demands on its interpreter: "To succeed in *Swan Lake*," Balanchine has written, "is to become overnight a ballerina." Many legendary ballerinas have left their mark on the dance, including Harvey's mentor at Ballet Theatre, Natalia Makarova, and the Russian prima ballerina assoluta Maya Plisetskaya, who danced with the Bolshoi in San Francisco when Harvey was a local teen-ager recruited to help fill the stage. Audiences and critics avidly remember these great performers of the past, their lineage reaching back to the original production: The Italian ballerina Pierina Legnani had insisted on appearing as both Odette and Odile, initiating a tradition of dual performance that has continued almost unbroken into the present day—sustaining the romantic tradition of the ballerina as both chaste, unworldly white maiden and dark seductress bent on destroying the romantic hero.

"As a person," Harvey says, "I'm more comfortable with Odette. When I'm on stage I feel I have an easier time with Odile. It's easier to hide behind flash than to hide behind subtlety." Flushed with the success of her last performance in Detroit, where Baryshnikov had returned from injury to partner her, she is worried now about her preparation: Coached by committees of ballet masters and mistresses rather than directly by an established ballerina like Makarova or Van Hamel, Harvey must make most of the important discoveries about the role alone. "There's a special terror before the performance—because of the unknown. There's a great feeling of the unknown for me." Makarova and Margot Fonteyn, who have each danced the role

Mikhail Baryshnikov with crossbow in the Royal Ballet production of *Swan Lake* in 1975. (© 1975 Martha Swope)

hundreds of times, agree. "In a sense," Rudolf Nureyev once remarked, "dancers are paid for their fear."

"Places," drawls the stage manager, pacing nervously.

A crowd of dancers, clad in the russet browns and deep burgundies of their Bruegelish peasant costumes, move suddenly from the wings on to the stage. The music rises to a crescendo then crashes down, an intimation of the coming tragedy.

The music settles into rumbling tympany as the stage manager receives a signal on his headset; he nods at two chunky stagehands clinging to a rope. Magically, the curtain rises at the Metropolitan Center on the opening act of Tchaikovsky's *Swan Lake*.

Rows of arching flats have been painted to resemble overhanging trees, and a backdrop with a turreted castle on a rocky crag many leagues across plains and mountains suggests the meadow near the castle, all designed by Oliver Smith. Peasants are hailing one another across long tables, for a celebration is in progress: It is Prince Siegfried's twenty-first birthday party, his coming of age. The Prince's friend, Benno (danced by Gregory Osborne, a company soloist since 1979), greets the first group of arriving guests—courtiers passing in promenades directly descended from pageants in Renaissance Italian courts. Siegfried's aging tutor, Wolfgang (danced by Terry Orr), flirts with the peasant girls before noticing the pitchers of wine spread along the tables. Most of the first act will pass through a *pas d'action,* with the dancers conveying the progress of the plot through dance, mime, and pageantry.

Suddenly the Prince arrives in his golden tunic, and Baryshnikov receives his obligatory applause. According to his mother's decree, Siegfried must choose a wife, but already he is resisting his biological and political destiny, turning away from tradition in a quest for some as-yet unnameable desire. Baryshnikov's care-worn Siegfried deigns to acknowledge the festivities out of noblesse oblige, and twelve peasant girls glide forward to present him with trailing flower garlands. The Prince offers a toast, and the aristocrats drink without touching their goblets to their lips. The first divertissement of the evening begins with Tchaikovsky's famous lilting waltz; the peasant girls arrange themselves for an appealing frolic, soon joined by six men with bolder footwork and double tours in the air. Petipa used these dance sequences—actual performances within performances—to develop the pure dance elements of classicism; today many of the steps and music appear as classroom exercises.

The Prince sets aside his cup to dance his own variation: Baryshnikov's slow, space-

The Act I pas de trois from *Swan Lake*. (© 1981 Martha Swope)

devouring leaps and gently suspended *assemblés* seem subdued somehow, as if Siegfried cannot renounce his vague melancholy even in a moment of celebration. *Swan Lake* is designed to showcase the virtuosity of stars, but Baryshnikov has dimmed his own physical brilliance to light his character's gradual dramatic progress.

The Queen Mother (Georgina Parkinson) appears suddenly with her retinue, upbraiding her son in pantomime, telling him that six maidens are coming and that he must choose one. In this expectant world of artificial drama, the pas de trois that follows proves the highlight of *Swan Lake*'s first act. Restaged to accord more closely with the Kirov version, the dance was once performed by Benno and two peasant women, but now the male role has been handed to an anonymous virtuoso presumably hired as an entertainer for the occasion. Rebecca Wright, a last-minute replacement for an injured soloist, flashes through her variation with a soubrette's pert correctness, prancing in a pizzicato rhythm, soaring into high *pas de chats,* then gliding into deep arabesques. Quick spins carry her into the wings, where she reaches for Danilo Radojevic's hand to apologize for some invisible gaffe at the beginning of the dance. Radojevic squeezes back, then hurtles through the wings for his own variation, with its hair-trigger leaps, kicking turns, and beats. Then all three dancers return for the codas and a final gallant pose to sustained applause.

Now the ballet changes mood abruptly, passing into a courtly promenade and toasts by the aristocrats—a grand polonaise known as the "Goblet Dance," or "Danse des Coupes," which closes the day's festivities without quickening the attention. Underneath the lavish staging, the dilemma of Siegfried's manhood remains vague, unfocused; as the last guests depart, the Prince has yet to cast off his strange morbidity. Almost as a projection of his state of mind, the plaintive melody of the swans rises from the pit—music said to have been written for Tchaikovsky's nieces and nephews—and a flight of swans passes in the distance. Seeking to comfort his friend, Benno suggests they go hunting that evening. Curiously elated at the prospect, Siegfried dances an urgent legato solo with his crossbow, a controversial interpolation at the Kirov some years ago, popularized at the Royal Ballet by Nureyev.

Throughout the first act the drama has seemed negligible, but no one has danced Shakespeare in Russian; the care and gusto of the young ensemble has been altogether pleasurable. The curtain falls on the ballet's prologue, as Benno and Siegfried race off together in anticipation of their visit to the Lake of Swans.

·   ·   ·

During the intermission, Baryshnikov rushes back onstage to consult with Gregory Osborne about some earlier difficulty; the artistic director is thinking ahead. The swans reconnoiter in the wings. Three minutes before curtain, the stagehands have finished lashing the rocky crags into place, and a fog machine begins to pump a thick billowy mist onto the stage. "Places, Places," cries the stage manager, agitated again for some reason.

Suddenly Baryshnikov begins to cry out in a muffled voice: "Props! Props!" His crossbow is missing.

Stagehands frantically search the wings and a crossbow materializes just as the curtain rises on Ivanov's "white" act, the single most famous scene in classical ballet.

Baryshnikov has altered the Act II opening: Now the evil Von Rothbart rises in moonlight from the fuming mists, sweeping his great black cape and musty locks. He vanishes suddenly as Siegfried swoops on- and offstage; Odette's famous entrance on the empty stage has likewise been re-formed. No longer the soaring pas de chat or grand jeté of a swan's magnificent alight, Cynthia Harvey as the plumed Odette bourrées gracefully onstage on full pointe—"as if stepping out of water and shaking off her feathers, I think."

Siegfried surprises the Swan Queen, and Odette rears up, trembling to her full height and simulating the motions of a swan attempting flight. Enchanted by this supernatural vision, the Prince dashes behind Odette who arches fearfully. After assurances that he will not shoot, Odette proceeds to tell her tragic story in mime. With the help of the libretto, we read thusly: "I am the Queen of the Swans. The lake was made by my mother's tears. A wicked enchanter has turned me into a wild bird, and so I shall remain, except between the hours of midnight and dawn, unless a man should love me and never love another. Then I will be released from my plight."

Deeply moved, Siegfried immediately raises two fingers to the heavens, pledging his troth to Odette forever. The fantasy he has craved suddenly becomes a glistening reality, and *Swan Lake*'s tragic melodrama is engaged. "You have to keep a little bit of that story in your head," Baryshnikov says of the Swan's mime. "You communicate a tremolo to the audience. It's something from the head and from the heart." Although Tchaikovsky swears the emotion is true, "It is a lie," says Baryshnikov, "but you have to pretend you feel it."

Reappearing suddenly across the glen, Rothbart conjures himself menacingly while Odette pleads with the sorcerer to be merciful. The heroic outrage of Siegfried evaporates in what follows, perhaps the ultimate image of classical ballet: the entry of the Swans, twenty-four in all, racing forward precipitously in a serpentine line, prancing for a few steps then stretching into flying arabesque *sautée,* winding four times back and forth the width of the stage.

The geometry of the dances that follow, their polyphonic relationship to Tchaikovsky's music, is breathtaking in its effect. Columns, concentric circles, and triangular wedges of dancers form and dissolve in a larger rhythmic persuasion that overwhelms all individual lapses. Mastering the organization of a small number of steps and images in a startling variety of ways, Ivanov, the choreographer of *Swan Lake*'s second and fourth acts, discovered how rapturous, lyrical dancing might convey both irresistible suffering and psychological depth, as the Swans' deep arabesques and beating wings suggest the tragic resignation of women who have been transformed into birds. Cowering in a staggered mass at one side of the stage, while Odette implores Siegfried not to harm her pathetic sisters, the Swans regroup in three columns for the beginning of the six linked dances that form the heart of Ivanov's choreography in Act II.

Only in recent years has Ivanov's contribution to Western ballet been fully acknowledged. Responsible for restaging Petipa's established works, he reputedly knew the entire Maryinsky repertory by heart; supremely musical, he could render a piece of music at the piano after hearing it one time, and once played an entire score from memory when a rehearsal pianist failed to appear. Petipa choreographed from an architectural rather than a musical impulse, but Ivanov wanted his own ballets to reflect the mood and inspiration of the composer, and to capture the music's emotional core. In creating his first ballet during the winter of 1875/76, Tchaikovsky had instinctively found a revolutionary means for resolving dance rhythms within a fully orchestrated symphonic score, creating musical

ideas that dancers could interpret as they would a role. Ivanov's understanding of Tchaikovsky's achievement signaled the beginning of the full-scale musical abstractions that would continue in the modern era, resulting in a modern classicism surpassing in its musical depth anything achieved in Russian ballet. The great *ballet blancs* of the twentieth century, Fokine's *Les Sylphides* and Balanchine's *Serenade,* descend from Ivanov's abstract display of movement to music.

·   ·   ·

In the wings, a very young member of the corps—a peasant girl in Act I, her dancing through for the evening—marks along with the movements and music on stage. Dressed in a red bathrobe over her tights and leotard, she is still learning the dance but will someday soon join the Swans in performance. The stagehands, the backstage doctor and his companion, even the fretting stage manager stop to gaze at her. Amazingly, the young members of the corps de ballet have given themselves to what Arlene Croce calls Tchaikovsky's "elated melancholy," and discovered something of its musical heart.

When Baryshnikov races back on stage, he searches for Odette among the rows of Swans framing the stage on either side. To an extended harp arpeggio, he leads the discovered Swan Queen to center stage, where Odette lowers herself submissively in the familiar image of the swan-ballerina popularized by Pavlova, with her arms swept forward as her upper body reclines over an extended leg. Siegfried tenderly helps her rise for the beginning of the White Swan pas de deux—telegraphed by an unfortunate collapse of tempo from the pit.

Although the idea of the pas de deux as a choreographic love poem reached its highest expression under Petipa, Ivanov's White Swan adagio is one of the great showcases in ballet, singled out by a critic at its first performance as "an expression of elegiac grief, continuing sorrow, and the illusion of love." The ballerina must trust her partner completely in her exposed multiple pirouettes, plunging arabesque penchés, and soft extensions; the two dancers must have perfect musical timing for her off-center balances

Cynthia Harvey and Mikhail Baryshnikov in Act II of *Swan Lake*. (© 1981 Mira)

and slow, supported jumps; at times they must sustain their communication instinctively, without exchanging a glance. The adagio must realize the ambition of romantic maturity: the possibility of a limitless freedom at the height of emotional and physical life.

One critic has spoken of Cynthia Harvey's "British restraint and Russian eloquence"; although her youthful quickness occasionally carries her ahead of the music, her phrasing remains elegant and tactfully scaled, her voluptuousness well tempered. Baryshnikov shelters her through six, seven pirouettes, holding her fingers high above her head until she dives into a deep penché arabesque, one leg lifted to the sky; held in his arms, she invites him ecstatically to continue,

melting into his grasp. We are witnessing the humanization of a swan. Baryshnikov is all gallant self-effacement as he makes his pictures with Harvey's body, guiding her discreetly under his wing. Ending in a high lift framed by a V-formation of swans in the background, tonight's pas de deux appears less a love poem than an initiation into artistry. Siegfried follows Odette offstage, and together they return for bows. The moment, as always, belongs to the ballerina.

All illusions of story and plot vanish. The famous "Dance of the Cygnets" is performed in unison with interlocking arms, with eight feet glancing and eight eyes darting to the four corners of the proscenium arch as the four Little Swans crisscross the stage. The lyric machinery is all in place, and as the dancers huff offstage in a clatter of toe shoes, four perfection-minded American kids are completely upset by the condition of the floor. Clutching a curtain, Baryshnikov has watched them dreamily from the wings.

"Too much?" he asks with a wan smile, facing them in his golden tunic.

"You're never satisfied," Cheryl Yeager retorts, gulping for breath. Deirdre Carberry, Christine Spizzo, and Yeager carry on in stage whispers about their problems, but Baryshnikov, continuing to smile vaguely in their direction, does not appear to listen.

Onstage, the four Big Swans are repeating a variation of their earlier waltz, their sweeping développés passing into deep lunges with wrists crossed, signifying their captivity. Odette's solo variation appraises the tragedy of her situation. Siegfried returns and, in the final image of the Swan Kingdom, holds Odette aloft in a euphoric vision of transcendence. Prince and Swan have fallen in love. But ABT's success tonight has not been based on the *frisson* of stars; instead, Boston has watched a major American company in the process of remaking itself from top to bottom.

Suddenly the plaintive swan theme returns, and Rothbart arrives to summon the maidens back to their daytime existence as birds. Odette cannot resist her fate: Swept away from Siegfried's grasp in a musical undertow, she is transformed before our eyes into a wild swan. Rothbart returns to relish his victory as the curtain descends.

· · ·

Two nights later, two other American Ballet Theatre stars have taken over the roles of Swan Queen and Prince. At the close of Act II, broken-winged, convulsed, struggling with every ounce of her being against her fate, Cynthia Gregory had shuddered and whipped her body to its full height—six feet one on pointe—before bourréeing offstage in a magnificent image of a pristine swan in flight. It is one of the great transformations in the American theater, a nearly

perfect marriage of classicism and show business, and as usual it brought down the house.

Gregory is one of the few American-born ballerinas embodying what Balanchine called "a force of unbelievable perfection." Because of her monumental height, the teen-age star with the San Francisco Ballet had to audition for Ballet Theatre three times before finally being accepted into the corps in 1965, at the age of nineteen. Two years later she became a principal dancer; the year following she learned Odette/Odile in two weeks and by 1972, the role made her a major star. A shy, sensitive woman easily slighted, Gregory has spent much of her career in the shadow of Russian superstars: "If you defect from San Francisco," she once said, "nobody cares."

Gregory's extreme height and American origins proved the greatest hindrance to her career until the arrival of thirty-year-old Alexander Godunov in 1979, not long after he had eluded the KGB in a Manhattan hotel lobby during a tour of the Bolshoi Ballet. Six feet three inches tall, with long blond hair and the sullen, almost brutal good looks of a rock star, Godunov was eagerly received by many Ballet Theatre fans, but his adjustment to work in America proved difficult. Once the partner of the legendary Plisetskaya, he found few roles in the ABT repertory well suited to a former Bolshoi *danseur noble*. Siegfried was no problem: *Swan Lake*'s Prince was the first full-evening role he had ever performed in Moscow, and he had danced it hundreds of times, in dozens of Soviet cities, on tour. "Same as Kirov production," he shrugged during an interview in his agent's office on the Upper East Side of Manhattan, "with little Grigorovich and Gorsky," referring to two Bolshoi choreographers who have restaged the ballet.

At the beginning of the Act III showcase for bravura dancing, trumpets herald Siegfried's fateful evening under the high arches of the castle's great hall. Aristocrats promenade on stage, and more trumpets announce the arrival of the Prince and his mother. Eligible princesses from around the kingdom perform a graceful if slightly vacuous waltz for him, and Godunov as Sieg-

Cynthia Gregory's transformation into a swan at the end of Act II of *Swan Lake*.
(© 1978 Beverly Gallegos)

fried wanders among them halfheartedly. Moving toward each of the princesses in turn, he at last faces his mother, his hands open as if to say, "You don't understand."

A third fanfare signals the arrival of Baron von Rothbart, his entourage, and his daughter, Odile. The swan theme returns at a fevered tempo, immediately impressing the resemblance between the Prince's Swan Queen and Odile, dressed in a black tutu and crown. Siegfried is smitten immediately. They dash offstage together—a new idea of Baryshnikov's that makes little sense—while Von Rothbart plays host to the national dances that Petipa used to deepen the texture of his ballets and provide contrasts to the *style noble* of the French academy. "Character dances are important," Baryshnikov said in 1980, "not so much in themselves but because they build the dramatic excitement of the ballet. I would say that Petipa created a classical character dance. He took steps from folk dance and transferred them to the Imperial Ballet in a more stylish way."

Baryshnikov has added a new *danse espagnole* by Bolshoi choreographer Leonid Lavrovsky; *danses hongroises*—Ivanov's marvelous czardas—are performed with passionate abandon by Leslie Browne, who starred in the film *The Turning Point,* Frank Smith, and others. Last comes the Polish mazurka; Baryshnikov has deleted the original's Neapolitan dance, but the rest are vastly improved over recent productions at Ballet Theatre.

Gregory and Godunov return for the famous Black Swan pas de deux, which follows the traditional pattern of a dance for both together, then a variation for the cavalier, one for the ballerina, and codas for each. Even with their fluid communication and obvious enjoyment of each other, it is Gregory's personality that dominates their partnership; her imperious dazzle is less an interpretation of Odile than an assault on the role. Presenting steps of extraordinary dimension and power, Gregory does little to hide each of her ambitious effects; even as Odile tries to convince Siegfried that she is the Swan Queen,

we forget Odette entirely in Gregory's histrionic, quicksilver turns and fearless balancés. Gregory as Odile casts a natural web of wickedness, rendering even her most vulgar effects entirely plausible and in character: As she leans on Von Rothbart's arm for whispered instructions, her glee is terrifyingly absolute.

With his naturally imposing presence, Godunov is still somewhat opaque; unable to create the illusion of devouring space, he dances his variations with enormous power, the arabesque of his scissor-kick tour jeté plowing upward like a broadsword a full sixty degrees; his series of double tours with no preparation in between appears effortless, ending in a perfect fifth position; six or seven pirouettes at a time, executed with even more force than Baryshnikov's, disturb not a hair on his head.

Godunov and Gregory have brought the tux-and-jeans audience at the Metropolitan Center to the edge of their seats, but the fireworks are just beginning. The ballerina returns for thirty-two prancing relevés-passés mixed with beats of the leg that hang in the air like showering diamonds; she closes with a series of piqué double turns whirling around the edge of the stage, arms glancing around her body like a pinwheel. Godunov appears at center stage for a series of booming turns at a rate of perhaps two a second, with a leg stretched parallel to his waist. After thirty-two, he brings a toe to his knee for a stunning eight or nine pirouettes that close in a textbook fourth position. Bravos erupt from the house but are silenced immediately as Gregory follows with the famous thirty-two whipping turns that the original Odette/Odile, Pierina Legnani, introduced from abroad. Makarova has said that Odile's virtuosity signifies her "already accomplished triumph" over Siegfried. Gregory and Godunov have outdone themselves tonight. The Boston audience is in an uproar.

Siegfried's mime is a foregone conclusion: "Mother," he gestures, "I want her." Von Rothbart steps in and insists he take an oath, and Siegfried moves downstage, two fingers pointed skyward. While an apparitional film of Odette bourréeing frantically to the sped-up swan theme appears on a rear scrim, Siegfried completes his oath, sealing Odette's fate. Odile seizes the wedding bouquet and gleefully scatters it in the air, then flees triumphantly with Von Rothbart into the night. The Queen faints; the Prince, hands clutched to his head, races into the darkness, insane with remorse.

.   .   .

At its best, ABT's *Swan Lake* has survived both as a forgery of a vanished past and as a celebration of American energy, for what remains indelibly in the mind is the dancing itself: the thrill of Cynthia Gregory's exquisite line in third arabesque, its lyrical sweep from fingertip to toe, and the surge of the corps shifting through the music like an ocean wave. Besieged by controversy since its inception, Ballet Theatre's full-evening production offers everything American audiences consciously and unconsciously associate with ballet as an art: Russian stars, glamour, pageantry, and dreams. Because of its popular and historic importance—and because it has helped to secure a Soviet-style approach to the classics at ABT—Baryshnikov has plans to restage it; but in a few months he will dismiss his old school friend Alexander Godunov, saying that there is little for him to dance at ABT except the classical Prince. The 1980s have become an age of transition not only at ABT but at City Ballet, the San Francisco Ballet, the Pennsylvania Ballet and elsewhere; the great warhorse ballets continue to sustain the memory of an art that received its one permanent consolidation in Petipa, Ivanov, and Tchaikovsky.

Act IV, again set in the gloomy lakeside dale: Lamenting their missing sister, the Swans dance to recall their former lives as women. Odette enters, and the Swans urge her to trust in Siegfried's return. When the Prince at last arrives, he begs Odette's forgiveness, which she immediately grants him. The two lovers' fates are now intertwined, and the immensity of the tragedy gathers in Tchaikovsky's massive music: Siegfried has given himself completely to a woman who must now remain a swan forever, while "the nature and fate of Odette," Makarova has written, "teaches her a forgiveness stronger than death."

In the original ending of Petipa and Ivanov's tragedy, Odette dies in Siegfried's arms, and the Prince casts her crown into the waters, which rise to immerse them both, resolving their love in death. In the Soviet Union—where ballet has become a phantom of socialist-realism—Von Rothbart is overthrown and Odette united with Siegfried in life. American Ballet Theatre has retained a version of the Imperial ending: Odette, unwilling to remain a swan forever, tosses herself into the lake, and Siegfried follows with a leap from the rocky crag. This final sacrifice spells the sorcerer's doom. Von Rothbart dies, shattering his power over the Swan Maidens. The two lovers are joined in death, riding a swan boat into the sky as the curtain plunges.

What Arlene Croce once called "the greatest unstageable ballet ever written" is finished, three hours after the first note of music.

Arranging themselves backstage for the curtain calls, the Swans tug costumes into place, wipe sweat from brows, and pat their hair into place. When the curtain rises again, they are neatly arrayed behind Gregory and Godunov, who are called back by the shouts of the audience again and again. A young woman in a tight evening dress runs awkwardly down an aisle, takes a clumsy swing and sends a single rose flying in the direction of Cynthia Gregory's feet. The rose lands in the percussion section of the orchestra, and the audience groans.

The curtain falls for the last time, and the dancers are transformed into young Americans again, hungry and nearly ready for sleep. Straggling downstairs to the dressing rooms, they strip costumes and makeup, change quickly into street clothes, and strike off in small groups for a hot meal. A few are so charged from the performance they won't sleep for hours. Tonight a young but vastly talented company sustained the American legacy of the Russian Imperial ballet, and became what George Steiner describes all of

American culture to be—"the archives of Eden," a storehouse for the cultural treasures of the Old World. Tomorrow class begins at eleven in the morning. The future, always the future.

THE
FELD
BALLET

· THE UNIVERSE OF ELIOT FELD ·

The Feld Ballet is an unusual occasion in American dance: an ensemble ballet company functioning with the intimacy of a modern dance troupe to produce the work of a single artist. In an age of ballet big business, the Feld Ballet has developed without the financial base afforded companies with a strong civic or regional identity; at a time when some critics have argued that American ballet is moribund as a choreographic art, Feld has kept alive one of the major talents in world dance. In 1979, *Dance in America*'s cameras visited his school, his rehearsal studios, and the theater that would shortly become his company's home, documenting the fruits of one man's persistent vision of an American performing arts institution.

Eliot Feld was a twenty-four-year-old soloist with American Ballet Theatre when he first began to assemble steps to Prokofiev's Fifth Piano Concerto in 1967. He tells his story in a gleaming studio in Manhattan's Chelsea district, where his company inherited the shambles of a former belt factory in 1976. The perennial boy wonder and bad boy of ballet, now approaching his fortieth birthday, speaks with the kind of effusive precision that marks his choreography as well.

"I didn't have a ballet in mind," he begins. "I just had this one movement—this very fast, staccato movement. I worked with dancers from the company, rented studios, and worked at Ballet Theatre when I could. And so I did a two-minute dance, which must have taken me about six months. Then I did another movement and thought, 'What am I doing? I have to have somebody look at this.' " Feld asked Jerome Robbins, whom he knew through his work as the original Baby John in the stage and film versions of *West Side Story*. "He was enormously encouraging," Feld continued. He said he would speak to Lucia Chase, the director of the company, and he must have, because I choreographed *Harbinger,* and suddenly I was a choreographer."

And more than a choreographer: Feld was immediately hailed as the new whiz kid of American ballet. *Harbinger* celebrated Prokofiev's music and the lyric exultation of neoclassical dancing with enormous insight and feeling. Feld had demonstrated an instinctive truthfulness in the expression of music and mood, sustaining inventive imagery and the youthful charms of the dancers themselves through a generous scrutiny of form—an inspired craftsmanship. "I'm talking about myself and the people I know," Feld explained. "It's like showing some of the kinds of personal games we play." Unfortunately, American Ballet Theatre was moving away from the task of nurturing new ballets and ballet-makers.

"They did *Harbinger* and *Swan Lake* that

Eliot Feld rehearsing *Santa Fe Saga* with Mikhail Baryshnikov in Feld's studios on Broadway and 18th Street in Manhattan. (© 1978 Lois Greenfield)

year," Feld recalls, without a trace of rancor, "and they chose their course. When you do *Swan Lake,* you can pretty much control who's dancing it, who's staging it, who's doing the costumes—it puts a lot of control in the hands of semi-artistic people. Having choreographers around is a threat to authority, and I think that has a lot to do with their choice." When Feld's second ballet, the poignant and introspective *At Midnight,* was used as a curtain-raiser for a grand performance of *Giselle* in Los Angeles—and flopped, after a successful world premiere in New York—Feld gave American Ballet Theatre his notice.

" 'You mustn't leave, we'll do anything! What do you want?' " Feld reports Oliver Smith, the company codirector, pleading. "I said, 'I want to control my own work, and I can't do it here.' He said, 'Specifically, what do you want?' And I said, 'If I could have the right to hire and fire dancers . . .' " Feld hoists his shoulders, then lets them drop. "Now I knew that was impossible. You can't have a subcompany within a company, and so I didn't really ask for it. So that's that sad tale. I wasn't intending to have a company of my own. I just left."

But it soon became apparent that Eliot Feld was one of those hair-shirt personalities willing to bear the emotional and fiscal burdens of put-

The Feld Ballet in *Intermezzo*. (© 1978 Lois Greenfield)

ting together a ballet company from scratch. After assembling a third ballet, *Meadowlark,* for the Royal Winnipeg Ballet in Canada, he announced the formation of the ambitious new American Ballet Company in 1969, with help from the NEA and the Brooklyn Academy of Music in his native borough in New York. Over the next thirty months, Feld churned out four or five new works annually with his youthful chamber ensemble—among them *Intermezzo,* earning praise from Arlene Croce as "the most brilliant piece of work by an under-thirty choreographer since Paul Taylor's *Three Epitaphs,*" created over a decade earlier. Seen in part on *Dance in America, Intermezzo* is an evocation of Brahms's romantic piano music, performed by three couples as a sensuous delectation of ballroom figures. Feld clearly had a gift for assuming as many different

styles of dancing as he liked, but "there was no money," Feld says today. "I mean *no* money. Nobody got paid." The company appeared in Brooklyn and on a few brief American tours, but in the end the American Ballet Company was forced to disband, and Feld reluctantly returned to the fold at Ballet Theatre.

This second stay lasted six months, Feld swiftly renewing his reputation for aggressive, angry, obstinate behavior in rehearsal and in his grapplings with the powers that be. Soon he was gone, free-lancing with the Joffrey, the Royal Danish Ballet, and a company in Sweden. Working with dancers he did not know, he left two new works unfinished. "Doing a ballet has always been so difficult for me personally," he explains, "that when you're in a foreign country where you have no friends and can't speak the language and are living in a hotel . . ." He pauses, casting a blithe look into the ether, then comes at his answer from a different direction. "Making a ballet is a kind of mystery trip. You start with a piece of thread and you're supposed to make a gown. It takes a great deal of courage just to start, and you need people who have faith in you, who trust you and know you'll do all right. But when you've got people saying, 'Look, I've been standing around here for three hours,' that's nearly impossible." And Feld was the kind of choreographer who needed to take his time: In 1975, his dancers crawled on the floor to Hindemith for a week, before he realized he couldn't think of a way to get them on their feet, and abandoned the work.

Forced to take another stab at a company of his own, Feld spent a year chasing around the country, meeting potential backers in several cities to discuss the possibility of sharing a company between them. In the end, the American-style quest for civic prestige meant that each city hoped for exclusive rights to a company they couldn't afford. Help finally came from home. The associate producer of the New York Shakespeare Festival, Bernard Gersten, offered Feld the use of a three-hundred-seat Off-Broadway house in the festival's Lafayette Street complex. The company would have to raise its own expenses through grants and donations, and even rent rehearsal space, but in the spring of 1974, the eighteen-member Eliot Feld Ballet was born. It was a much needed chamber-size company in the world's ballet capital, and its sold-out first season was extended to five weeks.

Comfortably in charge, Feld began moving with easy vibrancy through a gamut of styles, but always seeking to reconcile, in his own words, "the wonderful virtues of classical ballet with the way people actually live." His ballets bore a kind of witness to the memory of an American past, assimilating lessons from everywhere in a restless catalogue of effects: In "The Blues" section of *The Real McCoy,* aired on *Dance in America,* Feld and Michaela Hughes summon George Gershwin's romantic 1930s with a dusky love duet. Dolled up in a pale, slinky gown, Hughes

steps through a Ferris wheel of walking sticks manipulated by a chorus of five men—an ingenious image not always matched by the nostalgic sentimentality of the ballet's other vignettes. *Excursions* (1975), danced to piano music by Samuel Barber, opens with Christine Sarry's perky, skittering solo on pointe, magnifying the fearless vivacity of the company's best-known dancer.

Once again, Feld's repertory was largely successful, but the producing stratagems at the festival did not prove as satisfactory. Producer Joseph Papp "always asserted his territorial right over the space," Feld recalls. "This is a lesson I've learned in life: If you want to control your own fate, you have to have a place you've created yourself." By 1977, the Eliot Feld Ballet was without a theater and on the move again.

In the meantime, however, the company had acquired a rehearsal space of its own: a gutted ruin on the eighth floor of a run-down building on Broadway and Eighteenth Street, but with over two hundred feet of unpillared space, forty-five-feet wide, with only a single retaining wall. Clear, unobstructed space for dancing is a major find in Manhattan, and after six months of renovation—made possible by a gift from LuEsther Mertz, a well-known New York patron of the performing arts—the company had a modern, even luxurious complex of offices and three major dance studios. Feld had yet another plan, this one for founding his New Ballet School: With the cooperation of the New York public school system, he began to offer free dance scholarships to disadvantaged students aged eight to twelve from across the city—especially from Chinatown, Harlem, and the Lower East Side. Eighteen thousand kids had auditioned by 1982. "It was not done out of any liberal social conscience," Feld insists. "Letting people help themselves is ultimately the best kind of help you can give anybody. There's also a lot of talent among our 175 kids, and in several more years, believe me, the best are going to be helping us."

As the Feld company in its different incarnations approached its difficult tenth anniversary, with many dancers leaving and new ones

The Feld Ballet in *Danzón Cubano.* (© 1978 Lois Greenfield)

taking their places, the problem of where to perform continued to grow. The punishing costs of a first season on Broadway, with guest artists Mikhail Baryshnikov and Christine Sarry in the crowd-pleasing *Variations on America,* and two self-produced seasons at City Center nearly had the company on the ropes. At least new works had resulted: *La Vida,* a dreamy evocation of Mexico, danced with sultry femininity and delicate machismo to a score by Aaron Copland; and *Santa Fe Saga,* a branch-watered afterthought to Eugene Loring's *Billy the Kid,* which Feld had danced with Ballet Theatre. By the fall of 1978, expenses had pushed the Feld Ballet back to the New York Shakespeare Theatre, where more dances premiered: *Danzón Cubano,* a musically taut investigation of more south-of-the-border themes; and *Half-Time,* a good-natured show-biz spectacle, replete with athletes, cheerleaders, and drum majorettes parading about to

Morton Gould's *Formations* for marching bands. But costs being what they were, Feld was going to have to take one more step toward controlling his own destiny. If the existence of the company was not to be threatened by the essential act of performing before larger audiences than the Shakespeare Festival provided, then a new theater was clearly necessary.

A medium-size theater for dance in New York City had been spoken of since the mid-1960s, but none materialized until Bernard Gersten —the husband of Feld's executive director, Cora Cahan—learned that a crumbling forty-year-old movie house in Chelsea was on the market. In January 1979, Feld's nonprofit corporation purchased the Elgin Theater for $225,000 and began to complete its transformation for dance through an extensive package of loans, grants, and private contributions with a goal of $3.8 million. The Joyce Theater—named after

Mrs. Mertz's late daughter—finally opened on June 1, 1982, as a cost-effective theater for America's medium-size dance companies. With low weekly rentals, a dance company at the Joyce can conceivably turn a profit. But the first company to perform in its swank new confines was the Feld Ballet, making its first appearance in New York City in almost four years. Eliot Feld had completed his own universe.

"It's amazing how hard it is to build a ballet company," he told *The New York Times* in 1977. "It is easy to get it started, but when you get to the nitty-gritty, it is hard to endure. Talent is only one-tenth of what it takes to go on. And you have to suffer lean times, artistically as well as financially." Some of Feld's recent work has not met with the critical enthusiasm that greeted his earliest ballets, but freedom to an artist doesn't mean good reviews. It only means the ability to give it everything you have.

"When I start a new dance," Feld concludes, "I think I'm really trying to invent a language that expresses what I feel about the music and what the music evokes in me. The problems are problem solving. The most important thing when you choreograph is to create a great deal of trouble for yourself. You want to set up a serious problem—the problem must be there naturally, whether you can articulate it or not. And then you work because it's of interest to you. If you get something from it, that's wonderful. If you get a lot from it, that's great. But these are personal needs, and work has its own set of needs."

"And finally," he says, "it can't be answerable to anybody."

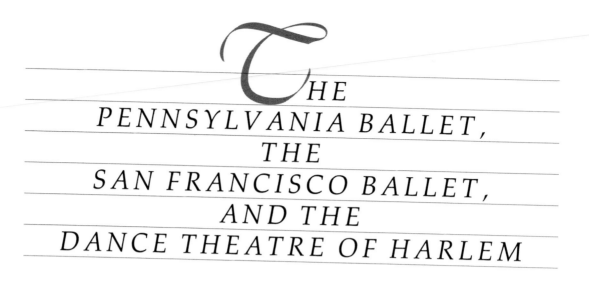

THE PENNSYLVANIA BALLET, THE SAN FRANCISCO BALLET, AND THE DANCE THEATRE OF HARLEM

· WEST OF THE HUDSON AND UPTOWN ·

The largest and most prestigious American ballet companies continue to make their homes on an island between the Hudson and the East rivers, where dance audiences attend as easily as the rest of the nation runs off to the movies. But "New York City is not America," as W. H. Auden once remarked. The growth of significant regional ballet companies in Boston, Houston, Salt Lake City, Seattle, Cincinnati, Columbus, Dayton, Pittsburgh, Oakland, Tulsa, and Cleveland has become the American ballet's most significant development over the past quarter-century. Professional and semiprofessional ballet companies have sprung up in virtually every American city with a population over 250,000, performing in established institutional settings just fifty years after Lincoln Kirstein compared the task of transplanting ballet to this country to trying "to raise a palm tree in Dakota."

In most cities, civic taste and prejudice have required a ballet to serve a cultural rather than an artistic or creative purpose, adapting its style to local audiences. But some companies have sought to transcend such parochialism, educating old and new audiences into an appreciation of ballet as a serious art form through repertories featuring works by established masters as well as the latest innovators. The Pennsylvania Ballet is both a representative and an unusual example of how the maturity of American dance academies and the rise in public and private fundings for the arts—especially the more than $30 million presented by the Ford Foundation to American ballet in the 1960s and 1970s—have come together to produce world-class ballet companies outside the nation's dance capital.

Philadelphia has a long history of ballet performance, beginning in the days of John Durang, continuing through the romantic era with Mary Ann Lee and Augusta Maywood, and culminating in the 1930s, when the "All-American" Littlefield Ballet presented a diverse repertory of classical and American works, including the nation's first production of a full-evening ballet, *The Sleeping Beauty*. But when the Littlefield company disbanded in 1941, the city was without a major ballet for over twenty years until the Ford Foundation implemented its carefully laid plans to provide massive support for ballet across the nation. The foundation's study, conducted over a period of years in cooperation with Balanchine and the School of American Ballet, had uncovered the fact that many regional companies were foundering because of a lack of adequately trained dancers. Regional training was too often conducted in studios isolated from the companies themselves, destroying the vital link between the classroom and stage that marked the achievements of Russian ballet and the New York City Ballet as well.

Now, with Balanchine's encouragement, W. McNeil Lowry, the architect of the Ford program, decided to build a major part of his funding efforts around instructors who could cultivate dancers as students, apprentices, and finally as full-fledged professionals. One of the teachers he approached was Barbara Weisberger. An early student of the Littlefields and the first child accepted for study at the School of American Ballet, Weisberger had given up her own chances for a performing career to become a wife, mother, inspired teacher, and occasional choreographer at her own school in Wilkes-Barre, Pennsylvania, where she often sent dancers on to Balanchine. In 1962, Weisberger moved her academy to America's fifth largest city, and two years later formed the Pennsylvania Ballet with a $295,000 grant from the Ford Foundation, as the youngest of the six companies in the Ford program.

Building a meaningful repertory swiftly becomes the essential problem facing any ballet company without a resident genius of its own: Choreographers must be brought in from outside or else developed within the company itself. Weisberger decided to gather a diverse range of nineteenth- and twentieth-century classics new to Philadelphia audiences, as well as works by younger choreographers such as John Butler and modern masterpieces by Paul Taylor, Doris Humphrey, and José Limón. Balanchine provided artistic and institutional support, and by 1966 the company enjoyed a successful season in Philadelphia with its own resident orchestra. In 1968, when the Pennsylvania Ballet appeared for the first time in New York, critics praised it as the nation's finest regional company. Guest artists appeared only on rare occasions; a strong group of young dancers performed Balanchine works with special authority. Nevertheless, the Pennsylvania Ballet was not met with overwhelming support in the city of Philadelphia: Many audiences continued to prefer the grand Russian-style classics danced by international stars.

In 1972, Weisberger was joined by a new artistic director, choreographer Benjamin Har-karvy, the founder of the Netherlands Dance Theatre, who arrived with a group of European choreographers and an often controversial approach to winning new audiences. Something less than a style, the Pennsylvania Ballet's new modern ballets were actually an approach to music, borrowing from Martha Graham's muscular, enigmatic romanticism as Europeans understood it in the 1950s. Harkarvy introduced the works of Hans van Manen of the Netherlands Ballet to Philadelphia audiences; Van Manen's abstract pas de deux to Beethoven, *Adagio Hammerklavier* (1973), borrows from the grand adagios of classicism but grafts a lush eroticism on the beautiful bodies of dancers Lawrence Rhodes and Michelle Lucci. Without presenting an encompassing vision of human behavior or emotion, the modern repertory of works by John Butler, Charles Czarny, Van Manen, and others offered Philadelphians at least proved successful in attracting younger audiences to the company. The 1977 *Dance in America* performances of the Pennsylvania Ballet suggested the continuing range of the repertory: In addition to Van Manen's *Adagio* and *Grosse Fugue* and Czarny's *Concerto Grosso,* the program featured Balanchine's serene and civilized *Concerto Barocco* and Harkarvy's own neoclassical *Madrigalesco,* to Vivaldi, a demonstration of the choreographer's scrupulous insight into the discipline instilled at the company school.

Meanwhile a series of financial near-disasters throughout the 1970s further plagued the artistic development of the company, as they would nearly every major American ballet company during a decade of economic hardship and inflation. Ford's generous support continued through the early 1970s, but by the latter part of the decade financial pressures had reduced the company's prospects for touring and a lengthy season at home. By 1982, after a forced suspension of activities threatened the very existence of the company, the board of directors asserted its power and Mrs. Weisberger resigned as director in March. Balanchine withdrew his repertory in her support; in part to reassert ties with the New York City Ballet, Robert Weiss, a City Ballet

The Pennsylvania Ballet in Charles Czarny's *Concerto Grosso*, with Jeffrey Gribler and Dane LaFontsee. (© Kenn Duncan)

The Pennsylvania Ballet in George Balanchine's *Concerto Barocco*. (© 1984 Paul Kolnik)

principal dancer and choreographer, was named the new artistic director in July, with Peter Martins as his artistic adviser. Calling the Pennsylvania Ballet "a good company with the potential to be great," Weiss laid out plans for preserving and expanding the eclectic repertory. A March fund-raising drive continued until August, garnering $2.1 million; a direct-mail campaign, new marketing techniques, and a quadrupling of support in the Philadelphia area suggest a little of what it takes to keep a ballet company alive in the American eighties.

Surviving within the creative orbit of the New York City Ballet, the Pennsylvania Ballet has initiated audiences into a spectrum of contemporary and historic dances drawn from across America and Western Europe. But as American dance copes with increasing financial hardships, nearly every company has sunk roots deeper into its own community, creating a style of institutional dance-theater paralleling the rise of resident theaters, operas, and symphonies throughout the United States since the 1960s. The San Francisco Ballet and Dance Theatre of Harlem illustrate an historic expansion of culture beyond former boundaries of geography and race, suggesting new standards of excellence that have emerged over the past two decades—one company thriving on the far side of the continent from New York City, the other only a few miles northeast of Lincoln Center but in a vastly different universe by force of history, culture, and racial discrimination.

· · ·

Celebrating its fiftieth anniversary in 1983 as the oldest professional ballet company in America, the San Francisco Ballet is one of the healthiest arts institutions in America, performing forty-

The Christensen brothers, America's first ballet dynasty (from right): Lew, Willam, Harold, and their father, Christian Christensen. (Courtesy Lew Christensen)

four weeks each year at the War Memorial Opera House and on numerous regional and national tours. Four-fifths of its dancers are trained at the company's own academy, the finest in the nation outside New York City. Along with twelve ballets by Balanchine and major works by Ashton, Robbins, and other twentieth-century masters, the repertory has added more newly commissioned ballets over the past decade—eighty—than any other American troupe, most contributed by a stable of in-house choreographers who have risen through the company with a special knowledge of its style and strengths. This unique repertory includes works by company dancers John McFall and Tomm Ruud, assistant director Robert Gladstein, the late artistic codirector Lew Christensen, and especially Michael Smuin, who has succeeded in creating hugely popular full-evening entertainments without abandoning the company's fundamental commitment to classical expression. But the saga of the San Francisco Ballet is finally inseparable from that of its founding family: Willam, Harold, and Lew Christensen, the nation's first

ballet dynasty and the fathers of American ballet west of the Rockies.

Born in the first decade of this century, the Mormon grandchildren of a family of Danish dance and music instructors who settled in Utah in 1854, the Christensen brothers had no occasion to doubt that ballet was a legitimate cultural expression for Americans. In the late 1920s, they adapted their Old World training to appear as "exotic" dancers on the vaudeville circuit, headlining with Jack Benny and W. C. Fields; by the mid-1930s, Harold and Lew were working with Balanchine and establishing reputations as the first important American-born ballet dancers and choreographers of their generation. Lew appeared as the original American Apollo, transforming the role into an indisputably American creation. "You're a woodcutter," Balanchine told him, "a swimmer, a football player, and a God." With Kirstein's Ballet Caravan, Lew also choreographed *Filling Station,* a "ballet-document in one act," one of the first widely acclaimed ballets on an American theme.

Three thousand miles away, in the city of

San Francisco—like Philadelphia, proud of a long and honorable history of support for dance—the white marble opera house opened during the heart of the Great Depression, with its opera ballet under the direction of former Ballets Russes star Adolph Bolm. After founding a small ballet company in Portland, Willam Christensen traveled south to dance in 1937; the following year he took over the San Francisco company, reorganizing it into an entity separate from the opera company, establishing a Western and Midwestern touring schedule and a school that would grow to over four hundred students by the end of World War II.

While choreographers in New York City concentrated on Americana and modernist experiments, Willam began introducing San Franciscans to ballet's nineteenth-century Russian past, with an American touch. After the success of his full-evening *Coppélia* in 1939, he set to work again for Tchaikovsky's centennial in 1940—reading, consulting with Russian teachers and émigrés who had seen productions in Russia, and finally assembling a tenable four-act *Swan Lake* without having seen a production himself. Four years later, struggling over the music and visual imagery of *The Nutcracker* one afternoon, Willam listened as a guest artist with the company, ballerina Alexandra Danilova, explained a few of Ivanov's original steps as they were performed at the Maryinsky. Another guest, George Balanchine, interrupted her, suggesting that Christensen discover the coherence and thrust of the dancing in the process of assembling it. The first American production of Tchaikovsky's full-evening Christmas classic proved a spectacular success; Christensen's *Nutcracker* would establish a tradition of winter stagings crucial to the future success of ballet in America. The late artistic director of the Cincinnati Ballet, David McLain, expressed the gratitude of many institutions in 1981: "We have survived as a company," he said, "because of *The Nutcracker.*"

Skillfully merging its Old World values and the unaffected virtues of a Western metropolis, the renamed San Francisco Civic Ballet—the largest dance company in America—became the nation's first city-sponsored ballet troupe in 1947, priding itself on an image of artistic seriousness in a culture-conscious city. Small but loyal San Francisco audiences enjoyed their Main Street ballerinas in romantic evocations of the nineteenth century and the Russian classics, but the Christensens never relaxed their commitment to Balanchine's abstract, plotless ballets, which continued to seem strange and experimental to uninitiated audiences. Neoclassicism was emerging as the American choreographer's climate of inspiration in the years following the war, and Lew Christensen, with his theatrical acumen and background with Balanchine, understood classical style in a way that enabled him to assert its boldest conventions unselfconsciously. To avoid charges of effeteness, the Christensens emphasized the health, discipline, and self-confidence that ballet dancing could impart. One late-1940s publicity photograph showed an overcrowded dressing room, with the caption: "As American as apple pie, these ballerinas are from Main Street themselves, and they live by the rule: All for one, one for all. 'Check your costumes, girls, and easy on the makeup!' "

In 1952, Willam returned to Utah, later establishing the Christensen brothers' other major creation, known today as Ballet West in Salt Lake City and currently the fifth largest ballet company in America. Lew assumed the directorship in San Francisco, with Harold running the school until 1975—training, Lincoln Kirstein insists, "the finest male aspirants on the continent." Under Lew and Harold, San Francisco Ballet deepened its relationship with the New York City Ballet through the exchange of repertory and dancers, and by the late 1950s reaffirmed its position as the nation's leading regional troupe.

Many American ballet companies in the 1960s and 1970s expanded rapidly to meet new audiences, then found themselves unable to sustain their new scale with the decline in public, private, and foundation support at the close of the decade. The old, established San Francisco Ballet faced its future sooner than most: The family-run operation had failed to cultivate the

Dancers from the San Francisco Ballet at the Golden Gate Bridge in 1958. (Courtesy San Francisco Ballet.)

younger, well-heeled art lovers in the city who would have been willing to patronize the ballet through a period of economic recession. Company members danced in offices and department store windows to raise nickels and dimes, and a "Save Our Ballet" campaign in the early 1970s rescued the company temporarily, but major changes in the structure of the administration were clearly called for. Professional administrators were brought in for the first time, institut-

ing aggressive new marketing and fund-raising techniques. And with Lew Christensen's blessing, Michael Smuin became associate artistic director in 1973, and later codirector.

One of Willam Christensen's ablest and most devoted students, Montana-born Smuin had first joined the San Francisco Ballet as an ambitious teen-ager in 1958. Dancing with the company for four years, he organized a young choreographer's workshop before leaving to form a nightclub act with his wife, dancer Paula Tracey. In a time of increasing ballet professionalism, it has become unusual for a future choreographer to gather skills from nonclassical styles, but Smuin followed the Christensens' example and immersed himself in show business—dancing for television and a Bob Fosse musical on Broadway, gaining insight into what lures an audience under a marquee. In 1966, he joined American Ballet Theatre, where he swiftly rose to principal dancer, choreographing a number of robust, modern ballets that left some critics lukewarm but many audiences delighted. "Ballet," says Michael Smuin, "is entertainment."

With Smuin in charge, the San Francisco Ballet became what it needed to become to survive: Between 1974 and 1977, the heart of the dance boom nationwide, a new, younger, audience flooded into the War Memorial Opera House, boosting attendance from just forty-one percent of capacity to very nearly twice that.

In 1976, the thirty-eight-year-old choreographer premiered the "new" San Francisco Ballet's flagship ballet, the full-evening *Romeo and Juliet,* choreographed to the celebrated Prokofiev score originally introduced by the Kirov Ballet in Leningrad thirty-six years before. In an age of "autonomous" ballets dealing with only those elements of the art of dance unique to itself, many choreographers have felt the mythic lure of the full-evening story ballet. *Romeo and Juliet* has attracted European choreographers especially, notably Sir Frederick Ashton and Kenneth MacMillan of the Royal Ballet, John Cranko in Stuttgart, John Neumeier in Cologne, as well as the ballet masters of the great Russian companies. Faced with such a contemporary tradition, the first impediment Michael Smuin of Billings, Montana, had to confront was a matter of faith. "Nobody believed that an American choreographer could pull it off," he frankly recalls. "There has always been a distrust of Americans—whether as actors or singers or choreographers—tackling Shakespeare."

Smuin exudes a Western-style confidence close to brashness; he is quite willing to measure the San Francisco Ballet of the 1980s against the Russian Imperial Ballet of the late nineteenth century and to announce that the American ballet mantle has passed from the shoulders of New York City to the city by the bay. In convincing his board of directors to spend the necessary money for his instant warhorse, Smuin refused to be daunted, proving his abilities through a series of shorter productions before attempting the full-scale version.

In Smuin's hands, Shakespeare became the basis for a contemporary classical ballet with all the traditional trappings: pageantry, mime, character dances, lavish divertissements, and sensual pas de deux for a noble Romeo, danced by Jim Sohm for *Dance in America* in 1978, and a shy yet passionate Juliet, tenderly realized by ballerina Diana Weber. With the scenario moving "now in the direction of family entertainment, now toward a sophisticated, 'modern' interpretation," as Arlene Croce noted, Shakespeare's fair Verona became fairly a bawdy house, with Montagues, Capulets, and a bevy of harlots brawling jubilantly in the street for sport, and flamboyant sword duels between the rival families celebrating the unusual strength of the company's men. More profusely danced than any previous treatment of the Prokofiev score, Smuin's familiar tale of star-crossed lovers didn't so much hinge on the choreography as lie impaled there, but as a fast-moving adaptation of Prokofiev's scenario it had high romance, melodrama, vivid action, and tragedy—an ennobling aura that audiences continue to look for at the ballet.

"Most audiences are interested in story ballets for some reason," Michael Smuin explains, "but for me it's always movement and music, whether there's a story in it or not. I don't know what *abstract* means—or *plotless*—and I never have. To me there's nothing abstract about dance. The minute there's a living, breathing human body on stage, there's nothing abstract about it—it's very definite. There's always some element of drama or story or atmosphere or location or idea." By choosing a story and music with universal cultural currency, Smuin had assured himself of a plot—a mystique, really—that

Michael Smuin's *The Tempest,* with Lynda Meyer and Vane Vest. (© 1980 James Armstrong, courtesy San Francisco Ballet)

audiences could relax and enjoy rather than struggle to understand. It became an instant story classic and the greatest hit in the history of the San Francisco Ballet: A ten-minute standing ovation greeted *Romeo and Juliet* at its world premiere.

Searching through all of Shakespeare for another dramatic idea, Smuin finally settled on the Bard's highly visual romantic fantasy of the New World as suitable material for his next full-evening superspectacle. *The Tempest* touches on "themes of sin, atonement, change, and reconciliation," Smuin has written, but the most fascinating of all "is that of illusion and reality, and it is this theme, also, that lends itself best to expression in this medium of ballet." More skeptical of the separation between the worlds of ballet and show business than any American ballet choreographer, Smuin called on set designer Tony Walton, an Oscar winner for his work on Bob Fosse's *All That Jazz,* as well as

costume designer Willa Kim, whose fanciful colors and extravagance are well known in the dance world; the choreographer himself set to work with co-librettist Philip Semark, while the company's resident composer, Paul Seiko Chihara, fashioned an original score around Henry Purcell's seventeenth-century incidental music for *The Tempest* and other works. "I was trying to make a very old-fashioned ballet," Smuin explains, "but done with the latest state-of-the-art mechanics that we could possibly afford. And that's what it was always supposed to be: in Shakespeare's words, 'a great entertainment.' And certainly that's what Petipa was about as well."

Like Petipa's *Sleeping Beauty* and Balanchine's *Midsummer Night's Dream,* Smuin's *Tempest* tells its story in Act I, beginning with a prologue appearance by Shakespeare himself, then passing into the colossal wreck of a ship on Prospero's enchanted isle—the huge vessel splitting asunder in a storm of billowy fabric raised by the magician's fairy sprite, Ariel, brilliantly danced for *Dance in America* audiences by David McNaughton. Alonzo, King of Naples, along with his entourage, are rudely tossed on a barren shore, ruled by the exiled Duke of Milan, who had lost his title to his brother Antonio, now a member of the shipwrecked party. The ballet's second act begins with a series of divertissements based on the form of the seventeenth-century masque, with Prospero conjuring up various mythological figures to celebrate the nuptials of his daughter Miranda and Ferdinand, son of the King of Naples. Just as the imperial theaters used national dances, Smuin employs American forms such as the tango, blues, fox-trot, and beguine—along with Spanish dancers, satyrs, and drunks, and the magnificent arrivals of Iris, Ceres, and Juno in her celestial car—to fashion inventive solos, pas de deux, pas de trois, pas de six, and a final grand divertissement closing the festivities. Smuin rightfully claims that the cornerstones of *The Tempest* are "those three rock-solid giants": Shakespeare, Purcell, and Petipa. What resulted was another blockbuster, the first full-evening *American* classical ballet—the creation of American designers, an American composer, and an American choreographer. When *The Tempest* was aired on *Dance in America* in 1981, it was the first time it had been seen outside the War Memorial Opera House: It was simply too expensive to move.

With the death of Lew Christensen in October 1984, an era ended in San Francisco, but the San Francisco Ballet continues to thrive under a new artistic director, Helgi Tomasson, formerly with the New York City Ballet. Guided by its president, Richard LeBlond, Jr., the company annually sells nearly 400,000 tickets at home and on tour, with box-office receipts providing over two-thirds of an operating budget of over $7 million—an unusually high percentage. Since December 1983, the company has worked in a new $13.8 million rehearsal, office, and school complex across the street from the opera house, training dancers for companies at home, around the country and the world. Recognition for company choreographers has grown: John McFall

created two original works for American Ballet Theatre, and Smuin's work for *Dance in America*—including *Song for Dead Warriors,* aired in early 1984—has brought the company to vast new audiences. As much a symbol of its city as trolley cars, the Golden Gate Bridge, and the TransAmerica Pyramid, the San Francisco Ballet has reached new heights of national achievement and recognition by responding to the conditions of mass culture, becoming a popular civic expression—the dream machine of the people.

·   ·   ·

If there is any single reason for the enormous strides taken by American ballet over the past quarter-century and for its rise in international importance, it is the dancers themselves. Once again, Balanchine's contribution assumes renewed importance, offering a vision of ballet training and initiation cutting across regional, class, and racial boundaries. "I don't take people because they are white or black," he once explained. "I take exquisite people that I like to see dancing."

Arthur Mitchell, who had trained first at the High School of Performing Arts then at the School of American Ballet, joined the New York City Ballet in 1955 as the first black American permanently a member of a major ballet company. In 1957, he danced unforgettably in the original *Agon;* later he created the role of Puck in Balanchine's *Midsummer Night's Dream,* and appeared on Broadway. But at the death of Martin Luther King, Jr., in 1968, he returned to his native Harlem, saying he felt a responsibility to rescue young people from the tragedy of the ghetto, recognizing in Harlem's vast untapped resources the beginnings of a new community identity through ballet.

Despite the success of dancers such as Mitchell, Janet Reed, and Carmen de Lavallade, among others, it was a long-held misconception in the ballet world that black people lacked the physiques to master a classical line. In fact what they lacked was the opportunity: Five black ballet companies have folded since 1937, in part because of reluctance of producers to accept them into their theaters. But the intense, charismatic

Dance Theatre of Harlem dancer Theara Ward with neighborhood children in 1981. (© 1981 Jack Vartoogian)

Mitchell—a self-described "controlled maniac"—proved to be both the inspiration and organizer of a real beginning for black classicism. Teaching free classes at the Harlem School of the Arts and later moving to the basement of a neighborhood church, Mitchell showed how ballet could be a proud, vigorous form of dancing, attracting 250 students in only two years' time.

"We gave lecture demonstrations every Wednesday afternoon at two," recalls ballerina Virginia Johnson, "sometimes to corporate representatives, sometimes just to local kids. Arthur took them all very seriously. No funny business. He told us that this was how we were going to improve." The school taught every aspect of theater production, from music and costuming to accounting; to attract more young men from the streets, Mitchell allowed them to take class only to ogle the girls, trusting that the fascination of classical training would lead them to more serious application. With help from the Ford Foundation, the school finally found larger quarters, this time in an empty garage in a notorious drug neighborhood on 122nd Street, a few blocks from where Arthur Mitchell was born in 1934. Here, the Dance Theatre of Harlem began in February 1969.

"Natural rhythm was all people saw at first," says Johnson. But Mitchell's aesthetic goals

Elena Carter and Joseph Wyatt in Petipa's *Paquita,* staged for the Dance Theatre of Harlem by Alexandra Danilova and Frederic Franklin. (© 1980 Jack Vartoogian)

were definite: His dancers reflected the disciplined courtesy, musicality, and correctness of Balanchine's Russian-derived training, but with an unmistakable Afro-American inflection. "There is such a thing as black classicism," Arlene Croce would note, "and it is a phenomenon, not an invention." The new company was extravagantly praised in Europe only a few years after its founding; by 1974, after its first extended New York season, it was famous on two continents.

In such classical one-acts as *Le Corsaire* and *Don Quixote*—restaged by DTH co-founder Karel Shook, a celebrated teacher and former direc-

tor of the National Ballet of Holland—Dance Theatre demonstrates its formidable dramatic flair and technical daring. Balanchine's *Bugaku,* a Japanese wedding night performed on *Dance in America* in 1977, featured Lydia Abarca, the company's earliest ballerina, in formal, spiderlike contortions of her body around her lover. Mitchell's *Holberg Suite,* originally choreographed to music by Edvard Grieg for a company lecture-demonstration, represents a continuation of City Ballet's neoclassicism. The black heritage has also helped define the artistic reach of the company: Arthur Mitchell's signature work, *Forces of Rhythm* (1972), contrasts the free pelvis and back movements of African and Caribbean dance with the prancing footwork and lavish extensions of Balanchine's style, as dancers dressed in tights, leotards, and T-shirts encounter others in African-style loincloths and full white skirts—and still another group strutting in the bowlers and gloves of black minstrelsy. Performed to funk tunes like "Doin' the Breakdown," and the soulful ballad, "He's Not Heavy, He's My Brother" by Donny Hathaway, this experimental merger of ethnic and social dancing with ballet served to illustrate the connections between classicism and more traditional Afro-American dance forms for new audiences in the black community. By the 1980s, the Dance Theatre of Harlem achieved its simplest goal: In Mitchell's words, "Blackness is now irrelevant in ballet." The thirty-nine–member Dance Theatre of Harlem has earned a reputation based on neither novelty nor tokenism, as an institution capable of representing American culture around the world.

Today, the company rehearses in beautiful studios located in a converted warehouse on West 152nd Street, near Harlem's Sugar Hill. Over a thousand students—future theater workers from thirty-one states and sixteen countries, many on generous scholarships—study annually at the school. Its alumni include doctors, lawyers, and business people, as well as dancers, musicians, designers, and technical crews working across America. The current repertory of the company is expanding in the direction of a new theatricality, with such high-stepping story ballets as Ruth Page's and Bentley Stone's classic

Frankie and Johnnie (1947), Valerie Bettis's *Streetcar Named Desire* (1948), and Caribbean-inspired extravangazas like Geoffrey Holder's *Dougla* (1974). "We proved we could count," says Virginia Johnson. "We could be in line. But we wanted to be *people,* too."

. . .

Early in 1982, Michael Smuin and Arthur Mitchell chatted together in San Francisco during a DTH engagement in the city. For professional rivals, the two men are unusually good friends; the San Francisco Ballet was sponsoring the Harlem company, sharing its audience in a gesture of unusual magnanimity. Mitchell pointed out how both of them had come up through the dance world "the hard way, working in a variety of dance fields." Now they run into one another in hotel lobbies in China and on dance panels in Washington, D.C.

"Michael, I know that in some past life we must have danced together," Mitchell teased him. "We would have made a great vaudeville act, too." He then spoke of their shared aesthetic purpose: "Some companies can be so 'artistic' that they lose the entire point. We'd say, 'In the long run, are the seats filled? Is the audience having a wonderful time? Okay, it works.' "

Michael Smuin agreed. "That's why our companies are so popular with audiences, I'm sure. . . . *Either you make the magic or you don't.*"

Theatrical entertainment and civic pride in modernism, merging in a new image of cultural vitality: The American ballet of the 1980s has become an inseparable part of the cultural expression of our age.

George Balanchine's **Serenade**, *performed by the New York City Ballet. (© 1983 Martha Swope)*

The Joffrey Ballet in Agnes de Mille's Rodeo *(1942).*
American dance has drawn on a range of popular styles,
including square dancing. (© 1981 Herbert Migdoll)

Mikhail Baryshnikov in the title role of The Prodigal Son, *by George Balanchine. (© 1978 Costas)*

Balanchine's staging of The Nutcracker, *an annual Christmas event at the New York State Theater, home of the New York City Ballet. (© 1977 Martha Swope)*

The Dance Theatre of Harlem in Geoffrey Holder's
Dougla. (© 1977 Martha Swope)

The Feld Ballet in Eliot Feld's Half-Time.
(© 1978 Lois Greenfield)

Peggy Lyman in Martha Graham's Lamentation.

(© 1980 Jack Vartoogian)

Alvin Ailey's Revelations. *(© 1977 Johan Elbers)*

Cunningham's Travelogue, *with decor by Robert*

Rauschenberg. It was performed to a John Cage score

of amplified Australian birdcalls and recorded

telephone messages, including horse-racing results.

(© 1977 Johan Elbers)

Taylor's Big Bertha, *featuring Tom Evert, Monica Morris, Carolyn Adams, and Bettie de Jong in the title role. (© 1980 Herbert Migdoll)*

Trisha Brown Dance Company in Opal Loop.

(© 1983 Johan Elbers)

THE MODERNS
AND BEYOND

THE ORIGINS OF MODERN DANCE

· AN AMERICAN GARDEN ·

Near the end of the nineteenth century, a handful of American women began to suspect that the dance traditions of the past had little to do with emerging realities in modern life. Enlightened, "artistic" dancing was still almost exclusively the property of touring ballet companies from Europe; with the American theater dominated by all-male minstrel shows, women who dared to dance in public places were usually considered little better than common prostitutes. Gradually, however, as female dancers and choreographers began to explore entirely new impulses to move, their struggles to invent an American dance for modern times became something more than a rejection of a classical past the nation had barely known. Rather they became the expression of a new state of mind, responding to uniquely American conditions with a social and artistic seriousness the stages of the Western world had never seen before.

The origins of this new American art had an unlikely advent in scandal: In 1866, the manager of Niblo's Garden, an otherwise-forgotten theater in lower Manhattan, decided to restage a clumsy cloak-and-dagger melodrama with a ballet company that had lost its own booking because of a fire. The resulting five-and-one-half-hour "spectacle-extravaganza," *The Black Crook,* caused riots in the streets, as hundreds fought to witness "the revel of sirens," "pas de demons,"

and fairy scenes danced in a vast stalactite grotto—and to gaze upon the dreamy flesh-colored tights of the Italian ballerina Marie Bonfanti and her half-trained English and American corps de ballet, as it giggled, talked, and leered at the audience from the stage. With the commercial triumph of this prototypical American musical, the craze for dancing women in the theater became nearly universal.

Indeed, throughout the Western world, as author Elizabeth Kendall has observed, late nineteenth-century audiences could enjoy "a glorious array of entertainment: operas, operettas, melodramas with music, giant spectacle-tableau, circuses, pantomimes, vaudeville, variety, music-hall, minstrel shows, cabaret, living pictures, dime museums, carnival midways—and in every show, there was some kind of dancing." By 1889, the demand for vaudeville entertainments that "mothers, sweethearts, and children" could attend had led to the introduction of a new form of feminine dancing from England. "Skirt dancing" blended the lively jigs and hornpipes of the British Isles with the svelte posturing and acrobatic feats of the ballet, allowing respectable girls to dance gracefully at public balls and cotillions without the least hint of impropriety. Here, then, was the foundation for an artistic dance in a nation ready to grant special significance to all forms of aesthetic expression.

American and English dancers in the original production of *The Black Crook*. (Courtesy Performing Arts Research Center, The New York Public Library)

The United States was approaching the twentieth century in the throes of a vast urban and industrial transformation—with an entire nation, as Alfred Kazin has written, "standing suddenly, as it were, between one society and another, one moral order and another . . . The sense of impending change became almost oppressive in its vividness." With Big Business in the saddle and new technology booming, newspapers and public speakers warned against the dangers of sensual pleasure and encouraged self-restraint. Noting the growing demand for urban amusements, social critics denounced as decadent such Old World preoccupations as theater and dance. Certainly ballroom dancing was a respectable avocation for any well-bred young Victorian woman, but many influential citizens believed that physical exhibitionism posed a threat to the moral economy of the age. The invention of the time clock and the closing of the frontier in 1890 marked the beginning of a new sense of American time and space; cities and factories were places of increasing toil and regimentation. And women were expected to be *home,* the tamers and civilizers of men, dependent, loving but without passion, providing husbands and children with havens from a heartless world. Not surprisingly, numbers of Americans began to

combat the poverty of their native situation—their sense of thwarted passions and limited horizons—with a new self-consciousness about the relationship between creativity and the body.

Physical fitness had long been intertwined with morality in America, and Americans' love of comfort noted by de Tocqueville decades before; both traditions resurfaced, merging with recent ideas about the spiritual value of art and the profundity of the ancient world. Greek statue posing became a fad; as a means to acquire the energy and freedom denied by the restrictive corsets and stays worn by American women of all social classes, systems of "aesthetic gymnastics" came to be practiced in fashionable salons and in working-class households across the nation. The work of a French music teacher, François Delsarte, had delineated the body into nine sections for the purposes of harmonious, expressive gesture—the first time that a system of movement had developed according to modern, "scientific" principles.

Out of this wide range of cultural influences, a new style of artistic dancing was born, its free-form leaps and skips and prances reviving a pastoral image of an America unviolated by the materialism of the late nineteenth century. Delsartean exercise, the imagination of ancient

"From her proceeds an expanding web—giant butterflies and petals, unfoldings—everything of a pure and elemental order," wrote Stéphane Mallarmé after an 1893 performance by Loie Fuller. (Courtesy The Stravinsky-Diaghilev Foundation)

Greece, and the swirls of the skirt dancers came together in an uninhibited continuity and flow, more a matter of lavish feeling than of talent. Barefoot "aesthetic" dancing may seem quaint and genteel to us now: "States of nature," as Irving Howe has written, "thrive only in the heads of civilized people." But in its day, such dancing embodied an instinctive rebellion against the oppression and frigidity of the Victorian era—a transgression worthy of denunciation from pulpits and lecterns around the country.

In the face of American prejudice against dance, the most intelligent, artistically inclined young women had no place except Europe to develop the new interpretive forms. One of the first was Loie Fuller (1862–1928) of Fullersburg, Ohio, who borrowed an innovation of Wagner's at Bayreuth to become the first choreog-

rapher to insist on a completely darkened theater during dance performances. Covering her stages in black velvet, she designed and implemented one of the first systems of projected stage lighting ever invented—complete with calcium and incandescent lights, magic lanterns, revolving disks, gels, and reflectors. Against this backdrop, Fuller draped herself in great swaths of flowing fabrics to dance as an illuminated butterfly, an orchid, a flame—an "instrument of light" capable of emanating the entire spectacle of the ballet-extravaganzas from a single body. Appearing as an impersonal yet entirely "natural" phenomenon, "La Loïe" was hailed as a genius in Paris for her invention of an entirely new art form. Her concept of "total theater" would revolutionize the presentation of movement in America and Europe, influencing even the future Ballets Russes; but her exotic sensuality, artistic seriousness, and commanding use of the solo figure in space commended her work immediately to contemporaries who followed her across the Atlantic. Among them was a charismatic young woman from San Francisco who arrived in England by way of New York in 1899. Unlike Loie Fuller, Isadora Duncan (1878–1927) learned to project her vivid personality through music, motion, and stillness alone, expanding the aesthetic ideal of beauty and self-expression into a dream of liberation, a total vision of life that came to symbolize the modern rediscovery of the dance.

· · · ·

Raised as a "pagan" nature worshiper in California, Duncan was immersed in Greek and Renaissance ideals of beauty in music and movement from the time she was old enough to move. The surge of the Pacific, Delsarte, and the image of Botticelli's *Primavera* inspired her earliest nature studies; at the age of eighteen, she headed East with her mother to dance in the popular theater and later performed pretty "aesthetic" pantomimes at the fashionable lawn parties and drawing-room soirées of the wealthy. When her pretensions to genius were ridiculed by the New York press, she fled to London, discovering firsthand the beauty of Greek sculpture in the British Museum, later learning from Loie Fuller the majesty of gesture. Within only a few years of her arrival abroad she could announce, "I am the dance," and half the continent agreed.

Her simple movements were fearlessly performed to great music by Bach, Beethoven, Chopin, Gluck, Schubert, and Wagner; merely walking barefoot or skipping gracefully across a stage, her supple arms and torso flowing in generous, expansive rhythms, Isadora could express fundamental feelings of joy, anger, fear, exultation. Her work was the fruit of a constant study of classical and Renaissance art, along with skirt dancing, Delsarte, ethnic dance forms, and the ballet she had learned from Marie Bonfanti. But most important, she had come to analyze the intimate rise and fall of her body's weight and breath: "For hours I could stand quite still," she

Isadora Duncan and her six adopted daughters, the Isadorables. Duncan founded the first school of modern dance in Berlin in 1905, and a second one in Moscow in 1921. "What I want is a school of life," she wrote. (Courtesy Performing Arts Research Center, The New York Public Library)

wrote, "my two hands folded between my breasts, covering the solar plexus. I was seeking and finally discovered the central spring of all movement, the creator of motor power, the unity from which all diversities of movement are born, the mirror of vision for the creation of the dance."

To Europeans, Isadora appeared as a miraculous vision of sensual innocence, an incarnation of a pagan America, and an evocation of the glories of ancient Greece in a single body. Canonized as a major artistic figure, Duncan came to symbolize the century's creative ferment not only in dance but in theater, sculpture, painting, and literature as well. Nevertheless, she met with only limited success on several tours to the nation she never disavowed: Many Americans deplored her profligate Bohemianism, her open liaisons with men, and her two illegitimate children; moralists scourged her as an amateur indulging in the most shameless kind of self-advertisement. In 1909, she achieved a *succès d'estime* at the Metropolitan Opera House in New York City; public sympathy shifted only after the tragic deaths of her children in a motor accident four years later. But there was a larger force behind her bittersweet triumph at the Met in 1914: In an insurgent spirit of free expression, the United States was sloughing off the gentility of the nineteenth century in a groundswell of popular interest in dance.

At home and in public, to live orchestras and the newly invented record player, Americans of all ages and social classes were beginning to move to the broad, elusive syncopations of ragtime and driving underworld rhythms of the ragtime-blues amalgam known as jazz. By mid-decade, Irene and Vernon Castle had popularized smooth exhibition tangos, one-steps, and hesitation waltzes, exemplifying a new age of urban sophistication. With social dancing a uniquely American form of expression, the originality and gusto of the Grizzly Bear, the Bunny Hug, the Fox-trot, and the Turkey Trot became sources of cultural pride. America's home-grown "classical" dancing also emerged for a time as a kind of national exercise, practiced on lawns and in parks around the country; but this pastoral vision of American grace and beauty received a mortal blow with the ascendance of urban jazz.

Still, Isadora clung to her ideals, scorning "the sensual convulsion of the Negro" and expanding her advocacy of physical culture to embrace the radical political causes of her day. Attacking her legions of imitators as "saccharine and sweet syrup," she danced as a tragedienne, composing monumental patriotic works, *Marche Slave* and "La Marseillaise," honoring the wartime heroism of Poland and France. Her support for the Russian Revolution linked her with the "red menace" of the 1920s, and after baring a breast at a curtain call in Boston—"that shameless hussy doesn't wear enough clothes to pad a crutch," cried Billy Sunday—she rarely traveled again to her homeland. Instead, in schools established in Germany and Russia, Duncan tested her theories and methods of training, seeking ways to make the body "become transparent" and "a medium for the mind and spirit." Her six adopted daughters, the Isadorables, performed around the world, establishing several companies and schools in America to promulgate her ideas. But Isadora never succeeded in establishing a rational technique for future generations; today, her cult survives only through the sensitive devotion of individual artists.

What does endure, however, is a spiritual legacy: Along with Loie Fuller, Duncan demonstrated that individual feeling could stimulate new and authentic ways of thinking about the body in space and time, departing from the dance traditions of the past to forge a vital link with the contemporary spirit. Isadora never sought a nostalgic or ineffectual beauty; her descendants were freed to evoke not a glamorous, ethereal world of fairies and sylphs but "the feelings and emotions of all humanity."

·   ·   ·

In June 1977, during a time of renewed reverence for the roots of an American art, "Trailblazers of Modern Dance," an epic history of American modern dance from the late nineteenth century to the 1930s, aired on *Dance in America*. The script was written by Elizabeth Kendall, and the massive job of assembling rare film footage fell to director/producer Emile Ardolino and producer Judy Kinberg, with research by Dell Byrne. Thomas Edison's hand-painted 1897 film re-created the effect of colored scarves swirling around a Loie Fuller imitator named Annabella; another film fragment revealed La Loïe herself, dancing in ambient regalia. The romance of darkest Russia and of Hollywood came together in a brief look at Anna Pavlova, skipping on those famous pointes during a visit to Los Angeles. Isadora's adopted daughter, Anna Duncan, improvised and her sister Irma's "aesthetic" dancers pranced through a Southern California garden for a 1932 newsreel, "Aesthetic Dancers Aid the Unemployed." Remarkably, Isadora Duncan herself—in her only known film, recently rediscovered in London—performed at a small garden party, where a camera had rolled furtively behind a tree for less than a minute.

Along with documentary footage, "Trailblazers" also included contemporary interpretations and reconstructions that have added immeasurably to our understanding of an era when dance was seldom preserved by any means. The great English choreographer Sir Frederick Ashton had seen Duncan dance forty years before: "She seemed to me a woman of tremendous personality and tremendous passion," Ashton told *Dance in America* audiences. "She had an incredible gift of stillness. She could stand there and hold an audience in the most wonderful way and then suddenly just move her hand—it was like a miracle, you know." In Ashton's *Five Brahms Waltzes in the Manner of Isadora Duncan,* ballerina Lynn Seymour of the Royal Ballet bounds across the space in a diaphanous gown, showering rose petals as she moves. Ashton and Seymour's idealized image of Duncan was based on nothing more than memory, but another dancer, the American Annabelle Gamson, performed a version of Duncan's actual choreography to Alexander Scriabin's Etude No. 8, Opus 12, recapturing the hardier joys of revolutionary commitment. Born a year after Duncan's death, Gamson was trained as a child by Julia Levien, a former member of Irma and Anna Duncan's companies; after a career in other forms of dance, she returned to Levien in the early 1970s to become not an impersonator of Isadora but an interpreter of her work and spirit. In a dance composed to Scriabin's Etude No. 2, Opus 1, Duncan had mourned the loss of her children and prayed for the future of the children she taught; Gamson's powerful dynamics, the communicative directness of the images she generates, suggest Duncan's anticipation of the modern dance of the future.

At the end of her life Isadora was essentially a tragic figure, her school in Moscow already closed for three years on the afternoon she climbed into a car rolling away from a party in the south of France. *"Je vais à la gloire,"* she said, and a few seconds later her long scarf caught in the spokes of a wheel, killing her instantly. The future of American dance did not rest with this self-appointed apostle of liberation, already drowned in the rising tide of modern times. As it happened, the fountainhead of the modern spirit lay instead within the mystic longings and shrewd

Annabelle Gamson dancing to Scriabin's Etude No. 2, Opus 1. "Duncan solos are like folk forms," Gamson has remarked. "You learn the outline and then you have to fill them up with yourself. . . . They spring from the gut—from the simple, human instinct to move." (© 1976 Lois Greenfield)

theatrical know-how of a young Irish-American named Ruth St. Denis (1878–1968).

·   ·   ·

Raised as a tomboyish country girl in New Jersey, Ruthie Dennis was the incarnation of her mother's progressive theories of feminine health, dress reform, and Delsartean exercise. But very early in life, she had encountered the sensual religion of neighborhood Catholic girls, and recognized in herself a need to be at the service of some greater thing. At age seven, she found P. T. Barnum's circus unforgettable, and six years later, a theatrical spectacle called *Egypt Through the Ages* suggested the possibility of dance as a career. By the time she was twenty-one, Ruth was a largely

Ruth St. Denis and Ted Shawn as Egyptians, 1923. (Courtesy Performing Arts Research Center, The New York Public Library)

her new name on her steamer trunk. A creature of the theater, she nevertheless heard in "the drama of her soul" the voice of a sacred calling.

In a Buffalo soda shop during a thirty-five-week Belasco tour, St. Denis noticed an illustration of the goddess Isis in an advertisement for Egyptian Deity Cigarettes, and at that moment resolved: "I will be Egypt." The 1893 Columbian Exposition in Chicago had introduced the dance of the Orient to America, but vaudeville was popularizing the art of the "mysterious East" without much comprehension of its artistry; visiting libraries and working with a group of Hindu "nautch" dancers living in Coney Island, St. Denis undertook a serious study of Oriental traditions. Her solo, *Radha,* "marked the first time in commercial theater," Elizabeth Kendall has noted, "that the body of a dancer had realized its own natural pace and began to occupy all the space and time it craved on stage."

Ruth St. Denis became an overnight sensation. In 1906, she took her ambitious new dances to Europe, where she performed for King Edward VII and was toasted by some of Europe's greatest artists. Unlike Loie Fuller and Isadora Duncan, however, St. Denis returned for good to "hurrying, money-making America" three years later, arriving during a time of renewed popular interest in the exotic East. She immediately set about fashioning lavish "ceremonies of the senses," sweeping audiences around the nation into the tumult of the bazaar and the ancient hush of incense-filled temples. Her first and most famous major work, *Egypta*—featuring the prematurely white-haired choreographer as its untouchable goddess, high-priestess, and seer—drew equally on Belasco's canny theatricality, her own exotic allure, and a sure instinct for the mystic aura. St. Denis's severe yet sensual spectacles were compared in their day to the works of the Ballets Russes and Pavlova; one contemporary critic saw in St. Denis's seductive saintliness "a universal rhythm beneath the broken chaos of our modern industrial life which shall infuse new joy and rhythmic harmony into our common life." St. Denis had rediscovered for popular American audiences the spiritual

self-taught skirt dancer with an impressive array of acrobatic tricks under her belt, working for New York impresario David Belasco in hugely successful pictorial extravaganzas headlining the greatest stars of the day. Noticing the gorgeous, full-bodied woman, Belasco pulled Ruth out of the chorus line and made her a protégée—although her willful girlishness once so infuriated the flamboyant producer that he cursed her as "St. Dennis." Recognizing an omen when she saw one, Ruth dropped one of the *n*'s and wrote

Students in an outdoor class at Denishawn. "I started the teaching day by supervising the students' exercise in stretching, limbering, breathing," Ted Shawn wrote many years later. (Courtesy Performing Arts Research Center, The New York Public Library)

origins of dance in ritual—and created thrilling entertainments to boot.

In 1911, a twenty-year-old former Methodist divinity student wept at his first sight of St. Denis on stage. Three years later, Ted Shawn appeared at Miss Ruth's studio in New York, and within months became her first dance partner and eventually her husband. Concealing his homosexuality from the public, Shawn offered a new image of the male dancer in America: an "Anglo-Saxon Hercules" with a powerful physique and a burning authority on stage. Working with an almost evangelical fervor to attract both men and women to dance, later choreographing his own free adaptations of ballet for a brawny all-male troupe, Shawn was also a skillful entrepreneur, and under his influence Denishawn—the first institutional dance theater in the nation—brought serious concert performances to new heights of popular acceptance in the United States.

With the first appearances of Pavlova, at least a few Americans had begun to suspect that dance required serious application. Yet dancing as a profession continued to carry an onus of immorality until this respectably married couple established an open-air school in Los Angeles, training dancers for their several touring companies and the new California film industry. Drawn by the bewitching Denishawn formula of good health and virginal spirituality, significant numbers of middle-class American girls were attracted to the dance for the first time—the same graceful girls next door glamorized in silent films, pursuing their naïve dreams of art in the hills above Hollywood. Because Shawn believed that "dance is too great to be encompassed by any one system," the school taught a host of techniques, ranging from barefoot ballet and "aesthetic" dance to "the ancient terpsichorean art" of Asia and the Near East. The stress on diverse, persistent study would become Denishawn's most important legacy to the coming generation of modern dancers.

One documentary clip of "Trailblazers" shows women gathering for outdoor classes at Denishawn; in another, hundreds of Denishawn dancers appear as Egyptians in the largest out-

Without questioning the fundamentals of movement, Helen Tamiris (1905–1966) opened modern dance to a new range of subject matter. After a brief career as a nightclub dancer, Helen Becker took the name of a ruthless Persian queen and brought "100 percent Americanism to American art," dancing to Negro spirituals and jazz, and even drawing on the movements of boxers for her *Prize Fight Studies*. With her good looks and combustible showmanship, Tamiris brought a much-needed glamour to modern dance; she also brought a social conscience, anticipating the modern dance of the 1930s. (Soiohi Sunami, Courtesy Performing Arts Research Center, The New York Public Library)

ation of works from the teens and twenties, presented by the Joyce Trisler Danscompany—captured for television the theatrical architecture of Denishawn's creations. Shawn's "music visualization," *Polonaise,* reconstructed by Norman Walker, was "masculine in principle and performance," Ted Shawn noted, and even further from the dreamy aestheticism of Denishawn: When his all-male troupe danced the ballet in brief flesh-colored trunks that made them appear nude, London audiences literally gasped in shock. In many respects, these Denishawn works linger as curiosities from an age when "exotic" dancers appeared in nearly every area of American entertainment. Nonetheless, they became the ground for a native American art.

• • •

Denishawn's eclecticism spawned an independent outlook among its brighter and more ambitious students, especially Doris Humphrey (1895–1958) of Oak Park, Illinois. Educated in progressive schools, Humphrey taught dance with her mother and even choreographed a ballet three years before traveling west to join Denishawn in 1915. St. Denis's own work, inspired by Isadora Duncan's music visualizations, had grown increasingly classical, reflecting the structure and mood of the music through plastic poses, flowing scarves and draperies that complemented the girlish loveliness of her dancers. In 1920, she chose Humphrey as her collaborator on *Soaring,* a visualization of a Robert Schumann score. Karna Pinska's re-creation of *Soaring* for Trisler's company captured little of the naïve abandon of the dance evident from the early Denishawn films and photographs. One former Denishawn dancer, Jane Sherman, insisted that *Soaring* was originally danced in flesh-colored unitards, not Grecian tunics, so that nothing would distract from the play of colored lights on a large billowing scarf. A balletic, lyrical work for five women creating an illusion of waves and clouds with the fabric, the new dance was reminiscent of the creations of Loie Fuller; but the elegant, carefully structured design suggests the budding analytical intelligence of a future modernist, Doris Humphrey.

door pageant in film history, staged for D. W. Griffith's *Intolerance* in 1915. St. Denis herself performs a Siamese dance, a Javanese court dance, and an Indian nautch dance in a 1932 film that suggests the substance if not the spirit of her art. The 1976 revival of "The Spirit of Denishawn"—a controversial evening-length re-cre-

In 1916, another young middle-class woman arrived at Denishawn: a vain, intense, not unusually attractive twenty-three-year-old Californian named Martha Graham. Sharing the discipline of Denishawn as a common ground for their rejection of the past, Graham and Humphrey would soon look beyond St. Denis's extravagant ornamental interpretations of foreign lands and the nostalgic pastoral themes of aestheticism. In less than fifteen years, a generation of modern dancers would leave behind the popular theater to create an approach to art characterized "like the true dance of any period of world history," as Graham would declare, "by a simplicity of idea, a focus directly upon movement, and behind and above and all around, a direct relationship to the blood flow of the time and the country that nourishes it."

What would the new modern dance look like? There would be as many different styles as there were individual choreographers—but unlike the dancers of Europe, who performed in ballet slippers and pointe shoes for an illusion of lightness, early modern dancers would move like "aesthetic" dancers, barefoot, in touch with the earth. The high carriage, calm center, and proud aerial leaps of the ballet seem to defy gravity—but some modern dancers would emphasize the body's actual weight and effort, the powerful tensions and countertensions of the torso and the limbs. Like the "aesthetic" dancers, the future moderns believed that dance was the supreme manifestation of spiritual life and sought the essential gesture—but they would examine the movements of bodies en masse and the visceral sensations, the clash and contrast of commonplace activities such as walking, running, falling, and the exhalation of breath. Direct experience and observation of how people actually move became an essential response to a society reinventing itself through the power and pulsing rhythms of the machine.

Influenced by the rise of abstraction in all the twentieth-century arts, modern choreographers would focus the aesthetic ideal of self-expression at its primary source—the movement of the body—and develop entirely new disciplines of training to serve their individual visions. The essence, the core of dancing would become the drama of the kinetic idea, for the moderns believed that if the dancer could only re-create the quality of an emotion, then the body would generate new, concrete shapes to reveal a world of inner experience. "Americans love only what is beautiful," declared Ruth St. Denis, but modern dancers would make their chief aim "the expression of an inner compulsion," wrote John Martin, America's first full-time critic of the dance; they would invent ways of moving never seen on antique friezes or on European ballet stages, borrowing from traditions around the world to create dances that would not necessarily be beautiful but which would be *significant*.

In the pursuit of their intuitive perceptions and elusive truths, early modern dancers also recognized the deep interdependence of movement, private emotion, and communal myth. Some works would develop as narratives reflecting the nation's historical experiences, while others bore the modern message through the patterned organization of movement alone. Doris Humphrey discarded her old-fashioned hoops and scarves to discover a starker lyricism in *Air for a G-String* (1928), one of her last dances for Denishawn. "Four abstract themes, all moving equally and harmoniously together like a fugue," she later wrote, "would convey the significance of democracy far better than would one woman dressed in red, white, and blue, with stars in her hair." Modern choreographers were preparing to announce their social, political, and psychological relevance to American society with a "candid, sweeping, wind-worn liberty," as Lincoln Kirstein noted, consciously engaging the most crucial issues of the age. The traditions of the past became more than an impediment to free expression; they now represented an abrogation of the present. A modern dance meant the abandonment of all former constraints of custom and style: "Make it new," as Ezra Pound advised.

Doris Humphrey left Denishawn in 1928 in the company of a gifted mime and character dancer, Charles Weidman, to form an *American* dance company in New York City. Three years

Doris Humphrey's *The Shakers,* performed by dancers with the José Limón Dance Company: Mark Ammerman, Jennifer Scanlon, and Laura Glenn. "The disposition of the sect was bound to appeal to her temperament, which was drawn always to the art of disciplined simplicity," Humphrey's biographer, Selma Jean Cohen, has written. (© 1975 Martha Swope)

earlier, she had observed Oriental dance first-hand during a Denishawn tour of Asia and returned to the United States convinced that any attempt to transplant a foreign tradition to the New World was fundamentally wrongheaded. A strict and inspired teacher, Humphrey began to investigate movement as an activity occurring between falling and recovery, in-breath and out-breath, balance and the loss of balance—"the arc between two deaths." Gradually she would discover in this stable patterning of "energy made visible" her own emotional relationship to the restless sway of modern life. Her earliest dra-

matic masterpiece, *The Shakers* (1931), was based on the ecstatic movement of the nineteenth-century Shaker sect, whose members shook their bodies to rid themselves of sin. The Shaker ritual "met all the definitions of great dance drama," Humphrey later wrote. "It had a lofty purpose, it was dramatic, communicative, and rhythmic, and in addition was truly communal, engaging every man, woman, and child in the colony." These qualities would preoccupy Humphrey for the next twenty-five years, even in her most abstract movement studies.

But it was Martha Graham who would

stand at the absolute frontier of the modern revolt. Graham's reaction against the frivolity and decorousness of her aesthetic training was total: "I did not want to be a tree, a flower or a wave," she later recalled. "In a dancer's body, we as audience must see ourselves, not the imitated behavior of everyday actions, not the phenomena of nature, not exotic creatures from another planet, but something of the miracle that is a human being, motivated, disciplined, controlled. . . ." Inspired by a painting by Wassily Kandinsky, viewing his stark red slash against a field of blue in 1921, she told herself, "I will dance like that."

Driven by a burning desire to feel, to know, to be aware of themselves and their world, modern choreographers would create a new tradition of radical individuality amid communal effort, finding in personal truths a physical expression of their time. But it was Graham herself, investigating the struggle between her own Puritan heritage and the new freedom of the twentieth century, who would discover, in the words of one early critic, "a tempo, a rhythm and attitude toward space which is peculiar to America and . . . unlike any other nation on earth."

Martha Graham's first New York concert in 1926 offered eighteen barefoot, exotically costumed dances in the classical-interpretative vein, including *A Study in Lacquer,* to music by Marcel Bernheim. (Courtesy Martha Graham Center of Contemporary Dance)

THE MARTHA GRAHAM DANCE COMPANY

· AN INNER LANDSCAPE ·

"There is no end of the things of the heart."
EZRA POUND

Piano music drifts through the narrow angled hallways and staircase, the quiet dressing rooms of an ivy-covered building on Manhattan's Upper East Side. Visible through one of the studio doorways, a group of dance students engage in a morning ritual that once seemed an essential initiation into the mysteries of modern dance expression. "Freedom to a dancer means only one thing," Martha Graham has said many times. *"Discipline.* The body is shaped, disciplined, honored, and, in time, trusted."

Developed through fifty years of choreographic necessity, classes at the Martha Graham School of Contemporary Dance are theater in their own right, an approach to movement that glorifies struggle, heaving up the ecstatic weight of the body, then surrendering it to the pull of the earth. The dancers are seated on the floor with the soles of their feet together, curving and lengthening their spines with a deep exhalation of breath. This contraction and its release provide a new command over the shape of the torso but, more important, become the impetus behind all Graham's movement, integrating limbs and trunk for the conquest of space. With a release of the spine, the dancers stretch their legs luxuriously to the side, then gather them up with another contraction; now curving tautly back, almost touching the floor, they arch up into a seated position again. Suddenly backs curve and

lengthen convulsively, legs lash open, ankles flex, and arms stab forward in cathartic gestures of surrender. "The open crotch school of movement," scoffed Ruth St. Denis. Another powerful rotation of the spine, and the dancers are seated at right angles to the mirror, swirling their arms overhead, sweeping their upper bodies in abrupt circles along the floor. They then sink slowly to the ground for a movement known as "the pleadings," which Graham first developed in the 1930s. Lying on the gray marled floor, they convulse orgasmically, lifting shoulders and knees so their bodies assume the shape of bowls. Whether luxurious or percussive, these movements have all originated in what Graham calls "the house of the pelvic truth," shaping images of an almost primal conviction.

When the dancers finally leave the floor, their spiraling falls and pitched turns, sliding splits to the floor, space-devouring leaps and "sparkles," and loping runs with arms akimbo comprise a kind of body language "composed solely of epithets," as critic Deborah Jowitt once observed. Each exercise was first invented for a dance, then formalized into a tool for training; many postures and inflections seem archaic, with suggestions of Egyptian profiles, Javenese flexed feet, Cambodian knee walks, and various other restructured Orientalisms that remain from Graham's years with Denishawn. "I am a thief,"

Martha Graham at the Metropolitan Opera House in 1980. "For me, the dance is life," she told a friend on opening night, "and I'm always hungry for more." (© 1980 Jack Vartoogian)

Graham has written, "and I glory in it." The expressive range of Graham's technique has made it the first lasting alternative to the idiom of classical ballet in over three centuries. But for the choreographer, technique is only a vehicle for self-discovery—and there is nothing more revealing than movement.

"I am interested only in the subtle being," the choreographer wrote in the late 1940s, during the years of her greatest achievements; "the subtle body that lies beneath the gross muscles. Every dance is, to some greater or lesser extent, a kind of fever chart, a graph of the heart. I do not compose ideologically and I have never considered my dances in any way intellectual. Whatever theory may be read into them proceeds from the material and not vice versa." Although the extraordinary sophistication of her style has limited her dances almost exclusively to her own company, Martha Graham's approach to movement—born from a Puritan's view of freedom as the recognition of necessity—has resulted in an entirely new means to measure the human heart, to probe the psyche in all its complexities and dark deceits. For the choreographer of 175 dances, a woman who is her most intense and characteristic self in rehearsal and on stage, the idea of casting off this "divine turbulence" has clearly been impossible.

For two hours each afternoon and evening, and sometimes long into the night, Graham works with her company of twenty-seven dancers, preparing new works for the coming season. In her tenth decade, a frail, arthritic woman with a scuttling walk, she enters the studio like some high priestess from another age. Perched in regal isolation by the studio mirrors, skin taut over her high cheekbones and calf eyes flashing, she talks through her dances now, commanding the room with runic utterances, at times deeply frustrated by her inability to dance herself. As a young woman, when her absolute command and audacity as a dancer made her a legend throughout the American theater, Graham sometimes practiced four hundred jumps in fifteen minutes to bring herself to a pitch of performance readiness. Now, working with a generation of dancers who have never seen her perform, she can only demonstrate with haunted energy a contraction and release, seated in her chair, to clarify the motivation of a dancer's movement. Stories about Graham's tearing a telephone off a wall and ripping dancers' costumes to shreds before a performance are part of her personal legend. But as she once remarked, "I have never destroyed anyone who didn't want to be destroyed."

"Every now and then she will save it up and deliver, believe me," says David Brown, a Jamaican-born principal dancer who began as a percussionist for dance classes. "She knows how to find someone's weak point, how to tear into people to give a dance life. Martha investigates personalities in time and space. Sometimes she'll say, 'I want you to hate me. I don't care if you hate my guts, let's see your guts on the stage.' The funny thing about her is she likes strong personalities, people who've investigated themselves and have strong responses and impulses. And at the same time she's such a domineering woman, someone who can't really respect personalities. But if you're good—strong—you can sacrifice some of your self-determination because she has the power to take you to another place. You feel a psychological dimension, you see the person unmasked—and the better they are, the more unmasked they are."

Graham's ability to draw out the psychological and emotional truth of gesture is unequaled. Movement must become a kind of personal immolation, a glimpse behind the curtain of consciousness. Graham's means for achieving this are sometimes abusive but more often intuitive, allusive, magical. During a rehearsal of the new *Dances of the Golden Hall*—a kind of homage to Denishawn inspired by a book Graham received from the Indian classical dancer Shanto Rao—Anna Kisselgoff of *The New York Times* was given the rare opportunity to observe Graham at work. The choreographer told a young dancer to press her foot "implacably" into a man's stomach: "It's a domination," Graham explained. "At that moment she becomes Kali. You know what I mean, the goddess of death. That doesn't mean dying, but killing in yourself the things you don't want. The commitment with that foot must be apparent or it's just dance positions, which I want to avoid. You must have a constant flow. Then you get something ritualistic. Unless you feel it passionately, it can be a very bad dance."

Because Graham can no longer generate new movement with her own body, she must depend on her dancers to produce movement within her codified style, shaping and reshaping their contributions into her latest dances. With growing numbers of classically trained, long-limbed performers entering the company, a new harmony and virtuosic strength has transformed not only Graham's new work but her older dances as well, so that many longtime observers of the company believe that the primal character of Graham's early masterpieces has been lost. The risk of becoming a period style is ever present. Graham herself assessed the differences between her present company and the sturdy, Amazonian troupes of the 1930s and early 1940s: "Slimmer, very much slimmer, with longer legs," she

Martha Graham's *Adorations.*
(© Herbert Migdoll)

said. "They're not built aggressively. They're built more for air, swiftness, not for argument."

Not only are bodies different but dancers *think* differently today: Recapturing the expressionist tension of one woman's struggle to transform herself into an artist is a difficult task. Amid company classes and work on new pieces, former dancers Linda Hodes, Yuriko Kikuchi, and Pearl Lang rehearse with the company to keep Graham's historic repertory alive, as true to its orginal conception as possible—from the stark, weighted ritualism of *Primitive Mysteries,* created in 1931, to the celebratory pantheism of *Acts of Light,* made half a century later. Occasionally Graham will marshal her energies to appear unannounced at repertory rehearsals. She may correct a step, rediscover a gesture's appropriate tension, or speak at great length—and with great beauty—of the emotions that stirred a dance at its formation. A video camera records these insights for future generations. Unlike a classical ballet, much of Graham's work is a kind of theatrical autobiography, a web of secrets known only to her; even here, within her company, certain dances have become shadows of a past beyond remembering, and will never be revived.

Yet the choreographer continues to believe that through the act of dancing, ancient emotions emerge—unconscious memories lingering in the nervous system, traces of "ancestral mood." Sometimes the sight of her own past stirs painful memories of earlier self-confrontations. *Hérodiade* (1944), originally titled *Mirror Before Me,* Graham once described as "a dance of choice . . . the doom-eager act of a dedicated being." Later she thought of it as a story of a woman facing the fact of her own aging. In recreating this ambiguous crisis for the first time in seven years, the company brought a new dancer to the role. Yuriko Kimura, born and raised in traditional Japan, found herself facing Graham's "thunder—as if her spirit were still trapped there."

"Sometimes dancing her roles," says Kimura, "I think maybe this is it: Once you fell in love very deeply and you burned your passion in the Other—this is a different time now and you can't burn that much, you can't fall in love with the same passion. This is like doing her parts and always recalling her through that inner language. Working with her is like living a life together. And that kind of strength gives me the

Martha Graham as *Xochitl*, 1920. (Courtesy Performing Arts Research Center, The New York Public Library)

ability to control myself, and I think I gain much more understanding of my life outside the studio."

Graham's recent work has not enjoyed the critical esteem of the past. Arlene Croce has described her image as "a bookish lady" creating "post-Victorian exhortations for the moral enrichment of mankind." And yet much of her art remains an expression beyond words, expanding her own technique as theater, passing into a fully codified modern classicism celebrating the eloquence of dancing with little of the transcendent pessimism that characterizes many artists' advanced age. "Truth is, you must love life," she has said many times in recent years. Working with the heroism of patience and pitiless self-examination, Martha Graham has made one of the great artistic odysseys of any era, moving

along a frontier between reality and myth and bringing "tragedy to the sense of touch," as Andrew Porter has written. The story of modern dance includes many others, but it is Graham's "lonely and terrifying gifts" that created an artistic revolution—a consuming expression of the thrust of modern times.

·   ·   ·

A tenth-generation American of Scottish-Irish descent, Martha Graham was born in Allegheny, Pennsylvania, on May 11, 1894, the eldest child of a conservative physician specializing in women's nervous complaints. She and her two younger sisters were raised by an Irish-Catholic nursemaid, a former patient of her father, who brought a playful sense of make-believe to a Presbyterian household where dancing was considered frivolous, though not a sinful preoccupation. By her own account, Graham was a difficult child. She would later claim that her first dance lesson came from her father, who told her he knew when she was lying by the way she held her body.

When Graham was fourteen her family moved to Santa Barbara, California, where the glorious weather and Spanish and Asian influences swung her "in the direction of paganism," as she recalled in an early interview, "though years were to pass before I was fully emancipated." Graham was a model student in high school, untouched by the popular theater and preparing for life in her station, when her father took her to see Ruth St. Denis in Los Angeles. Her inner existence was changed forever. After her father's death and two years of study at the Cumnock School of Expression in Los Angeles, Graham began her dance career at Denishawn in 1916, enrolling at the rather advanced age of twenty-three.

Asked to perform at her first audition, Graham claimed to have answered shyly, "But Miss Ruth, I've never danced, I don't know anything about it." Busy organizing a concert tour, St. Denis didn't know what to do with this abrupt, angular young woman, so she passed her along to Ted Shawn, who was assembling his own vaudeville touring company. Graham's commitment and bottomless capacity for work astonished everyone, and in 1920 Shawn made her a star as the furious princess fighting for her maidenhood in his "virile" Aztec spectacle *Xochitl*—the century's first dance created on an American theme. Although Graham stood only a few inches above five feet, the massive Shawn came off the stage literally bruised and bleeding from the beatings she administered. After three more years of touring, Graham left the company when St. Denis claimed the coveted role of Xochitl for a European tour, and took a job as an "artistic" dancer in the Greenwich Village Follies. She had been living and working with Shawn's company in New York since 1921, under the spell of a city unlike any she had ever experienced.

New York City was alive with the kinetic provocation of the streets and nightclubs, the parade of body-revealing fashions, and the excitement of Broadway, movies, and spectator sports. Graham was vividly aware of a gathering artistic and intellectual ferment as well—"a revolution of things colliding," in Wallace Stevens's phrase. Greenwich Village had been a bohemian mecca since the turn of the century, but by the 1920s it was the meeting ground of a young generation of artists stimulated by the most progressive ideas from Europe. "We are provincial no longer," said Woodrow Wilson, even before America's entry into World War I. Stanislavsky's Moscow Art Theater visited New York in 1923, bringing a new psychological understanding of acting: a desire to reveal on stage intimate knowledge of how men and women actually think and behave. Stanislavsky had been deeply impressed and perhaps even influenced by Isadora Duncan during her early visits to Russia; he in turn would affect the course of modern dance by proposing the body as a concrete agent of emotion. Freudian psychology—its recognition of the inner life and the importance of self-revelation—became another tool for younger artists, opening new access to the relationship between the mind and body and suggesting that sexuality was no longer something to be deliberately ignored or repressed.

Along with these ideas, a modern American sensibility was growing in defiance of the cultural supremacy of Europe. At the Neighborhood Playhouse and Theater Guild, the modern theater movement searched for America's folk roots, while the Provincetown Playhouse developed the work of a serious new American dramatist, Eugene O'Neill. For some artists it was a time of disillusionment caused by the disastrous war in Europe, a failed peace, and the larger inability of American progress to provide truly satisfying lives: "The capacity of this generation to believe has run very thin," wrote F. Scott Fitzgerald. But others were committing themselves to their art as a pathway to personal and social redemption. Everywhere, younger artists were insisting that if modern experience were left to act on the deepest sources of the self the result would be revolutionary new forms of expression. Out of a need to sustain the urgency of primitive feeling in the face of modern sophistication, life was to be lived in the present, and art was to nurture the direct, even vehement treatment of immediate perceptions and feelings.

Graham's initial attraction to the theatrical exoticism of Denishawn had been fueled by her own desire for grandeur, her need to escape the severity of her Presbyterian upbringing. But she was also alert, disciplined, able to approach the best new art unselfconsciously. At age thirty, a star of the Greenwich Village Follies, and living in reasonable comfort, she decided to begin her "adventure of seeking" at the experimental Eastman School of Music in Rochester, New York. Only half-realizing it at the time, she was searching for a modern dance.

·   ·   ·

Teaching movement to drama and music students, Graham almost immediately began her own intellectual and emotional investigation of choreography. "The first morning I went to class, I thought, 'I won't teach anything I know,'" she recalled years later. "I was through with character dancing. I wanted to begin not with characters or ideas but with movement. So I started with the simplest—walking, running, skipping, leaping—and went on from there. By

Mary Wigman (1886–1973), the primary exponent of Central European modernism and an important influence on the development of a modern dance in America. As early as 1913, she began to create strident, jarring, angular dances, striving with a scientific fury to exact the right movement for each emotion she wished to express. (Courtesy Performing Arts Research Center, The New York Public Library)

correcting what looked false, I soon began creating. I wanted significant movement. I did not want it to be beautiful or fluid. I wanted it to be fraught with inner meaning, with excitement and surge. I wanted to lose the facile quality. I did not want it to *leak* out, so I concentrated in a small space. Gradually, as I was able to force out the old, little new things began to grow."

After a year, Graham returned to New York to develop her work with the aid of a close friend, the former musical director at Deni-

shawn, Louis Horst (1894–1964). For Graham, Doris Humphrey, Charles Weidman, and other early moderns, Horst created "a landscape to move in," not only providing musical accompaniment for concerts but also promoting a disciplined, uncompromising approach to form, the antithesis of aestheticism's uninhibited freedom. He spent nearly three decades helping to structure Graham's instincts especially—introducing her to German philosophy, contemporary experimental music, and primitive sculpture, which had inspired Picasso and Braque in the early development of cubism. And it was Horst who, after a visit to Vienna, brought Graham photographs of a muscular young German dancer named Mary Wigman (1886–1973). Wigman's abstract dances—perhaps the first modern dances of our time—were alternately boneless and bursting with nervous tension, using the pure motion of the body to express primordial urges of joy, ecstasy, and horror, driven by a will of almost superhuman intensity.

Graham denies the influence of German expressionism, but soon her own work began to move along similar lines: She would strike the modern note for the first time in *Revolt* (1927), a stark, earthbound solo casting daunting new movements in the image of her own body, its gestures sharp, dissonant, angular, requiring a long, flexible spine and little jumping ability. As usual, Graham announced the seriousness of the occasion by renting a legitimate New York theater rather than a recital hall, where "artistic" dancing was usually consigned. From the beginning, Graham did not want to entertain audiences; she intended to *move* them with a style of theater encompassing lighting, costumes, music, and a serious artistic theme.

In order to support herself while developing her choreographic ideas, Graham resumed teaching in 1928 at the Neighborhood Playhouse in New York, where she possessed—or was possessed by—an extraordinary ability to spellbind and inspire. Her newly formed company of sturdy young women—built more along the lines of fieldworkers than temple virgins—held down jobs as secretaries, elevator operators, and salesgirls during the day for the privilege of toiling until midnight with Martha in the sacred groves of art. Capable of terrifying rages, Graham demanded total commitment from everyone around her, renouncing her private life in a fanatical desire to create dances that might "give voice to the fully awakened man." Nurturing a "mysterious, faintly lofty aura resembling that of Ruth St. Denis," notes biographer Don McDonough, she came to be considered hopelessly neurotic even by her friends.

Yet to her adherents, Graham was all things modern, teaching strength and virility through the phenomenon of her nearly inexhaustible energy and vivid psychological insights into movement. By now, she was thinking fundamentally about the body: Inspired by the floor exercises of a dancer named Ronny Johansson and by training methods that St. Denis had used in her Asian dance classes, she began to develop the floorbound contraction and release of the spine as an abstraction of the natural cycles of breathing—to motivate the movement of the limbs, to draw out unconscious feeling, and to instill in dancers her own instinctive sense of presence. A new percussiveness and nervous vitality entered Graham's work. "Her jumps are jolts," wrote Lincoln Kirstein after one early concert; "her walks, limps and staggers; her runs, heavy blind impulsive gallops; her bends, sways. Her idiom of motion has little of the aerial in it, but there's plenty of rolling around on the floor."

Setting her dances to dynamic contemporary music, Graham had come to identify with the very forces that drove the age, fusing the energy and power of her body with the chiseled lines of the machine. "Life today is nervous, sharp, and zigzag," she wrote in 1929, the year of the stock market collapse. "It often stops in midair." The term *modern dance*—"a genuinely primitive expression," Kirstein claimed—came into increasing usage, along with attacks on her work as ugly and self-indulgent. To those outsiders who knew of her dances, Graham was a "new barbarian," a "dark soul." Drama critic Stark Young suggested that if she were to give birth it would probably be to a cube. To these detractors, Graham replied that her movement proceeded not from thought but from instinctual feeling, and "fits me like a glove fits me. . . . Ugliness can be beautiful if it cries out with the voice of power."

And yet Graham's unique confrontation with her time never entirely transcended an image of herself as a feminine hero burning at the center of some essentially private crisis. Her discovery of self drew deeply on Ruth St. Denis's austere sensual grandeur as well as her longing "to ennoble man's concept of himself." But now Graham was moving beyond conventional images of the dancer to find some purer resolution between her emotions and their expression in movement. With the 1930 solo *Lamentation* she discovered the communicative power of a new approach to choreographic form and a new means for dissolving her inner tensions in an absolute realm of art.

Performed by Peggy Lyman for *Dance in America* in 1976, *Lamentation* presents an abstract distillation of the experience of grief. Shrouded in a long tube of stretch jersey, an unnamed woman never rises from a low bench: Her torso pulses, rocks, and twists; her limbs tug and push at the fabric, focusing intense scrutiny on its sculptural shapes and angles. The alternating distraction and concentration of her gestures suggest pleading, agony, and a final surrender to bereavement, and yet only the gnarled feet, the fretting hands, and the Madonna-like pathos of her face gazing from under the cowllike hood betrays the dance as an expression of human emotion. An image of grief depersonalized, *Lamentation* gains its force solely from the rigors of its design. Whatever experiences Graham recalled in creating this cameo masterpiece, her oldest surviving dance, the quality of the emotion had transformed into the shapes and energy of the dance itself.

Graham's formal mastery had evolved to the point that she could begin to approach choreography and performance as an exploration of the emotions binding all humanity. Later in 1930, after her company's first tour of the West Coast, Graham and Horst visited New Mexico, where

Graham in *Primitive Mysteries*. "I can say that it is one of the few things I have ever seen in dancing," wrote drama critic Stark Young, "where the idea, its origin, the source from which it grew, the development of its excitement and sanctity, give me a sense of baffled awe and surprise, the sense of wonder and defeat in its beautiful presence." (Courtesy Performing Arts Research Center, The New York Public Library.)

they observed the cruel rituals of the Penitentes, a Hispanic-Indian religious sect that blended paganism with the ritualistic Catholicism of Latin America. The fruit of her research was the epoch-making *Primitive Mysteries,* Graham's sixty-third dance, choreographed in 1931. The exaggerated restlessness of her earlier work had vanished entirely, as dancers moved in stiff vertical postures or at acute angles to the floor, framing the virginal central figure—Graham herself—like a saint in a shrine. Angular, cold, stylized, *Primitive Mysteries* was a new kind of ecstatic theater,

a miracle play that brought a purer flow to the emotions than any previous work, chastening its own fierce, aggressive patterns and weighted gestures with an enigmatic simplicity that seemed an ideal embodiment of ritual feeling. *Primitive Mysteries* was immediately recognized as a masterpiece of modern art and an indisputably American creation.

The adventure of the new American dance was only beginning. In the 1930s, choreographers and companies would use their newly disciplined freedom to probe the archetypal myths and social rituals of a nation coming into its own, holding a mirror to reality to reflect "the shapes of ancestral wonder." Only four years after *Primitive Mysteries,* Graham would create *Frontier,* a remarkable vision of feminine endurance celebrating America's vigor and tenacity in the settlement of a new country. "High Priestess Martha Graham and her surrealist fence act," cracked *Time* magazine, but Graham was moving with a new exhilaration and intimacy. The taut mask of her earlier work melted, and she smiled for the first time, dancing in the homespun of an American pioneer. Modern dance had begun to realize in movement a fundamental American truth—that the nation was not a place for starting but a place for starting *over.*

·   ·   ·

Although the early tours of the Ballet Russe de Monte Carlo exposed American audiences to the best ballet that Europe had to offer, modern dancers adhered to their distrust of foreign glamour and elite, escapist entertainments. Few choreographers believed they could ignore a world shaken by the Great Depression, unemployment, and the rise of fascism in Europe, viewing their art as a populist expression at last raised to the level of society's best dreams and aspirations. Some of the more radical labor unions established their own modern dance troupes as a means for exposing social ills and celebrating the collective destiny of the masses; the Federal Theater Project, a wing of the Works Progress Administration, hired 185 dancers at mid-decade and ended up ousting most of them as leftists.

Modern dance wedded itself easily to the adversary politics of the time, but the leading artists in the modern movement remained political liberals, not radicals. Graham herself was more concerned with "unlocking the fetters that bound the spirit, not those twisting the social fabric," as Don McDonough has noted, but even she made her sympathies known, refusing to let her company, with Jewish members, accept an invitation to the cultural Olympics in Berlin. She also voiced her outrage against the Spanish Civil War in *Chronicle* (1936) and *Immediate Tragedy* (1937), dances exposing "the ugly logic of imperialism, the need for conquest, the inevitability of conflict."

At Bennington College in Vermont, a kind of modern-dance Bayreuth established in the summer of 1934, Graham, Humphrey, Charles Weidman, and a recent émigré from Germany, Hanya Holm, dedicated their art to the creation of disciplined affirmations of faith in pluralistic, democratic society. Humphrey was considered by many the greatest choreographer of the group; her full-evening trilogy, *Theater Piece, With My Red Fires,* and *New Dance,* celebrated the possibility of individual fulfillment through the development of society "from disorganization to organization." John Martin called the work "the crowning achievement of American dance thus far." Martha Graham was viewed first and foremost as an unforgettable soloist—"a flaming obvious flower," wrote Humphrey, but nonetheless a dancer whose extraordinary self-possession on stage exerted a strange power over the rapt and enraptured audiences who filled her annual concerts in New York City. "Strangely enough, the impression she has always made is essentially feminine," Agnes de Mille noted in the early 1930s. "She is small—five feet, three inches. On the stage, she seems tall, gaunt, and powerful. She looks starved, but her body is deceptively sturdy. She has probably the strongest back and thighs in the world . . . the hands are heartbreaking, contorted, work-worn, the hands of a washerwoman. All the drudgery and bitterness of her life have gone into her hands. These are the extremities, roped with veins and knotted in

the joints, that seem to stream light when she lifts them into dance. But . . . it is the face one sees first and last, the eyes and voice that hold one. . . ."

After the success of *Primitive Mysteries,* Graham continued to create abstract, ritualistic dances, but with limited artistic success. Gradually she too was swept up in the largest current of the American arts in the 1930s—music, literature, and the visual arts as well as dance—and began to search for the *feel* of American reality through works reflecting the nation's historical experience. Beginning with *American Provincials* in 1934, three-quarters of Graham's work over the next decade bore on American subjects directly, including a major watershed in her career, *American Document* (1938). A programmatic dance-theater work based loosely on the format of the minstrel show, with spoken texts taken from the Declaration of Independence, the Gettysburg Address, the sermons of Jonathan Edwards, the Song of Songs, the works of Walt Whitman, and other important American letters, *American Document* signaled the beginnings of work directly addressing plot and character: dance-drama.

Graham's interest in theater had always been strong: She taught movement for actors at the Neighborhood Playhouse for years (Bette Davis and Gregory Peck were among her students) and sometimes choreographed for the commercial stage. The emergence of clear dramatic themes in her own work was further stimulated by the first appearance of a man in her company: the solid, classically American presence of Erick Hawkins, who was soon managing the troupe and living with Martha as well. Hawkins helped spur Graham to address issues of sexuality, to consider the dramatic conflict between woman's traditional cultural role as nurturer and her personal responsibilities as an artist. The stark percussiveness of her earlier work began to soften, and her dances grew more lyrical and varied, with airborne leaps and smooth transitional phrasing—like "ballet going against the grain," Edwin Denby suggested. At the age of forty-four, Graham began to leave behind what

Graham and the second man to join her company, Merce Cunningham, in *Letter to the World*. (© 1980 Barbara Morgan)

she later called her "period of long woolens," named after the shapeless fabrics of her company's sack dresses, and to embrace the full resources of the stage. By 1940, she had created her first great dance-theater work, *Letter to the World,* based on the life and poetry of Emily Dickinson: an ordered phantasmagoria employing cinematic flashbacks to explore the mysteries of a singular human heart.

"This is my letter to the world/that never wrote to me": *Letter* was unmistakably Graham's inner autobiography—"a documentary of the artist in a Puritanical culture," writes Marcia Siegel, "of woman caught in convention, and of

the beauty such a person can perceive and give back to her culture." The success of this and other dramas of conflict and resolution led to greater acceptance of her work among critics and audiences alike, and a week-long run at the National Theater on Broadway. In later years, Graham would wonder how she had managed to hold an audience for as long as she had. With her new dramatic approach, she was ready to enter a creative cycle that would result in America's most important dance-theater legacy.

·   ·   ·

Appalachian Spring (1944) is "essentially a dance of place," Graham said thirty years after its cre-

Janet Eilber, Ross Parkes, Yuriko Kimura, and Rudolf Nureyev in *Appalachian Spring*. (© 1975 Martha Swope)

ation. "You choose a place . . . part of the house goes up . . . you dedicate it. The questing spirit is there, and the sense of establishing roots." Performed for *Dance in America* during the bicentennial year, *Appalachian Spring* celebrates American values within an imaginative space that is at once a haven and an unfinished frontier homestead on the edge of a terrible wilderness. "If you have ever seen spring come," Graham once remarked, "the first shimmer of one of those willow trees in the light, or when you have seen the ground break for the first moment—it is that moment that I hoped would come out of the words 'Appalachian Spring.' "

Hoping to arrive at "an essence of the stark pioneer spirit," sculptor Isamu Noguchi designed a two-dimensional outline of a roof and walls, a section of unfinished wall with a narrow bench, and a porch with a slim rocking chair to one side. In the foreground, a high-railed fence sketches the border of the new homestead. "It's a structure on which the house is built," Graham explains, "and behind the structure is the emotion that builds the house, which is love." Louis Horst insisted on a specially commissioned score, and Graham worked closely with Aaron Copland for over a year on the Pulitzer Prize–winning music. With its steady tempos, odd rhythmic contrasts, and imaginative orchestrations of folk songs such as the Shaker hymn "Simple Gifts," Copland's *Appalachian Spring* has become both a landmark in dance-music collaboration and an American classic in its own right.

The choreographic structure for Graham's most popular work is splendidly simple and episodic, her genius for storytelling never more fully realized than in this unified setting of a housewarming marriage, placed in an unspecified earlier time in American history. The dancing itself displayed a genius for evoking the heritage of the nation through movement: "America," Graham wrote in a letter to Copland, "is forever peopled with characters who walk with us in the present in a very real way." The Husbandman suggests a practical character and an inflexible turn of mind with his broadshouldered, rolling gait, his careful slides across the ground, and his restrained yet proud leaps and turns. The Bride—unique among Graham's roles, an equal of the other characters—begins as a child-woman barely able to restrain her joy over her impending marriage; later she dances with nervous excitement, as if fearful that her future might be threatened by faithlessness or human

Takako Asakawa in *Cave of the Heart*. (© 1978 Beverly Gallegos)

frailty. Worn and remote, the Ancestress is an older version of the pioneer in *Frontier,* dignified by hardship and finding some inner wisdom gazing across an empty wilderness. The sanctimonious Revivalist appears forbidding and spiritually vain, strangely dependent on the submissive chorus of worshipers who flock around him in their frilly blue dresses. In his solo, he preaches against the evils of conjugal love, flinging himself to the ground and flailing his arms like thunderbolts, warning the young couple not to depart from the paths of righteousness. The fearful Husbandman looks to the Ancestress for support, but the Bride seems independent of formal religion. In her passion for the land, she embraces the earth, then turns unabashedly to her husband for strength. The marriage ceremony ends, and Husbandman and Bride dance their jubilant jigs and reels; the final moment finds

them facing the future alone, sitting on their porch steps at the beginning of a new life.

Rich with nostalgia, *Appalachian Spring* never condescends to the values it seeks to affirm; rather it seems to make visible the eloquence of inarticulate emotion, to make heard the silence of a uniquely American feeling. The dance summons the daring self-sufficiency and pride of an older America: Graham places the dancers in curious isolation from one another, interconnected, as Marcia Siegel has suggested, only "by means of their common ceremonies, myths, and aspirations." Beneath the joyous surface of the work, sustaining its dramatic power, seethes a hell-fired terror: The dance takes its title from a line in "The Dancer," part of Hart Crane's poem *The Bridge,* which tells the story of a newly married Indian brave captured by an enemy tribe and put to death at the stake, merging himself with his tormenters' ecstasy as they dance around his burning body. The Graham dancer must experience a similar symbolic immolation—and yet, ironically, the pioneers in *Appalachian Spring* conquer fear and isolation through open innocence, creating an enduring vision of American pioneer times with special significance during the hardships of World War II.

By the close of the war, Martha Graham was in her early fifties, her creativity at its height. Many of the other early figures of dance modernism were no longer creating their own work on a regular basis: Hanya Holm, Helen Tamiris, and Charles Weidman ventured in and out of Broadway and film choreography; Doris Humphrey had stopped dancing altogether, due to an arthritic hip, becoming artistic director of a new company established by her protégé, the Mexican-born dancer-choreographer José Limón. With her unrivaled mastery, Martha Graham became the focus of increasing deification that she did little to discourage.

And yet her personal life was in turmoil: Hawkins left her for the first time in 1945. Soon afterward she entered a Jungian analysis that deepened her long fascination with archetype and dream. Jung's view of myth as a kind of psychology to the ancients, his vision of humanity

Created at the first American Dance Festival at Connecticut College during the rainy summer of 1948–"when I thought an angel would never come out"—Martha Graham's *Diversion of Angels* was an unusual work at that period in her life—sunlit, nonliterary, celebrating the lyrical aspects of Graham's movement style and her dancers' idealized commitment to one another. An athletic corps of men frame three women, each representing "a different aspect of women in love," Graham later told *Dance in America* audiences. *Diversion* is one of Graham's best-known works, and one of the few that has been performed by companies other than her own. (© 1980 Lois Greenfield)

ruled not by reason or will but by the manifestation of primeval universal patterns, appeared to confirm the ideas she had explored from her earliest days with Denishawn. Now she would suddenly turn away from themes rooted in an American place and time to probe "the soul at a moment of agonized choice," dancing as the tragic-triumphant heroine at some supreme moment of illumination—seeking "to pierce through the strata of the trivial . . . to the roots of human experience."

In January 1946, Graham premiered one of her greatest works, *Dark Meadow*, casting herself as One Who Seeks, audaciously and eternally, for the dark sources of creativity and the promise of rebirth. Her first major work on a Greek theme, *Cave of the Heart*, appeared just four months later. Derived from the legend of Medea, the dance tells the story of the Sorceress of Colchis, who murders her own children and her husband, Jason, in a fury so exalted that it thrusts her beyond conventional morality into tragedy.

Originally titled *The Serpent Heart, Cave* does not tell Medea's entire story but rather locates its essence in "a dance of possessive and destroying love," Graham noted, "a love which feeds upon itself and when it is overthrown, is fulfilled only in revenge." The theme and music were developed through careful collaboration between Graham and composer Samuel Barber, with Isamu Noguchi designing the golden tree in which Medea enmeshes herself, branches trembling like serpents, at the end of her "Dance of Vengeance." Performed for *Dance in America* audiences by Takako Asakawa, Medea quivers and shakes in a violent tremolo, spewing from her bodice a long red ribbon and devouring it again and again: disturbing, unpredictable flashes of movement are repeated with maniacal intensity. When Graham unclenched her fury in the role during a visit to Burma in 1955, one audience member compared her to "an elephant run amok." Graham's ritual purification of emotion, evolving from the anonymous mourner in *Lam-*

José Limón (1907–1972), a former Humphrey-Weidman soloist who emerged as modern dance's finest male performer during the 1940s and 1950s. He swiftly became a major choreographer as well, seeking, in his own words, "man's basic tragedy and the grandeur of his spirit. . . . I reach for demons, martyrs, apostates, fools, and other impassioned victims." Limón's *The Moor's Pavane,* a distillation of the tragedy of Othello, has become the modern dance work most often performed by ballet companies. (© 1983 Martha Swope)

Erick Hawkins in his most important early work, *Here and Now with Watchers* (1957). Beginning with the realization that "taut muscles cannot feel," Hawkins has explored, a direct, free-flowing, sensual style, refusing to glorify the alienation of contemporary society. (© 1976 Lois Greenfield)

entation to the American longings of *Appalachian Spring,* now distilled a terrifying archetype of human consciousness.

In *Errand into the Maze* (1947), Graham portrayed a woman confronting a nameless terror in the Cretan labyrinth; that same year, *Night Journey* told the story of Oedipus from the point of view of his mother and wife, Jocasta. Graham's intellectual dance legends were expressions of very private passions: the isolation of artistic consciousness; her complex sense of immersion, awe, and fear in the act of creation; perhaps even her pangs for a receding past. But by presenting these themes through the mythology of the ancient world and insisting upon their truth as universal statements of the human condition, Graham ceased to confront the material of her own heart directly. In the future, she would create dances no longer "about herself in reference to mankind," Marcia Siegel suggests, but rather "about mankind as represented by herself and her company." With a fully established technique, a beautifully trained company of men and women, and her own presence absorbing and reflecting her meanings, her new ambitions had a chance to be realized. But with an aging body, Graham grew increasingly unable to generate movement herself, thus ending her direct, intuitive search into "the inner landscape which is the dancer's world." Her long period of experimentation and self-discovery would draw to a close during the 1950s—and at the same time modern dance itself entered its first crisis of faith.

·   ·   ·

The triumph of the Graham company on its 1955 world tour made it clear that modern dance had become a phenomenon capable of representing "highbrow" American culture around the world; by the end of the decade, the modern détente with ballet would be symbolized by the joint appearance of the Graham company with the New York City Ballet in a shared program at City Center. But with its growing recognition and cultural stature, many younger critics began to announce that the old modern dance had passed from the creative vanguard. Indeed, much of the work that followed in the footsteps of the mod-

Alwin Nikolais's expressionist brand of "total theater" is a multimedia blend of lights, sounds, spectacle, and the intriguing theatricality of bodies in abstract motion. Expanding the analysis of movement pioneered by Mary Wigman and her student, Hanya Holm, Nikolais explores a playful and mysterious world of human action with a showman's flair, controlling an audience's intuition and mood through illusion, games, and the suggestion of a mystical presence. (© 1980 Daniel Cande)

ern masters lacked their force and originality, celebrating skill rather than inspiration. By the mid-1950s, only Graham and Limón's companies were performing with any regularity.

Now there were new choreographic directions: Erick Hawkins embarked on his own work, rejecting Graham's emotional violence to develop a sensual, free-flowing movement style derived from his study of anatomy, kinesiology, and the dance forms of primitive cultures. Alwin Nikolais, a former puppeteer, musician, and student of Hanya Holm at Bennington College, established his own company in New York, preferring to think of man as "a fellow traveler within the total universal mechanism rather than the god from which all things flowed." Creating abstract dances dependent on lights, costumes, ambience, and mood, Nikolais departed from modern dance's traditional impassioned psychology, puzzling and even angering many longtime observers of the art.

But by far the most promising new work was being developed by a former Graham dancer, Merce Cunningham, who initiated a break within modern dance as radical as its earlier departure from Denishawn. Cunningham replaced modernism's passionate concern with message with the rhythms of the dancing itself, choreographing from a pure movement impulse having little to do with Graham's expressive motivations. And just over the horizon was the work of a dancer who had joined the Graham company in 1955: Paul Taylor, "a tall young man in perfect command of himself," wrote one slightly baffled critic at the close of the decade, "knowing what he wants to do and doing it, though not telling why."

Graham was not only passing out of the avant garde; even by her own high standards, her work in the 1950s was growing increasingly decorative and angst-ridden, inevitably focused on Graham herself, making one last push toward glory and self-extinction. Her close collaborations with Horst ended bitterly in 1948, her marriage to Hawkins two years later; increasingly alone and miserable, Graham managed to create only five new works between 1951 and 1958, including her popular *Seraphic Dialogue* (1955), based on the legend of St. Joan. But at mid-decade, she summoned her declining energies to spend three years creating her first evening-length dance, the most ambitious work of her career.

Presented in a ninety-minute version on *Dance in America* in 1979, the three-hour dance-drama *Clytemnestra* (1958) derives from the *Oresteia* of Aeschylus as imagined by the wife of Agamemnon, the king who led the Greeks in the long war against Troy. Clytemnestra is a woman driven by a great passion and a great bitterness: Two voices comment on the action while Clytemnestra wanders in the underworld among the dead, tormented by her memories of vengeance, lust, and power. She begins to remember—at first with panic, then with increasing clarity—the events that surrounded the Greeks' expedition to Troy and its tragic fruits.

In order to remain a ritual presence on stage without having to dance much, Graham had developed a compositional technique through which the story seems to unfold within the panorama of her own consciousness. Leaping from scene to scene in time fractured by memory, Clytemnestra watches the abduction of Helen by Paris; Agamemnon's sacrifice of their daughter, Iphigeneia, to procure favorable winds for the voyage; the fall and rape of Troy; and Agamemnon's triumphant return with Cassandra, the captive Trojan princess and prophetess. Through Clytemnestra's eyes we see her vengeful murder of her unfaithful husband and the seeress, aided by her new lover, Aegisthus; finally we observe Clytemnestra's own death at the hands of her son, Orestes, encouraged by his sister Elektra. If the dance sounds complex, it was; Graham was only able to draw the work together with the help of a company of dancers who had worked with her for nearly fifteen years. At the close of the work—performed in an eerie psychic landscape designed by Isamu Noguchi—Orestes meets his mother once more in the underworld, and Clytemnestra acknowledges her complicity in the colossal crimes that have unfolded, thus achieving a kind of spiritual rebirth. For all its sweeping monumentality and operatic emotion, "the theme of Clytemnestra is simply salvation," wrote John Martin, "perhaps in a Freudian rather than a religious sense."

The long-awaited premiere of the work Graham considers her masterpiece marked her

Clytemnestra, with Yuriko Kimura. (© 1984 Martha Swope.)

last great performance as a dancer. Although she danced the Bride with youthful veracity for a filming of *Appalachian Spring* the following year, by the early 1960s critics began to notice that she was having trouble rising from her knees. Fighting the inevitable, Graham choreographed increasingly immobile roles for herself, holding the stage through sheer force of will. All modern companies are dangerously dependent on their creators, but Graham believed that her own presence in her work was indispensable. At her company's urging, she reluctantly revived a few of her older works and recast the leading roles with younger dancers, but rehearsals grew increasingly chaotic, with Graham seeking to control them as she always had since the early 1950s— through cajolery and cunning. By the late 1960s, with the Graham company revered as a kind of national treasure, the repertory was clearly los-

ing its dramatic power. Graham's intense indentification with her achievement was threatening its very survival.

The morning of the company's 1970 opening at the Brooklyn Academy of Music, Graham read on the front page of *The New York Times* that she was retiring from the stage after a fifty-year career. It was unclear who had planted the story. That night, she arrived by limousine to tell her audience that the report was false, but she did not perform—and people knew the truth. She was seventy-six years old. After the season ended, Graham left New York for the Connecticut countryside, ostensibly to write a book. Her life as a performer had ended.

Graham entered a period of private agony. Over the next eighteen months, intestinal problems hospitalized her twice; denied alcohol, she undertook a special diet and strict medication. Back in New York, meanwhile, some dozen company members past and present were busy reconstructing from memory some 26 Graham dances—out of the 153 she had choreographed— then performing them for preservation on film and video.

One day Graham appeared unannounced at the studio on Sixty-third Street. She had passed through another personal rebirth, in part through the assistance of a thirty-year-old former law student and photographer named Ron Protas, who swiftly became the new company manager and later the associate artistic director. The 1973 Broadway season, which included a revival of *Clytemnestra* with Pearl Lang and Mary Hinkson alternating in the title role, proved a major success. After a 1974 tour of Asia, led by the resurgent eighty-year-old choreographer, the company went outside the school for the first time to hold auditions, and a number of technically superb young dancers entered the company— among them Takako Asakawa, Janet Eilber, David Hatch Walker, Peter Sparling, and Tim Wengerd. Although Graham had trained few of these dancers herself, the new company emerged in May to an enthusiastic Broadway reception.

·   ·   ·

Americans love tragedies with happy endings, and the Graham saga after 1974 has a certain ambiguous quality of triumph. Under Ron Protas's leadership, the profile of the company shifted in the direction of a glamour formerly reserved for the highest reaches of ballet. In 1975, the Martha Graham Dance Company held its first-ever gala opening, as the first modern dance company ever to conduct a season at New York's Metropolitan Opera House. The ceremonies were presided over by Jacqueline Onassis and First Lady Betty Ford— a former Graham student who had actually performed with the company as an apprentice in 1938. Graham vowed, "I am interested only in the star thing," and choreographed a new ballet, *Lucifer,* for Rudolf Nureyev and Margot Fonteyn, who also performed the crowd-pleasing Act II pas de deux from *Swan Lake.* Fonteyn had not danced barefoot since 1940.

For Graham, personal accolades contin-

ued. In October 1976, she was awarded the Medal for Freedom, the first dancer to receive the nation's high civilian honor since the ceremonies began in 1945. President Ford and Betty Ford hosted the reception at the White House, where Graham had first performed at the invitation of Eleanor Roosevelt thirty years before. The former artistic revolutionary had become part of the nation's most traditional cultural institutions: For the 1976 season at the Met, Graham created *The Scarlet Letter,* her first work on an American theme in thirty-two years, featuring Nureyev in the role of Reverend Dimmesdale; two years later, *Frescoes* honored the opening of the Egyptian Temple of Dendur at the Metropolitan Museum of Art. One way of assimilating a nation's artistic giants is to enshrine them as living treasures. Martha Graham has "survived into her own posterity," in Siegel's phrase, honored as the matriarch of the many who created a new era in American dance. Late in 1984, the Martha Graham Institute opened at the University of California at Berkeley, providing the company with an annual nine-week residency; in January, the company appeared at the Paris Opéra, now under Nureyev's direction, as the first American troupe ever to dance on the home stage of the world's first chartered ballet company. Graham herself was knighted by the French Legion of Honor.

For her ninetieth birthday season in New York, Martha Graham undertook one of the most ambitious projects of her career—her own version of Stravinsky's *Rite of Spring,* begun "with reluctance and fear," as she told *The New York Times.* "She's overwhelmed by it sometimes," says dancer Janet Eilber, who left the company to pursue a career in television, film, and theater. "She'll walk into the studio and all the sets are there and the crates before a season opens, and she'll say, 'Where did all this stuff come from?' And she'll wonder what her little company of three dancers has turned into."

Reaching across epochs in American dance history, Martha Graham's "divine dissatisfaction" has been essentially an investigation of her own spirit, and through it, the spirit of the age.

Her art remains difficult and "avant-garde" to many audiences, but her rethinking of the body has become the single most important fountainhead of new dance in this century, affecting the development of concert dance around the world. Virtually every major native-born American choreographer before the mid-1960s—from Jerome Robbins to Twyla Tharp—has touched on her training, and several former dancers have gone on to internationally recognized choreographic careers of their own. Ensuing generations may have moved in new directions, renewing the fundamental investigation of movement that was the distinguishing characteristic of early modern dance in the late 1920s, when Graham's odyssey began. But the need to be ruthlessly true to the spirit of the time—a tradition that Graham more than anyone inaugurated—has remained the point of departure for the dance of the present day: a tradition of change, of constant conflict between received ideas and the quest of the New.

And yet Martha Graham rejects her identification with the experience of this century alone. Denying that she was even a revolutionary, she has recast her tumultuous art as a search for a universal wisdom transcending the perspective of her era. Six decades of struggle and achievement have resulted in one of the world's great lyric theaters, and a legacy synonymous with the search for artistic passion and truth. Against loss and regret—and what Joseph Campbell calls "the ultimate passage of the dark gate"—Graham offers the world of the gods.

"A seashell is not modern," says dancer Tim Wengerd. "A mountain is not modern. It simply *is*."

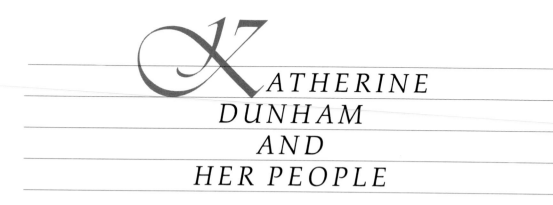

KATHERINE DUNHAM AND HER PEOPLE

· DIVINE DRUMBEATS ·

Modern dance has made a distinctly American contribution to world culture. But unlike jazz and so many other American popular entertainments, from minstrelsy to black Broadway musicals, early modern dance was largely developed by white, middle-class Americans. Afro-American shapes and rhythms have been the basis for nearly all American popular dance innovation, from the Cakewalk to Disco and beyond. Blackness has been the principal American *difference* in concert dance as well—with the presence of black attitudes and energy suggested in countless works by white choreographers all the way back to Adolph Bolm's *Crazy Cat* in 1921. But discrimination and lack of opportunity kept black Americans in the background throughout modernism's formative years, even if modern dance was easier to penetrate than the world of ballet, where five black companies went under.

A young woman named Edna Guy took private dance lessons from Ruth St. Denis, whose Hollywood center was segregated; she and Helmsley Winfield formed the Negro Art Theater Dance Group in 1931. That same year, a white choreographer named Lester Horton, whose modern duet *The Beloved* (1948) was presented on *Dance In America* by the Dance Theatre of Harlem, founded a fully integrated modern troupe in Los Angeles. Charles Williams and his all-black

Hampton Institute followed, and black Americans participated in the Federal Dance Project and at Ted Shawn's summer festival at Jacob's Pillow, Massachusetts, during the 1930s. But the brilliance of hoofers like Bill "Bojangles" Robinson, the Nicholas Brothers, and John Bubbles was closer to the genius of black dancing in that decade of extravaganza, as the great tradition of the tap reached its apogee. Such dancing seized the moment, sparkled and entertained, but the full cultural depth of the nation's largest racial minority remained largely untapped in concert form until the late 1930s, when a young University of Chicago–trained anthropologist named Katherine Dunham began her careful explorations into the origins of black dance in the Americas.

Born in Chicago and raised in the prison town of Joliet, Illinois, Dunham brought a vivid sense of cultural pride and a background in modern dance and ballet to bear on her study of the so-called primitive dances of the Carribean—dances largely ignored, misunderstood, or even banned by authorities in their own homelands. Antebellum slaves in the United States had incorporated European dance elements into their own to stave off cultural domination; in the Carribbean, where black culture had developed in greater isolation, dances remained much closer to the religious and cultural functions of the Af-

Katherine Dunham in the mid-1940s, dancing in *L'Ag'-Ya,* part of her world-famous 'Tropical Revue." (Courtesy Katherine Dunham)

rican originals. Now Dunham saw something fundamental to human nature in the village rituals of Martinique, Trinidad, Jamaica, Haiti, and the Lesser Antilles. The natives there chided her, saying she was a girl from the lost tribe of America who had forgotten the African gods. The advice changed her life.

Beginning in the late 1930s, Dunham recreated and popularized Afro-Caribbean dances in a series of hugely popular revues and extravaganzas, "Ballets Nègres," which some critics compared to the Ballets Russes of Diaghilev. *Choros* (1943) was based on a Brazilian quadrille; *L'Ag'Ya* (1944), a story of love and jealousy, used a West Indian fighting dance banned in Martinique; *Shango* (1945) drew upon Haitian voudun ritual. Touring America and the world with her "Tropical Revues," collaborating with Balanchine on the Broadway musical *Cabin in the Sky,* Dunham danced with her trademark cigar, hip-hugging wraparound skirts, and flamboyant energy as one of the great performers of a generation. "The High Priestess of the Pelvic Girdle," Martha Graham called her, she even developed her own technique, incorporating the hip-shaking, pounding feet, and undulating spine of African and Caribbean dances with the extensions

and turns of Western forms. As a teacher at her school in New York, the mother of a distinctly Afro-American concert dance stood at the center of a resurgence of cultural awareness that has touched every corner of Afro-American art and entertainment.

When public interest in Caribbean concert spectacle waned with the rise of television and "cooler" forms of entertainment in the 1950s, Dunham resettled abroad, returning in 1969 to live and work in East St. Louis. Here, in a community torn by poverty and crime, she swiftly demonstrated how art can break through the apathy and violence resulting from generations of discrimination and blighted ambitions: Her Performing Arts Training Center of the University of Southern Illinois has proved enormously successful in getting young people off the streets and moving in the direction of constructive lives.

Dunham has remained a living legend among many Americans, but *Dance in America* undoubtedly introduced an essential figure in American dance to millions who had never seen or heard of her work before. "Divine Drumbeats: Katherine Dunham and Her People," aired in 1980, resuscitated one of her most important early works, *Rites de Passage,* originally choreo-

Katherine Dunham's *Rites de Passage*. (© 1985 Don Perdue)

graphed in 1941. Adapted from the puberty and fertility rites of African tribes, with music from a Haitian drum theme, *Rites* was scheduled to open at the Boston Opera House in 1944, but the civic censor ordered it off the stage. Reconstructed at Yale University in the 1970s, with costumes and sets by Dunham's husband, the distinguished designer John Pratt, *Rites de Passage* was performed for *Dance in America* by former company members of her long-disbanded troupe, along with students from her East St. Louis school.

But for many years, Dunham's spiritual home has been Haiti, "the Land of High Mountains," where she lived, studied, and finally achieved recognition as a voudun priestess, or Mambo. Voudun—with its African gods, traces

of Catholicism, and reverence for the forces of Nature—is a cultural holdover from Haiti's colonial times, when a half million African slaves first picked coffee and sugar for the French. Since 1804, when the slaves overthrew their masters, Haitian culture has evolved in isolation and poverty. Katherine Dunham learned its secrets from a ninety-seven-year-old great-great-grandfather she calls Papa Denisier, whom she met on her first trip to the island in 1936. *Dance in America* visited Haiti with Dunham and also taped voudun dances of possession at her center in St. Louis that proved to be the most controversial piece the series has ever produced.

As Mambo, Dunham sat on a modest throne overlooking the dancers, serving as liaison between her people and their *loa*—the gods

in a shower of new ideas for dance in the postwar era.

.   .   .

The "triumph of American painting" was in the making, with the gestural energy of abstract expressionism transforming the artist's canvas into an arena of spontaneous physicality. A painting was to be conceived as a field of action producing not a picture but an *event* informed by the artist's existential confrontation with the materials of craft. The "content" of the artwork, as Willem de Kooning noted, "is a glimpse of something, an encounter like a flash," subordinated to the quality of energy and emotion the work expressed. Cunningham was also structuring dances to the rhythms, shapes, and momentum of the body alone. Sympathetic painters, as well as composers, were among the audiences for Cage and Cunningham's early concerts. Cage's renovated floor on Monroe Street on the Lower East Side—"one of the most spectacular rooms in New York," author Calvin Tomkins notes, with views stretching south to Wall Street and east to the river—became the scene of late-night parties and wide-ranging discussions on the new aesthetics; with the skyline providing the idea of the city, its liberating modernity a stimulus for new directions. Nowhere other than New York, Jean-Paul Sartre wrote in 1945, "will you ever have a stronger feeling of the simultaneity of human lives . . . the anguish of solitude, but never that of oppression."

Over the next several years, Cunningham and Cage survived hand-to-mouth, arranging small tours to colleges around the country. Cunningham's plotless, enigmatic solos danced to the odd plinks and plunks and silences of Cage's "prepared piano"—altered by placing nuts, bolts, and strips of leather between the strings—made for a new and difficult experience; audiences were often at a loss to interpret the artists' intentions. In many respects, Cunningham's choreography was still conventional, dependent on emotional and psychological connotations that his dramatic gifts as a dancer naturally sustained. One of his most successful early solos, *Root of an Un-*

focus, was concerned with fear, beginning "with a conscious awareness of something outside the individual, and after its passage in time [ending] in the person crawling out of light," Cunningham has written. "But the main thing about it—the thing everyone missed—was that its structure was based on time. It was divided into time units."

Cunningham was beginning to explore a new basis for choreographic organization: Time itself had become a material, ordering the luminous quality of each step and gesture and suggesting a new relationship between music and dance as well. In Graham's ballets, music was often composed expressly for the rhythms her choreography had generated; with Balanchine, music was the ground on which the dancers moved. But Cunningham was extending Cage's ideas on the possible discontinuity of music and dance to move free of specific sounds and notes—and, like a dancer in a Balanchine ballet, he no longer pretended to be a character in some obscure modern ritual. He was simply himself, dancing with a structured freedom utterly new to artistic dance in the West.

As his ideas continued to evolve through the late 1940s, Cunningham kept up his studies at SAB and even taught modern dance there for a few years at the end of the decade. In the spring of 1947, while Balanchine was in Paris, Lincoln Kirstein arranged a program of work by young choreographers for Ballet Society and commissioned Merce Cunningham to create a new ballet. Naturally Kirstein hoped for a dance with a beginning, a middle, and an end, but Cunningham wanted "to catch moments that might exist in life or in any fraction of human time." With a chamber orchestral score by John Cage and décor by Isamu Noguchi, *The Seasons* was a wash of serene, fractured, repetitive imagery. "Nothing in it," wrote the music and dance critic B. H. Haggin, "made any sense to me." In fact, the ballet was inspired by decisive Western and Eastern notions about the cyclical nature of time, reflecting insights of increasing importance in Cunningham's artistic evolution: Two years earlier, Cage, along with the choreographer on occasion, had begun studying Zen Buddhism with a recognized master, D. T. Suzuki.

Modern dance from Denishawn onward had borrowed inspiration, ideas, and even some of its spiritual aura from the Orient. But now the simplicity of Zen, with its emphasis on direct thought and action and the importance of self-transformation in artistic expression, suggested a new path through the inflated, sometimes turgid emotionalism of modern dance in the late 1940s. Zen Buddhism emphasized the transitoriness of history and social change, suggesting that the primary concern of art was simply to awaken people to the richness of the natural world. Cunningham and Cage became more convinced than ever that many of the traditional concerns of modern dance—its passionate need to communicate, its instinct to guide an audience's response—were products of neurotic need. They now began to explore the possibility of a less hampered view of the mind and creativity.

The discovery of Zen paralleled the introduction to America of ideas from European art and thought once sacrificed to the self-conscious Americanism of the 1930s and 1940s. Since the late 1930s, artists and intellectuals escaping the catastrophe in Europe had flooded into New York City, bringing with them what Elizabeth Hardwick calls "the wide, elusive, variegated sensibility of modernism" in all its facets, especially its more radical attempts to glorify irrationality and the unconscious. Beginning in 1942, Cage had formed a particular friendship with a major figure from the European avant garde, Marcel Duchamp, a kind of patron saint to the dadaist movement, and the most elegant and sublimely idle of men.

Duchamp advocated a constant self-questioning of taste, the abandonment of familiar ideas, the breaking open of all artistic taboos; he urged artists to move beyond the pathos and egotism of artistic "inspiration" to embrace the accidental, the arbitrary, the autonomous gesture. Duchamp proposed a new kind of artistic practice: In his view, art was completed by the eye of the beholder, and what was needed were not new objects but new thoughts for objects that already existed. His earlier "ready-mades"—a notorious reproduction of Leonardo's *Mona Lisa* with a mustache drawn in, a commonplace porcelain urinal with the signature "R. Mutt" inscribed, among others—had elevated ordinary, manufactured objects to the status of works of art, precipitating a gradual shift in twentieth-century aesthetics away from the demands of self-expression toward the service of the mind.

These ideas collided head-on with home-grown American modernism, which had always made an absolute distinction between art and the event. But Cage and Cunningham recognized the similarities between dadaist ideas and Zen Buddhism's vision of enlightened mind; indeed, the connection had been emphasized by their earliest teacher of Buddhism, Nancy Ross Wilson, in Seattle. By the late 1940s, John Cage was ready to make the momentous decision to substitute what had always been considered the sine qua non of Western artistic practice—the artist's subjective aesthetic judgment—for chance.

His first effort, *Music of Changes,* was determined entirely by the tossing of coins, a procedure suggested by his recent introduction to the Chinese *Book of Changes,* the *I Ching.* Cage's *Sonatas and Interludes* was generated by a similar method, and Cunningham employed this music for an evening-long epochal work, *16 Dances for Soloist and Company of 3,* in 1951. Chance operations determined the order of all sixteen dances, including nine solos based on the nine permanent emotions of Hindu mythology. "Anger," "Humor," "Sorrow," and so forth were placed in sequence according to the throw of coins; for the interlude after "Fear," the fourteenth dance, Cunningham used "charts of separate movements for materials for each of the four dancers, and let chance operations decide the continuity."

The use of chance rather than artistic choice proved not to be an indifferent method. Chance provided a concrete, elegant, and inexhaustible means of bypassing the limits of inspiration, moving artists beyond taste and memory, inviting the acceptance of sounds and movements in themselves. Disrupting conventional ideas about the nature of creativity, chance operations would gradually end the long hegemony of self-expression in modern dance, opening more new procedures for dance-making than any previous choreographic method. To some critics, chance seemed an abrogation of responsibility, but for Cunningham, "What is meant is not license, but freedom—that is, a complete awareness of the world and at the same time a detachment from it."

For Cage, the use of "aleatoric" or accidental methods of composition proved an even more radical departure from tradition than Cunningham's. To determine pitch, duration, volume, source, and occurrence of each sound, Cage has employed dice and the unpredictable choices of performers using scores without specific beginnings and endings; he has composed music based on the random fall of thrown objects (a procedure Duchamp had used on canvases) and marked transparencies of star charts to score an orchestral work, *Atlas Eclipticalis*. His fascination with "found" instruments has led him to make music from the sounds of running water, alarm clocks, thundersheets; for the *Dance in America* "Event for Television," he assembled a new score, "Branches," using percussion instruments made from various kinds of plant material, including a rattling pod from the poinsettia tree. Consistently viewing his work as an effort to restore people to a proper relationship with nature, he has even brought the natural "silence" of the world—its rich textures of ambient sound—into the concert hall: Cage's famous *4′33″* in 1952 was simply four minutes and thirty-three seconds of silence, during which a pianist, David Tudor, moved his arms three times before a piano. "My favorite piece," Cage has said many times, "is the one we hear all the time when we are quiet."

With his lively theoretical writings, Cage has become the father of an entire school of American composition, his seemingly random, atonal, often cacophonous compositions continuing to stimulate debates about the value of boredom in the musical experience. But in the early years most progressive music listeners, as well as the modern dance establishment, were

Cunningham in *Lavish Escapade* (1953), one of a series of solos choreographed in the mid-1950s to music by Christian Wolff. (Courtesy Performing Arts Research Center, The New York Public Library)

convinced that both Cage and Cunningham had taken utter leave of their senses. Cage's work was condemned as "an intellectual zero," an abandonment of music's traditional stature within Western culture; dance critic Walter Terry called *16 Dances* "closer to self-indulgence than self-expression." The movement seemed random, pointless to many observers, but Cunningham was deepening his realization that a dance could be held together by the natural drama, the unconscious imagery, the shapes and patterns of movement itself. Throughout his career, the syntax of chance has actually enriched the essentially lyric impulse in his imagination: "My use of chance operations," he has said, "is not a position I wish to die defending. It is a present mode of freeing my imagination from its own clichés, and it is a marvelous adventure in attention."

Chance operations found a new application in 1951, when Cage organized a group of musicians and engineers at Brandeis University in Waltham, Massachusetts, to assemble the first electronically generated sound studies out of cut-and-spliced audio tape; the invention of magnetic tape recording in the mid-1940s had literally transformed the time length of music into inches, which Cage now manipulated like scraps for a collage. A year later, Brandeis commissioned Cunningham to create a new work to Pierre Schaeffer's *Symphonie pour un Homme Seul,* an example of Cage's electronic *musique concrète.* Working with trained and untrained dancers from the university, the choreographer created the aptly titled *Collage,* incorporating snatches of ballroom steps and everyday behavior, just as Cage was working with the entire spectrum of audible sound. It had occurred to Cunningham that nondancers "could do the gestures that they did ordinarily. These were accepted as movement in daily life, why not on stage?" Announcing that the legitimate demands of choreography could be met by any conceivable movement at all, Cunningham broke completely with the ideal of a coherent style that choreographers had subscribed to throughout the century. Although he would never entirely surrender his commitment to the traditional possibilities of the trained body—that would be left to a new generation of dance-makers in the 1960s—Cunningham would continue throughout his career to juxtapose commonplace, vernacular movement with more stylized dancing. In *Collage,* he liked the effect: "The event was realistic, rather than forced," he wrote, "and [the performers] could enjoy it."

The summer of 1952 proved to be of crucial importance in the development of Cunningham's work and of what would later come to be called a "postmodern" aesthetic in the American performing arts. In 1948, and again in 1952 and 1953, Cunningham and Cage spent summers in the Great Smokies of western North Carolina, working as instructors at Black Mountain College. Founded in the 1930s by progressive European scholars and artists, Black Mountain was an interdisciplinary community of intellectuals and artists living and working in dedication to the "whole" human being. Here, Cage masterminded a forty-five-minute event now referred to as *Theater Piece #1,* which would become a prototype for the Happenings of the 1960s and a whole new style of art performance. The work emphasized procedures over results: Each participant was given two segments of time in which to perform, and many events happened simultaneously, without any causal connection. Movies and slides were shown; David Tudor, the major interpreter of Cage's work and "co-conceptualist" of the event, performed on piano and poured water from one bucket to another; a young painter, Robert Rauschenberg, displayed his all-white paintings on the ceiling and played music on an old gramophone; poets Charles Olson and M. C. Richards read from their works; Cage delivered a text from a stepladder and Cunningham improvised, chased by a barking dog that had somehow wandered in from outdoors. Unrehearsed, the results were "purposeless" in the sense that they were unanticipated—and in Cage's view mirrored the complexity of the contemporary world.

The spirited evolution of Cage and Cunningham's aesthetics had reached a point where the seemingly random events of such a performance could no longer define an absolute distinction between "life" and "art." It can be argued that modern change had so loosened the traditional bonds between art and value that audiences were now—whether they liked it or not—thrust into a reality experienced as isolated bits of information, with each individual free to synthesize his or her impressions. By the 1960s, younger audiences in particular would welcome this new kind of perceptual freedom, recognizing what humanist scholar Erich Auerbach had anticipated some forty years earlier: that it is precisely the preception of the random moment that everyone shares.

Cunningham's artistic direction was beginning to clarify. *Suite by Chance* (1953), performed to commissioned electronic music by Christian Wolff, was incubated over a period of months while the choreographer constructed elaborate chance-determined charts outlining the number of dancers to be used, the movement and stillness, the phrasing, the spacing, and how all the elements would be combined. Most important, "the dance was conceived to be seen from four sides, and was presented so whenever possible. Any angle of vision was permissible, as in the streets"—shattering the classical perspective inherited from the dance of Europe, in which action radiates from a fixed point center stage. That same year, Cunningham made his total break with modern expressionism. Constructed by tossing coins to fix the movements of isolated body parts, *Untitled Solo* was a steady accumulation of details—the first time that a dance had been systematically stripped of any preconceived dramatic intention. The modern choreographer as magnificent artificer, forging through intuition and impulse the uncreated conscience of the race, had been replaced by a kind of grand assembler abandoning all memory of what feels instinctively, humanly natural. Cunningham had pursued modernism's analytical impulse to the outer boundaries of logic, and yet *Untitled Solo* had "dramatic intensity in its bones, so to speak." Realizing that the body, mind, and spirit could become disciplined enough to accept more than what they had previously felt and thought, Cunningham overflowed the banks of contemporary modernism and discovered the essence of his future direction. With only a few exceptions, he would henceforth abandon wholly intuitive procedures to investigate dancing as "a continual preparation," says director Peter Brook, "for the shock of freedom."

In residence at Black Mountain during the summer of 1953, Cunningham at last began to put together a company that would endure beyond a single performance. The seven members included the daughter of a former Denishawn teacher and a Phi Beta Kappa graduate from Wheaton College named Carolyn Brown, Viola Farber, Remy Charlip, and, briefly, a former Syracuse University swimming star named Paul Taylor. In December, Merce Cunningham and Dance Company appeared Off Broadway at the Theater de Lys, presenting a complete repertory of work during a sold-out season. Not a single critic reviewed the event, but thanks to a 1954 Guggenheim Fellowship, the company survived. Working with a steady group of dancers, Cunningham began to make dances that were at least in part efforts of affection, exploring families of movement, themes, and variations that would foster an ambiguous quality of poetic emotion—allowing his ensemble of soloists to become, he hoped, "just as human as they are."

The year 1954 marked the introduction of a crucial new dimension in Cunningham's theater. At a time when Diaghilev's once-revolutionary notions of fully integrated choreography, sets, and costumes still dominated American dance, Cunningham decided to grant a designer nearly total freedom to function as partner in the creation of a new work, *Minutiae*. The collaborator was Robert Rauschenberg, not yet recognized as one of the major figures in postwar American art. Just as Cunningham and Cage had purged their work of symbolism and self-expression, Rauschenberg was jettisoning the tortured passions of an earlier generation of abstract expressionists, assembling lighthearted, ironical paintings with a genius for improvisation with found materials. For the first of many collaborations with Rauschenberg in the 1950s, Cunningham simply requested a piece that dancers could move around and through; the artist responded with a construction that needed to be hung from theater flyspace, which would have been impossible in most college auditoriums where the company performed. Returning to work, he assembled a freestanding structure out of discarded wood, then splattered it with bright paint and pieces of mirror. Cunningham later recalled how "one critic didn't know whether it was supposed to be a bathhouse at the beach or a fortune-teller's booth. That was what I liked about it."

In future years, Cunningham's open-minded approach to collaboration would result in some of the most imaginative design innovations in contemporary theater. But in the mid-1950s, his company could seldom afford the luxury of a set. With money Cage won on an Italian

(From right): Chris Komar, Meg Harper, Karole Armitage, and Ellen Cornfield in Merce Cunningham's *Minutiae,* with its Robert Rauschenberg set. The dance uses "small, abrupt movements," Cunningham has written, "arising from an observation over a period of time of people walking in the streets." (© Herbert Migdoll)

quiz show for correctly answering questions about wild mushrooms, Merce Cunningham and Dance Company purchased a new Volkswagen bus, which they used "as Denishawn used Pullmans," touring Eisenhower's America and premiering works throughout the rest of the decade.

Functioning as a kind of extended family, the young company even socialized regularly outside the demanding schedule of tours and rehearsals. Cunningham himself was enormously satisfied—"despite his unwavering need for seclusion," wrote Carolyn Brown, for twenty years his greatest dancer, "and his refusal to reveal any more about himself than that which he willingly offers." Stimulated by articles he had read, conversations that interested him, the observation of men and women in the street, even animals in a zoo, he restructured his movement ideas according to chance operations, then helped his dancers to shape the material within given constraints of space and duration. His concentrated, faunlike intensity during rehearsals did not inhibit laughter, yet Cunningham appeared to lack any obvious emotional commitment to the moods and images his dances evoked. Chance proce-

dures had removed from his hand many of his most important aesthetic decisions; but freed from the heaven and hell of self-expression, Cunningham became arguably more fascinated with the sheer *process* of making dances than any choreographer before him, exploring new ways of looking, seeing, and listening, and abandoning himself to his work with a practical, releasing pleasure.

His approach was beginning to result in genuine masterpieces, setting off reverberations in every area of American dance. Performed simultaneously with Cage's *Music for Piano, Suite for Five* (1956) was a series of linked dances later subtitled "At Random," "A Meander," "Transition," "Stillness," "Extended Moment," "Excursion," and the final "Meetings." "The events and sounds of the dance," the choreographer noted in the program, "revolve around a quiet center, which, though silent and unmoving, is the source from which they happen." Two years later, *Summerspace,* with a score by Morton Feldman, appeared as Cunningham's now-completed vision of dance as movement in time and space. Rauschenberg and his friend Jasper Johns had painted a forty-foot backdrop in pointillist drops, then dyed leotards and tights in the same pattern; immersed in a blur of pastel dots, the dancers moved with the serene aerialism and swiftness of classical dancers, simultaneously shattering and redefining the air with their bodies' motion. Premiered at Connecticut College, a bastion of the old modern dance, *Summerspace* rendered the materials of ballet in an impressionistic light, sketching its essential forms and patterns with eccentric even bizarre new accents and rhythms. In later works, Cunningham would continue to revoice the ballet's past, breaking open "kernels of academic wisdom," Croce has written, "and here, too [discarding] all but essence." *Summerspace* would be performed by the Boston Ballet and the New York City Ballet, while other Cunningham works have appeared in the repertories of American Ballet Theatre and the Paris Opéra.

The following summer, Cunningham returned to a more dadaesque spirit: Studded with satirical allusions to the work of Martha Graham, *Antic Meet* (1958) included sequences for Cunningham dancing with a chair strapped to his back and struggling to escape from Rauschenberg's seven-armed sweater. An "indeterminate" musical score, performed differently at every performance, offered no reference points

Carolyn Brown and Cunningham in *Suite for Five* (1956). (Courtesy Performing Arts Research Center, The New York Public Library)

Cunningham's *Antic Meet,* with its seven-armed sweater by Rauschenberg. (© Herbert Migdoll)

at all for the dancers, but Cunningham's company had mastered the ability to dance within a few seconds of three-minute intervals of time, attuned to the speed and rhythms of their bodies alone. With the enormously complex *Rune* (1959), the goals of Cunningham's neoclassical technique were fully resolved: "To move with speed, flexibility and control," Carolyn Brown has written; "to move with the sustained control of slow motion; to move free of any particular style."

With the emerging cultural freedom of the 1960s, wider American audiences began to look more closely at what Cunningham was up to—certainly after the lavish attention bestowed upon his company in Paris, London, and Venice during their first European engagements in 1964. In Vienna, Cunningham had responded to a booking in an unwieldy museum space with the first "Event," which led to more performances in unlikely spaces during the company's subsequent six-month, thirty-city world tour. Despite their patina of high art, Cunningham's dances were anarchic, impure, a response to a culture of instant disposability and excitement; the repertory's success abroad, paralleling the emergence of a postmodern American dance in both Europe and the United States, reversed the traditional pattern of contemporary companies who first achieved major recognition at home, only later to convince foreign critics and audiences of the value of their achievement. Nevertheless, the tour proved difficult in other respects: The company returned home exhausted and $85,000 in debt, and several key dancers departed. When the troupe finally made it to its feet again, much of the old family feeling was gone.

Cunningham's work after the mid-1960s moved in the direction of a new kind of total theater, incorporating elaborate music and scenic elements in brash, exhilarating amalgams of sound and sight. Freed from the constraints of naturalism and the need to illustrate Cunningham's dance with music, collaborating artists were left alone to contribute their own portions of a larger event: Two generations of American avant-garde composers—including Maryanne Amacher, David Behrman, Meredith Monk, Christian Wolff, and LaMonte Young—created music that sometimes clashed vividly with the choreography, fundamentally altering its impact in unpredictable ways. Increasing numbers of visual artists were invited to create work that would not need to support the dancing in any way, with Cunningham offering only the barest hints of the quality of movement the dance would contain. For the multimedia *Variations V* (1965), video guru Nam June Paik's TV installations and films by Stan VanDerBeek shared a space with twelve antennalike poles, each triggering a different sound and light effect whenever dancers passed within a four-foot radius. Frank Stella asked to create a set in 1967, and Cunningham reportedly answered, "Oh, good!" requesting only that it be portable; Stella responded with a series of narrow, colored strips of stretched canvas in blue, green, brown, and orange as a backdrop for *Scramble,* which appeared in part on *Dance in America* ten years later. For *Walkaround Time* (1968), Jasper Johns, the company's artistic adviser since 1966, conceived the idea of translating Marcel Duchamp's *The Large Glass* for the stage; seven images, originally etched on freestanding panes of glass, were silk-screened twice on semitransparent, air-filled vinyl boxes; Duchamp attended the world premiere in Buffalo a few months before his death. In *Canfield* (1969), Robert Morris's dark vertical column mounted with a white light swept slowly across the downstage area, casting shadows from the dancers' bodies and occasionally blocking the audience's view. Bruce Nauman placed rows of industrial fans on poles to create the gentle breezes of *Tread* (1970); and painter Morris Graves, an old friend of Cunningham and Cage from Seattle, designed the décor for *Inlets* (1977), which suggested the landscape around Puget Sound. From 1974 to 1984, the British painter Mark Lancaster served as the company's resident designer, helping to assemble *Sounddance, Rebus,* and *Torse,* among others; more recently, visual artists William Anastasi and Dove Bradshaw have arrived as artistic advisers in the creation of

Karen Attix, Catherine Kerr, and Karole Armitage in Cunningham's *Scramble,* with set by Frank Stella. (© Herbert Migdoll)

Walkaround Time (1968), with its Jasper Johns assemblage set, based on Marcel Duchamp's *Large Glass.* (Courtesy Performing Arts Research Center, The New York Public Library)

Merce Cunningham, a master of the public media of the age. (© 1983 Terry Stevenson)

lighting, costume, and scenic elements. Through the influence of the Cunningham company, the expressive power of independent design and choreography—"the American thing," wrote Gertrude Stein, "the *disconnection*"—has become the dominant style of artistic collaboration in contemporary dance, conveying the most advanced art of the present to stages around the world.

Universally recognized as a contemporary master, Cunningham has continued to flaunt his revolutionary unpredictability. Separating movement from the rise and fall of music and the demands of storytelling and psychology, he has shown American audiences how to relax before a spectacle of constant change, to surrender the need to interpret, censure, foresee, possess. In his dismantling of received ideas, he has granted all kinds of permission for other avant-garde experiments over the past three decades; as the maker of over one hundred dances, he has fundamentally altered our habits of seeing, restored to dance the drama of the natural world, and taught us more about the body's expressiveness, critic Dale Harris has noted, than any other choreographer except Balanchine.

·   ·   ·   ·

In many respects, Cunningham's aesthetic is a product of an age of television, a response to a postmodern era of information and technology in a nation where people create their own montages merely by switching the television dial. Since 1974, he has acknowledged his relationship to what he calls "the medium of the times," creating a series of remarkable video tapes and films largely as an investigation of movement possibility—in order "not to make pictures," he says, "but to make *dancing.*"

"With Merce, you just back away," says Merrill Brockway, who directed Cunningham's "Event for Television" on *Dance in America* in 1976. "He knows what he wants to see, and about the strongest he ever gets is, 'I prefer not.' " Brockway, Cunningham, and Cunningham's film and video associate, Charles Atlas, spent four weeks planning each shot and camera angle for an Event that included excerpts from *Minutiae,* with Rauschenberg's colorful freestanding sculpture; the choreographer's animal *Solo;* an early video/dance, *Westbeth;* the 1950s classic *Septet; Scramble; Sounddance;* and *Antic Meet,* with its Martha Graham spoof and Rauschenberg's problematical sweater. *RainForest* was danced in its entirety but with accelerated timing, so that a twenty-four-minute work was reduced to nineteen; Cunningham knew that everything needs to be faster on television. And the choreographer created a new work, *Video Triangle,* involving background color changes keyed in postproduction to the dancers' many changes in costume. What audiences saw was fifty-eight minutes and forty-five seconds of dancing in time and space, within the confines of the video rectangle.

But two years before the *Dance in America* taping, Cunningham had recognized that television was an inevitable extension of his interests as a choreographer: "On TV," he said, "it is a commonplace that several things can happen at once." With Atlas, a designer, filmmaker, and video artist as codirector, he assembled his first half-hour black-and-white tape, *Westbeth*, working around afternoon classes in the Westbeth studio—the first of a series of tapes that would challenge the traditional terms of dance on television in entirely new ways.

Their aim, Atlas told *The New York Times*, was "to 'energize' the camera as much as possible and thereby create a greater variety of rhythm, pacing, and spatial design than could be obtained by simply filming choreography originally intended for the stage." The images in *Westbeth* would shift kaleidoscopically between long-shots and close-ups, with numerous changes of speed and motion as the choreographer sometimes wielded the camera himself, dancing alongside his company. "Ever since Einstein and now the astronauts," Cunningham said, "we've realized something wholly different about space—that everything is moving. Well, I apply that idea to dancing. On television you see people moving and the camera still, or people still and the camera moving. But it seems very logical to me that the camera and the people should move, both at the same time. If this is disorienting, I think that it is simply a matter of seeing it more and more, and gradually, it becomes part of what you know." Cunningham and Atlas's wide-ranging "choreography" for the camera captured sculptural effects of massed bodies, lingering profiles, and still moments of intimacy, creating a very different impression from what the same choreography later made in live performance. The camera took in juxtapositions of movements impossible to see in the studio, and the magic of video postproduction further restructured the continuity of everything, superimposing dancers on different planes of action through a process known as chroma-keying.

Because television tends to flatten space, Cunningham and Atlas decided to exploit this flatness as the theme of their next exploration in video technology. In *Blue Studio: Five Segments* (1976), Cunningham appeared as "a solitary dancing decal," in critic Richard Lorber's phrase, chroma-keyed on a solid blue background and then on a street scene in Caracas, viewed through the rear window of a moving car. Even the most weighted movements transposed to television can look like a walk on the moon, so *Blue Studio* acknowledged the physicality of bodies in groundless space: Occasionally a dog, a frog, and a baby gorilla passed across the screen. In another section, five Merce Cunninghams danced together, an effect created by superimpositions involving instant playback in the studio so that Cunningham could move to a spot on the floor where he wouldn't block his video doppelgängers.

In 1978, Atlas and Cunningham created the masterly *Fractions*—the choreographer joking that he wanted its two versions shown side by side "to really confuse everybody." *Fraction's* title refers to its mix of "live" dancing and images re-recorded on the original tape: Three black-and-white and one color camera shift back and forth between monitors set up in the performing area and the action occurring around them. "Merce wanted to make a piece rather than something in sections," Atlas told *The Village Voice*, "even though it falls into several sections. But even between the sections, we wanted to make it *not end*. We'd stop shooting but we'd try for a transition that would keep it flowing." The following year *Locale* used the film camera as an integral part of the choreography: The portable steadicam swept over and through the dancers as a participant rather than an intruder in the work, resulting in one of the few great dance films ever made. The 1982 film/video/dance *Channels/Inserts* conveyed a sense of simultaneous events occurring in different shapes; and *Coast Zone*, filmed in January 1983 at the Synod House of the Cathedral of St. John the Divine in Manhattan, explored extreme spatial depth to explore the possibilities of deep focus, foreground and background figures, and a mobile camera.

Filming *Coast Zone* (1983) in the sanctuary of the Cathedral of St. John the Divine in New York City. (© 1983 Terry Stevenson)

Cunningham's video and film projects may finally be about dancing first and foremost, and not just about making pictures. But if dance is an art of the possible, then video has created an entirely new art form at the "impossible" interface between live bodies and electronics. Most of Cunningham's video/dances are later adapted for live performance, but the problems of the television screen remain unique: "There are no cadences in television," Cunningham once said. "There are no traditional ways of changing from one thing to another." Such an approach is ide-

ally suited to Cunningham's own gifts: By the 1980s, some of his most exciting new work has been reserved for media other than live performance.

· · ·

Cunningham works today in much the same fashion as always, arriving at Westbeth rehearsals fully prepared, speaking to his dancers only when necessary, and sometimes hardly at all. His enigmatic silences occasionally seem a preoccupation, at other times a voluntary act of listening. "There's no thinking involved in my choreography," he says. "I work alone for a couple of hours each morning in the studio. I just try things out. And my eye catches something that looks interesting, and then I work on that." He records the results of his chance operations in one of the innumerable notebooks he uses to teach his company his movement. "I have a tendency," he says, "to deal with what I call facts."

Virtually none of Cunningham's early work is in repertory, which currently features works from the 1970s and 1980s alone; much of this new choreography appears to be Cunningham's gloss of classicism. Everywhere his dances have grown increasingly swift, eliminating obvious transitional moments, responding to his dancers' technical gifts with more intricate unison and support work. Images from older dances reappear, as Cunningham repeats himself in new ways—"playing with older forms, past sequences, dredging up and interlocking past melodic elements, phrasing, line and fugal interpolations of old pieces," critic Jill Silverman has noted. Many of his dances express a style, an unmistakable look, built around an established repertory of experimental techniques and approaches. *Torse* (1976) uses Cunningham's classroom technique as its overt subject, moving one critic to describe it as "barefoot Balanchine." Thoroughly grounded in ballet training, the current crop of dancers with the Merce Cunningham Dance Company are excellent tools for the choreographer's present interests.

Some longtime observers of the company believe these new emphases have changed the nature of Cunningham's work: Carolyn Brown has argued that he was formerly interested in a "total human being" on stage but now tends to orchestrate his dancers to create more massive effects. Cunningham answers that he has always made "dramatic" works rich with emotional content. His dances remain fundamentally "about" the movement of the body: *Winterbranch* (1964) is about falling; *Sounddance,* about packed activity; *Landrover* (1972), about traveling over landscapes; *Trails,* ten years later, about partnering. Within the development of these movement ideas, Cunningham mirrors a thou-

sand different perspectives, freeing audiences to develop their own play of thoughts and feelings. "There seems to be a progression," Marcia Siegel once suggested, "from *Winterbranch,* where the dancers are crushed by merciless light and total darkness and a maniacally screeching sound track; to *Place,* where they rush frantically at the boundaries of some nameless enclosure and finally break out of it into some other unknown darkness; through *RainForest,* where they seem poised between their humanness and some nonhuman existence that could be either animalistic or artificial, and that they cannot attain in either case. Now, in *Canfield,* the dancers seem to have become resigned to a bland, computerized state in which both the joy and the rebellion have been diminished to faint emotions that can be easily countermanded by the more powerful hand of technology."

For his part, Cunningham, like Balanchine, never offers interpretations of his own work: "I don't have ideas, exactly." Working beneath the cathedral ceiling in the functional, well-lit studio at Westbeth, above the hum of the city streets, Cunningham assembles dances that remain, in his own words, "not a matter of reference but of direct impact."

· · ·

St. Patrick's Day, 1983. On the streets outside City Center, a *New York Post* headline announces, MERCE CUNNINGHAM STILL AVANT GARDE. Preparing for the opening of their spring season between legs of a yearlong tour through Asia, Europe, and South America, dancers in practice clothes are hovering across the shiny black floor on the empty City Center stage stripped of its rear cyclorama, exposing a dirty white wall, bare pipes, and twin rows of radiators. The dancing is a stream of empty, restful activity under the green wash of lights; a quiet voice on a loudspeaker is calling enigmatic dimmer cues: "22 to 20 . . . 37, 39 and 41 . . . 44 and 46 and 48, and 20. . . . You like these little JBVs?"

Merce Cunningham is seated alone in the darkened house, watching the stage, occasionally speaking in a high, clear voice, which cracks slightly.

"I'm looking to see about the connections," he tells the dancers, referring to new material that will join together excerpted sections of tonight's Event, one in a season of repertory work. "We'll take care of the other problems when we get to them. Until then, keep going."

Cunningham consults a stopwatch and a notebook while the dancing resumes. Some members of the company stretch in the wings, where some kind of commotion is going on, like the clang of radiator pipes. "What's that banging?" Cunningham finally asks.

"It's John," says a voice, and everyone laughs.

After the dance is over, Cunningham calls the company to center stage to discuss familiar last-minute problems: cues, spacing, counts.

Robert Swinston and Helen Barrow listen intently. "Robert, you begin behind her and, whatever you do, go directly off. This is for the solos," he says to everyone. "Now the trio . . . if you come in, the three of you . . ." He walks to the extreme downstage, and his voice becomes inaudible in the empty space. Cunningham's natural respect for the environment and the sanity of his dancers' discipline renews a deliberate relationship between nerve and muscle: The dancing resumes with an elemental leanness that is at once simple, beautiful, and profound. Cunningham presents a world fraught with contingency and contradiction, some moments a pastoral Arcadia, at others a reflection of the hectic, anxious rootlessness of modern life. But what is consistently true is his sense that a particular time and place is habitable, and that through movement we might begin to see with fresh eyes.

"I think it is that *enjoyment,*" he once said, "that deep enjoyment that lets dancers continue. It's a chance to play at something that interests you and, difficult as it is, can renew you each day."

"Working on a new piece, it is always the same feeling. At last I'm beginning."

POSTMODERN DANCE

· LIFE AS ART AS LIFE ·

During summers in the late 1950s, a young San Franciscan named Ann Halprin conducted a series of movement workshops outdoors, near Mount Tamalpais in Marin County. A former Humphrey–Weidman dancer, Halprin asked her students to pay close attention to the sensation of their bodies through easy, relaxed, improvisational actions and gestures. Emphasizing the free association of mental imagery to stimulate these movement ideas and drawing on her careful study of Gestalt psychology, kinesiology, and anatomy, Halprin invited visual artists, poets, musicians, and architects as well as dancers from across the country to share what she called "a common language through movement experiences."

What emerged from these experiments were often entirely commonplace activities: Sitting in a chair, sweeping a broom, crawling, walking, and running were stylized—*aestheticized*—through slow motion or repetition, then joined together without any obvious dramatic connotations. Startlingly, the resulting "dances" had an unpretentiousness and intimacy foreign to the modern dance of the time. Halprin's belief in thoughtful analysis and free expression had succeeded in creating a communal consciousness that audiences could share—one that a student, Simone Forti, later described as "a state of enchantment." These open, inquisitive investigations of physical actions accelerated a major shift in American dance experimentation: The great-grandchildren of Isadora were beginning to investigate gesture and action in their most unadorned expression, gathering inspiration and ideas from every quarter of the American avant garde.

By the 1960s, very ambitious and very controversial acts of affirmation were opening new vistas of experimentation throughout the contemporary arts, revealing the motion of bodies stripped to essentials—what Gertrude Stein called "the color and shape of the thing seen." The experimental theater was repudiating the authority of the playwright and the written word to emphasize a sensuous *mise en scène,* the gifts of the director, and the physical arts of the actors themselves; painters and sculptors were moving off the walls and gallery floors to fashion walk-in installations and environments where artists might roll their bodies in paint, throw great gobs of pigment at clear plastic, and even invite audiences to partake in the free-for-alls. These Happenings—the garden parties of an age of affluence—were transforming the gestural energy of abstract expressionism, pop art, and surrealist assemblage into rampant celebrations of the art-making of people in "real" time, rejecting the manipulated, illusionist time of traditional performance.

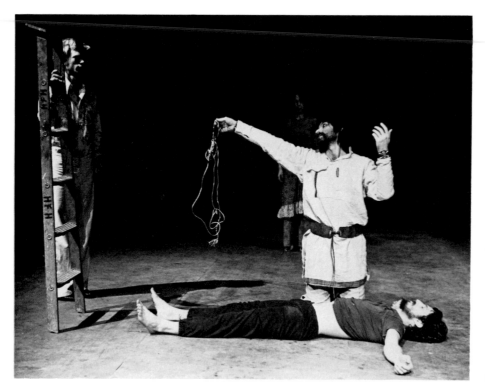

Grand Union, an early 1970s collaborative improvisational company. Its freewheeling verbal and physical horseplay incorporated a variety of everyday objects with intimate, frequently anarchical environments of movement and sound. (From left): Douglas Dunn, Nancy Lewis David Gordon, and, lying down, Steve Paxton. (© 1975 Johan Elbers)

With genres of art blurring and the past accelerating away, a youth culture had come into being, with antimaterialism, antiauthoritarianism, and the sheer velocity of social change fueling a new climate for innovation. United by the collective energy of rock music, millions of American youths were sharing in a popular dance renaissance that has continued unabated into the present day; communal styles of living, a new sexual freedom, drugs, the philosophy and practice of Eastern religions, and a larger dissatisfaction with the middle-class pursuit of happiness; mass communications, jet-age travel, widespread college education, and the inflamed politics of the time all contributed to a new vision not only of culture but of the nation itself. The urgencies of racial and sexual oppression and the Vietnam War, along with the aborted promise of a New Frontier and a Great Society, meant that most young experimental artists felt compelled to identify themselves with the nation's cultural protest, whether their work was expressly political or not. The vaunted aesthetics

of the recent past—such traditionally "modern" ideas as the perfectibility of form and the sacred purposes of art, intertwined with what Susan Sontag calls "the over-oxygenated hopes of modernism"—now seemed hopelessly outdated. Cunningham's liberation of dance from the demands of plot, character, and psychology had been taken to heart, but needed to discover a more intimate scale. The sheer physical immediacy of the decade had resulted in a more radical sense of *what counts* in art and life than at any time since the 1930s.

Naturally, America's traditional dance nexus in Manhattan became the center of this new experimentation, beginning in 1960, when John Cage invited Robert Dunn, a former student in his experimental music theory course at the New School for Social Research, to teach a course in movement composition at Cunningham's Westbeth studio. Dunn welcomed the participation of visual artists and musicians as well as dancers, embracing a down-to-earth confusion of art and life along Cagean lines: Refusing to evaluate work as "good" or "bad," Dunn emphasized instead the concrete analysis of structure and the use of ordinary objects as props in dance-making. Projects ranged from raw explosions of physical energy to suppressed slow-motion studies, along with such novel conceptual events as Lucinda Childs's dance on the street, observed by workshop members from a fifth-floor window. But always, as author Sally Banes notes, Dunn and his students asserted "the primacy of the body as the vital locus of experience, thought, memory, understanding, and a sense of wonder." In July 1962, with a three-hour performance at a liberal Greenwich Village church on Washington Square, the Judson Dance Theater was born.

Judson concerts welcomed the unruly processes of life itself into events: Such mundane activities as taking a bath, calisthenics, painting a wall, or roller-skating became new occasions for making the ordinary extraordinary, for exhilaration and the beauty of surprise. Fusing dancers and audience in one problematic field, Judson shattered the separation of audience and spectator that had dominated dance presentation since the age of Louis XIV, mingling viewers and performers in every nook and cranny of the church. Abandoning the modern dancer's soul-searching gaze across the horizon and the neutral, pulled-up look of a performer in a Cunningham ballet as well, Judson choreographers created dances out of pure task-mastering or else set loose streams of highly personalized, spontaneous horseplay that glorified the sheer exuberance of the body in motion. Nurturing chaos, enigma, and permissiveness at every level, musicians, visual artists, filmmakers, and writers appeared alongside trained dancers in tennis shoes, pointe shoes, combat boots, and bare feet; in old clothes, new clothes, and extravagant, unwieldy costumes (art objects, really), as well as tights and leotards—and sometimes nude, which nearly cost the Judson Memorial Church its affiliation with the American Baptist Conference. In 1966, Judson dancers journeyed to the 69th Regiment Armory on Twenty-fifth Street to collaborate with engineers from the Bell Telephone Laboratories on a series of multimedia experiments in new technology, creating environments of multiscreen projections, walk-through plastic bubbles, and extravagant lighting displays. Many choreographers addressed the social issues of the day, using movement, spoken texts, and slides to create abstract, multimedia statements of political belief. "Nothing but the exercise of puerile egocentric minds in the quest of shocking the unshockable," wrote Clive Barnes of *The New York Times,* but until it dissolved in 1968 Judson produced a barrage of public events that opened new avenues of kinesthetic delight, marking the beginnings of what many now call a postmodern era.

The choreographers of the 1960s were "in a somewhat beautiful way, touching in their use of natural movement," Merce Cunningham allowed two decades later. "But it all struck me as very limited. The instant they attempted something outside that, it didn't work, because they didn't have the training." Still, their experiments suggested that styles of perception have changed beyond what even Cunningham had anticipated. The constant exposure to raw information in postindustrial society—the multitude of signs and symbols, the innundation of stimuli on television, in advertising, and in our public lives—has created a receptivity toward physical actions poised in their boldest contexts. Inspired by an American pragmatism and delight in evidence, a generation had challenged the agreements of all previous ones to fashion a new interface between dance and life.

From this high tide of artistic faith, choreographers in the 1980s have been freed to approach traditional styles of dance prowess with an expanded sense of adventure. New forms of game-playing and athletic exertion, new images of violence and grace, even the precise articulation of beautifully crafted phrases of movement are increasingly nourished by choreographers emerging from the companies of Merce Cunningham and Twyla Tharp, especially. Postmodernism remains a catchall term, defining no single community or ideology or temperament, embracing a profusion of styles that defy the very

Yvonne Rainer. "I love . . . the duality of the body," she has written, "the body as a moving, thinking, decision- and action-making entity and the body as an inert entity, objectlike." (© 1980 Johan Elbers)

idea of a unified aesthetic for our time. Nevertheless, some twenty years after Judson, it has become the dominant movement for artistic innovation in American dance—a third wave of experimentation as radical in its assumptions as "aesthetic" and modern dance were in their own day, with continuing implications for the dance of the 1980s and beyond.

Dance in America's "Beyond the Mainstream" program in 1980 provided a reasonably complete look at several aspects of the postmodern achievement, including work by four early participants in the Judson revolution: Yvonne Rainer, Steve Paxton, David Gordon, and Trisha Brown.

·   ·   ·

Rainer was the principal aesthetician of the Judson group. A former modern dancer and student of Halprin, her work oscillated between structured improvisations, quiet, meditative stutterings, and fierce eruptions of energy; she finally responded to her downtown stardom with a dance that seemed to anthologize the major thrust of the postmodern impulse. Originally presented at Judson with Rainer, David Gordon, and

Steve Paxton executing the material simultaneously, *The Mind Is a Muscle, Part I,* known today as *Trio A* (1966), is an ingenious four-and-one-half-minute assemblage of distorted quotes from athletics, modern dance, classicism, and pedestrian behavior, executed in silence and with averted eyes. *Trio A*'s heterogeneous actions evoke no definitive emotional state; they require only a steady, unstressed continuum of effort, rather like the progress of a person in the street, proceeding from one configuration to the next without any irresistible momentum. Rejecting the "impoverishment of ideas, narcissism, and undisguised sexual exhibitionism of most dancing," Rainer had created a work that could be performed acceptably by almost anyone who made the effort; reacting against "an age without limits" and the chaos of Judson's total freedom, she consciously excommunicated sensuality, glamour, make-believe, drama, theatrical magic, and the seduction of spectacle in order to present dancing as an *objective* human activity. The cool, cerebral qualities of contemporary art in the late 1960s found an ideal correlative in dance departing entirely from the traditional neoprim-

Frank Conversano, Sara Rudner, and Bart Cook, at work on Yvonne Rainer's *Trio A*. (© 1979 Don Perdue)

itivism of modernism. Abandoning the sense of instinctive urgency that even Merce Cunningham's dances sustained, *Trio A* paradoxically revealed the human body in all its facets—"its actual weight, mass, and unenhanced physicality," Rainer has written—and the transparent physical personalities of the dancers themselves.

For *Dance in America, Trio A* was re-created by three very dissimilar performers: the bearlike, unconventionally trained Frank Conversano, who felt his way through the dance with a blunt, purposeful dignity; Sara Rudner, a choreographer and longtime dancer with Twyla Tharp, who executed the movements with robust yet exquisite feminine candor; and Bart Cook of the New York City Ballet, who danced with a sleek, fastidious attention to impulse and line. *Trio A* has been danced literally by dozens of people, some learning it fourth- and fifth-hand; it took Rainer years to meet "a *Trio A* I didn't like." This democratic ethos may appear dry and didactic to audiences who prefer the "magic" of virtuosity and theatrical illusion; certainly the irony of Rainer's choreographic career is that she abandoned it for film. But

throughout the 1970s and into the 1980s, choreographers have continued to explore the possibilities of natural, uninflected movement, creating dances not as a matter of feeling alone but of thought, and in the process generating new rationales for dance-making through the sheer mutability of the thinking body.

The desire *to show a thing being done*—to present dances at least in part about the dancer's experience of doing them—need not always result in calculating formal exercises. Improvisation invites another kind of immediacy, asking audiences to share in the ambient hesitations, rough edges, on-the-spot decision-making and unexpected revelations usually reserved for the privacy of the studio. Improvisation has been a means of generating new ideas in all forms of artistic dance for centuries, but the holistic impulse in postmodernism—its pursuit of enchantment—has elevated the act into an art in itself. Rather than rely entirely on the inspiration of the moment, dancers often improvise like jazz musicians, wedding themselves to carefully plotted structures nurturing unusual styles of virtuosity, as when Simone Forti transforms the

David Gordon and the Pickup Company in *Not Necessarily Recognizable Objectives.* "I refer to my work as my work, I refer to dancers as performers," Gordon says. "I think of myself as an artist who deals with movement. I say things are constructed, and I don't think of myself in dance history at all." (© 1978 Johan Elbers)

simple acts of crawling, circling, and animal "empathy" into elemental human events.

Beginning in 1972, Steven Paxton and other dancer/choreographers developed "contact improvisation," a dance style exploring the spiritual and communal implications of spontaneous movement as a way of life. Today, a network of participants thrives in North America and England, practicing what amounts to a rough-and-tumble exercise in attention. "Contact" is a populist dance-sport in which two or more partners share impulses and momentum along shifting points of physical contact; lavish if fleeting sculptural impressions arise and vanish as the dancers tumble, shift, wrestle, support, slide, and roll together in response to one another's movements. "The understanding of it comes through the physical experience you have of it," Paxton explained to *Dance in America* audiences. "It's a communication through the skin." An audience watches egalitarian relationships unfold between partners, an interaction naturally susceptible to the fluctuations in any kind of personal intercourse. "Both partners are surviving a dance moment," Paxton continued. "And they have to be pretty open for almost anything to happen. . . . They can't preplan, they can't hold on to what they've just done, or consider it; they can't be too much in control, because the minute you start to try to control what you and somebody else are doing, you've taken away from them their ability to interact with you." Some-

times crude and chaotic, sometimes as appealing as child's play, at other times bacchanalian in its jubilance, contact lends new definition to the dance's ephemeral, fleeting moment.

While improvisers throw ordinary caution to the wind, other choreographers are consciously attempting to manipulate a viewer's perceptions. David Gordon provokes laughter and pause in a no-man's-land between what an audience actually *sees* and what it might imagine his dances signify. To explain: In *Chair* (1974), Gordon and his partner, Valda Setterfield, move in staggered unison on, inside, and around two bright blue folding chairs, using them matter-of-factly as platforms, scenery, beds, toys, gadgets, launching pads, jungle gyms, weapons, and wearing apparel. With the musical accompaniment for the final section—"Stars and Stripes Forever"—played *con gusto* by a military band, the audience sits suspended between the dry yet playful inventiveness of the movement itself and the gorgeous absurdity of the entire enterprise. *"Chair* is an interesting piece to me," says Gordon, "because it is a very strange example of the way that I present an image and undercut it until I have almost destroyed it, and then pull it out from way down deep and make it theatrical again."

Like many choreographers of his generation, Gordon "accumulates and organizes multiple views of a single phenomenon into one composition," as Banes has written. But with

Duchampian irony, Gordon's play of perspectives becomes a means for delighting audiences with the conundrums of thought and perception. Incorporating punning spoken narratives, radical shifts in text and music, offstage behavior, and cagey repetitions and permutations of form—even honoring his own egotistical domination of proceedings—Gordon manages to charm, subvert, and finally recast a viewer's experience on his own terms.

Arlene Croce described a rehearsal of Gordon's *Close-Up* (1979) in Minneapolis, performed by three members of his "permanently temporary" ensemble, the Pickup Company: Keith Marshall, Susan Eschelbach, and Margaret Hoeffel.

"From the beginning," they all said together. Then they spoke separately.

KEITH: Keith as Keith.

SUSAN: Susan as Susan.

MARGARET: Margaret as Margaret.

They executed a series of small moves, naming each move as they went. Next, each dancer performed a full rotation and displaced another.

MARGARET: Margaret as Keith.

KEITH: Keith as Susan.

SUSAN: Susan as Margaret.

This motif returned in various guises, set to appropriate movement.

KEITH: Keith as lifter.

MARGARET: Margaret as support.

SUSAN: Susan as victim. *(As she is lifted)* Oh, no!

KEITH: Susan as pendulum.

MARGARET: As Tower of Pisa.

SUSAN: Susan as bread.

There were casual-sounding interjections ('Can you do this?' 'Wait till I put my hands here.') and still more transformations, as when

Margaret and Susan presented Keith as "father, brother, husband, son" and, while he bounced full-length on the floor, "Boun-cing ba-by boy!"

The actual dynamics and design of what Gordon calls his "constructions" are often casual and uninflected, executed with the deliberate ease of everyday encounters. Gordon suggests that it may be difficult for audiences "to understand that what they're seeing is not a second-rate, under-rehearsed dance company, but in fact another way of looking at performance," provoked by an acutely active sense of the responsibilities of performers on stage.

David Gordon's work represents the finest example of the new conceptual dance-theater that has evolved from the 1960s revolution. In contrast, the recent work of another Judson original, Trisha Brown, has been built around reams and reams of luscious movement—"articulate and silky," she says, "so much so that sometimes while I'm working I think I will slip off the air if I don't insert another kind of movement that is kind of mechanical, straightforward, four-square . . ." Brown's sense of *kinesthetics*—the sensation of the body in motion—has become as sure and sensitive as any choreographer's in America today. But along with the intuitive richness of her swift, unhurried style, Brown has also explored an enormous range of dance-making strategies over the past two decades.

Line-Up (1977), performed to Gordon Lightfoot's "Early Morning Rain," sung by Bob Dylan, is frank about its whimsically reductive mechanics: A dancer at the end of a long line of dancers begins to move forward in a hip-slinging shuffle and finally presses her body against the next dancer, who catches the movement impulse. The procedure continues until all seven dancers are packed like sardines against a far wall. In the palindromic *Solo Olos* (1976), responsiveness to the unexpected becomes a highly sophisticated structural element, as dancers reverse their progress through the dance at any moment, on the command of a caller. Fascinated by such

Dancer/choreographer Trisha Brown. (© 1981 Lois Greenfield)

mind-body complications, Brown has scored a dance on paper—*Locus* (1975)—then assembled the movement at a later time. "Developing a skill to fit an occasion," she once asked performers literally to walk on the walls of the Whitney Museum and up the side of a six-story building in SoHo, exposing the ropes, harnesses, and pulleys that made such defiance of gravity possible. Theoretical procedures constantly find their way into her dances: Brown made a tender art of accumulation in *Accumulation* (1971). The dance begins with a gentle, rotating thrust of the fist, then the thrust and a turn of the left thumb, then both movements repeated with a lifted foot, and so on in an A, A–B, A–B–C pattern that con-

tinues adding gestures, into the lower reaches of the alphabet. During all this, she tells two different stories, alternating sentences from each. Interleaving the dance with *Water Motor* (1978), she performed both dances and stories at the same time—"like driving my grain harvester while reciting French," she says.

Through such cool-headed, often mathematical calculation, Brown projects an amused intelligence and an improvisatory naturalness that heightens her image of the dancer as an ordinary, thinking person with extraordinary skills. Moving without the obsessively pointed feet and lifted chest of the classically trained dancer, Brown has nonetheless developed an extremely

POSTMODERN DANCE · 187

Kai Tekai's Moving Earth appeared on *Dance in America*'s "Beyond the Mainstream," presenting another view of the primitivist impulse in postmodernism—integrating everyday movement like walking, crawling, and stamping, child's play and Sisyphean task mastering in a desolate dream landscape. "I smell earth," Tekai has written. "Stage change/to riverside;/Lighting change to sun;/Little stone lead me/Place I never been,/They lead me to/Old Time/ Imagination/Universe/I dance there." Not long after she arrived from Japan in the late 1960s, Tekai began a kind of spiritual diary, *Light,* that has since expanded into eighteen different dances. Here is *Light, Part 18 (Wheat Field),* presented in 1983. (© 1983 Johan Elbers)

elegant and sophisticated movement style—deliberately casual, sensuous, thrown-away, "with a bit of a lunatic look," she once acknowledged of her *Glacial Decoy* (1978). While four vertical panels of rear-projected photographed landscapes and still-life montages by Robert Rauschenberg pass serenely across a rear scrim, four women in billowy, bell-shaped dresses flit in and out of the wings. The sense of life displaced by the proscenium arch—it was Brown's first dance designed expressly for a theater rather than an open space—was a calculated response to the arrogance implied in isolating art within a frame.

Glacial Decoy suggests that the dancing continues even when you can't see it anymore.

. . .

Although some critics argue that postmodernism from Judson onward is actually an extension of modern dance, emphasizing individual expression and the open investigation of movement possibility, new dance has continued to find many of its most potent influences in the visual arts. Conceptual art and its "dematerialization" of the art object, along with contemporary formalism in painting and sculpture, have stimulated dance-makers to deepen their investigation of structure and design; following the examples of "minimalist" artists such as Donald Judd, Robert Morris, and Sol LeWitt, along with composers such as Philip Glass and Steve Reich, a number of choreographers have assembled repetitive "pattern dances" wholly dominated by their visible architecture and rhythms.

Since the mid-1970s, Lucinda Childs has made dances out of synchronized walks, skips, glides, and leaps adapted from ballet, rhythmically shaped and altered over the course of an evening until the slightest changes in pattern cause tidal shifts in mood and perception. Molissa Fenley has adapted ideas from the minimalism of the 1970s beyond all previous limits of speed and endurance, pushing herself and her company through patterns of motion borrowed from modern dance, ballet, and a range of ethnic dance forms. Combining the systematic and the organic, Laura Dean—whose work appeared on "Beyond the Mainstream"—develops her patterns from folk steps and the spinning of Sufi dervishes, performed to the pulsing polyrhythms of her own musical compositions. Dean is not interested in what the body *does* so much as "where the energy goes," she says, and "with what quality it goes." Her shifting circles within circles represent a postmodern breakthrough to the spiritual harmony of older dance forms and the ecstatic abandon of ritual celebration.

As postmodernism becomes an academy of its own, more new and significant works are being assembled than can possibly be discussed here. Most emerging choreographers continue to present their work in open, nonproscenium spaces with minimal lighting and little emphasis on décor and costume; most dance audiences around America are still learning to look at contemporary dancers dressed in something other than modern leotards and tights. But increasingly, through performances at Danspace and P.S. 122 on Manhattan's Lower East Side, the Kitchen in SoHo, and the busiest dance venue in the world, Chelsea's Dance Theater Workshop, postmodernism has attracted new support from funding agencies and European producers. Several choreographers from the Judson era are now gaining recognition as contemporary masters, with Trisha Brown, Lucinda Childs, and David Gordon presenting their work on opera house stages, especially at the Brooklyn Academy of Music; younger choreographers such as Karole Armitage, Laura Dean, Senta Driver, Douglas Dunn, and Kai Tekai have choreographed for major ballet companies either at home or in Europe. The emergence of a postmodern avant garde has created a sense of having entered, by the late 1970s, a new era in American dance performance.

Pluralism and populism have continued as the essence of the postmodern movement during the six years since *Dance in America* looked "Beyond the Mainstream." The breakdown of boundaries between artistic genres—between dance and theater, high art and popular entertainment—has vastly expanded the theatrical range of postmodernism, with the intermedia operas of Meredith Monk, a member of the Judson group during the late 1960s, representing the finest examples of a new, imagistic, nonnarrative dance-theater. Other artists have returned directly to narrative story-telling; the long collaboration between Bill T. Jones and Arnie Zane, especially, has resulted in a unique fusion of modern dance and jazz, contact improvisation, structured game playing, vaudeville, improvisation poetry, and self-revelation. A broad-based expressionist resurgence has taken place: Pooh Kaye, for instance, fashions witty, energetic pieces with a spare, almost naïve movement vocabulary, incorporating child's play with commonplace hardware, boards, bricks, fire, and whatever else happens to be handy. New Wave styles in contemporary music, visual arts, and fashion have engaged a range of choreographers—most visibly Karole Armitage, whose "drastic-classicism" deconstructs the legacies of Cunningham and Balanchine in a maelstrom of bold, frenzied movements.

"A world neither structured by authority nor held together by tradition," as Suzi Gablik has described the contemporary visual arts, postmodernism represents the dissolution of a

Laura Dean Dance and Music in *Tympani,* 1980. (© 1980 Lois Greenfield)

long historical process and a radical change in our cultural ambitions. The fundamental task of the avant garde has remained the same: the invigoration of perception, an existential enrichment fulfilling Gertrude Stein's prophetic injunction that "the business of art is to live in the actual present, that is the complete actual present, and to express the complete actual present."

But increasing numbers of experimental choreographers are learning to view the past as a legacy, not a burden—"under our belt, not on our backs," as novelist John Barth has written of postmodern fiction. The evolution of modern dance that culminated in Merce Cunningham and postmodernism has released an extraordinary range of styles into the melting pot of American dance; the need to give individual shape to this welter of possibilities has moved at least two American choreographers beyond all labels. Paul Taylor and Twyla Tharp have embraced intensely personal visions of the classical and modern past, developing a formal mastery that enables them to invoke many different styles at will. Their sense of the richness of tradition has been infused with the modern desire to break through all limits, to aspire to a mythic dimension—to create dances that at once illuminate and disturb our images of ourselves and the world.

The nation's greatest periods of dance creativity from Denishawn onward have usually coincided with the breakdown of distinctions between elite art and popular entertainment; the popular acclaim that has greeted the achievements of Taylor, Tharp, and the emerging postmodernists suggests that the real challenge facing American artists today rests with the creation of new risks and new possibilities for popular art. Working toward what Helen Vendler calls "that harmony of form that can enclose and mediate the disorder of life," they are proposing their own ambitious alternatives to the past and future of dance in America.

TWO CONTEMPORARY MASTERS

THE PAUL TAYLOR DANCE COMPANY

· AMERICAN GOTHIC ·

Beneath the contoured ceilings of an 1823 Manhattan town house, an uncategorizable master of modern dance lives as quietly as any retired Southern gentleman, guarding the unimpeachable good manners of a former age. Half-buried in an overstuffed chair by a crackling fire, Paul Taylor reaches over his paunch to warm a visitor's coffee, placed on a low glass-covered coffee table enshrining a hand-picked collection of seashells. In his early fifties now, Taylor seldom ventures out of this slightly shabby bastion of gentility except to work—constantly, obsessively—in his nearby studio on lower Broadway, to putter in his backyard garden, or to seclude himself in his hideaway on the north shore of Long Island, overlooking the Sound.

"I have never liked being *seen*," he suggests with a trace of a Virginia accent, lighting his fifth or sixth cigarette of the morning. "I never got over stage fright the whole time I danced. I'm not tempted to perform again. Even when I stopped I wasn't tempted. It was more of a relief. I can see what I'm doing now when I make a dance, and I don't have to get everybody to move like I do.

"I do remember I could always *hear* very well when I was dancing," he adds, flashing his famous Cheshire-Cat grin while his devoted mongrel, Deedee, nuzzles her head against his thigh, waiting to be scratched. *"That* was nice."

Taylor's conversational style is funny, phlegmatic, and occasionally self-deprecatory, colored by a vague, almost rueful affection for the work he has fashioned in the thirty years since he first decided that dancing would be "a nice way" to spend his life. And yet a disturbing ambiguity has marked Taylor's career as one of the most curious and unpredictable in American dance: Along with some of the tenderest, most *civil* dances in the modern repertory, choreographed to masterpieces of classical music, Taylor has also fashioned some of the most macabre, coolly unburdening himself of a nightmare vision of human hypocrisy, monstrousness, and degradation without precedent in the American theater. "I have always had ten thousand ideas about everything," he says in passing. "I have always been very confused."

His *Big Bertha* (1971) presents a "typical" American family caught in the grip of a mechanical fortune-teller and band machine, who induces Mom to dance a striptease and Dad to rape, then murder his daughter before replacing Big Bertha himself. "I have an instinct for evil," says the choreographer. In contrast, *Diggity* (1978) is a good-natured, almost bland celebration of interspecies affection, performed on a stage littered with tiny cutout depictions of Deedee. *Private Domain* (1969), half invisible at any time behind a series of downstage panels, is an escha-

Ruth Andrien, David Parsons, and Elie Chaib in Taylor's *Le Sacre du Printemps (The Rehearsal),* a dance that returned to themes central to all the American narrative arts: grotesque comedy and projected dream, an insight into the marvelous, and an apocalyptic finale. (© 1980 Jack Vartoogian)

tological glimpse into a world of meaningless lust; *Public Domain* (1968), danced to a hilarious collage of familiar popular music and advertising jingles, is an absurdist rendering of the most inconsequential American behavior. *Cloven Kingdom* (1976) burlesques the Darwinian boundary between human nightlife and animal behavior; *Dust,* the triumph of a 1978 tour to the Soviet Union, is a study of affliction, deformity, flagellation, and umbilical dread that cartoonist Edward Gorey, a friend of the company, thought the funniest dance he'd ever seen.

In the passionate strangeness of his work, its range of mood, and its genius for cannibalizing everything from classical ballet to the most radical dance experimentation, Paul Taylor could be called the last artistically viable choreographer in the modern camp. His signature choreographic style of quirks and oddities draws unique inspiration from the circus, vaudeville, and sports; the movements of lions, insects, dogs, and people in the street "doing what they usually do: waiting, swarming, even lying down, in an array of primal and ageless riches." Originally trained as a painter before rejecting the canvas

for "real space," Taylor has brought a painterly awareness of collage to the composition of movement; like many postwar visual artists, he has escaped choreographic formula through an ordered, associative randomness governed by his own "clear illogic"—creating dances "like gigantic crossword puzzles in three dimensions," as he once described them.

Before it is anything else, dance is play. But for all the charm, wonder, and cathartic violence Taylor pours into his work, he nevertheless succumbs sometimes to an unpredictable pessimism about the value of his achievement. His moods have helped to make him a grand master of the sinister stir, the rosy apocalypse, but now he worries that he has reached a point where everybody knows what to expect. "The tradition of modern dance is to move ahead," he says, "and I get bored doing the same things. I get bored doing different things, lately."

Taylor's instinct for surprise found dark expression in his 1980 masterpiece, *Le Sacre du Printemps (The Rehearsal),* a reconception of Nijinsky's frenzied vision of pagan Russia that had shocked and stunned Parisian audiences in 1913.

For decades, Nijinsky's epochal work has existed in memory only, as numerous choreographers failed to comprehend "the broken rhythms and jagged harmonies" of the Stravinsky score and its neoprimitive theme; even Balanchine called it "impossible, terrible" and consciously left it alone. Taylor first attempted the music for his *Scudorama* in 1963 but, dissatisfied with the results, threw the accompaniment overboard; *Profiles,* completed in 1979, was based loosely on Nijinsky's two-dimensional movement style. Finally, some sixty-seven years after the legendary evening when Diaghilev shouted above the tumult, commanding the ballet to continue, Paul Taylor brought his own *Rites* to Broadway and created a very different order of surprise: An icon of the European avant garde had been translated into a comic strip/American detective yarn and a masterpiece of dance storytelling.

Taylor's cunningly innocent melodrama navigates with astonishing ease through the rhythmically treacherous Stravinsky score, reducing its four-hand piano version to a transparent silent-movie accompaniment. Alluding to the pulsing, asymmetrical gymnastics of the Nijinsky original, the dance begins with a young mother approaching a world-weary shamus (Christopher Gillis) for help in recovering her child, kidnapped by a gang of Chinatown thugs; the action moves back in time to a bar where a mysterious dance rehearsal is in progress, conducted by a grim Russian ballet mistress (Bettie de Jong). The baby is snatched, and the Private Eye arrested in the confusion of an ensuing police raid. The head crook's Chinese Moll (Monica Morris) becomes infatuated with the purloined infant; the Crook (Elie Chaib) and his Stooge (Lila York) begin plotting to bump her off. Meanwhile, the young mother visits the detective in his jailhouse dreams, giving him superhuman strength to escape and rescue the baby in the middle of the Stooge's bungled assassination attempt. With the Keystone Kops in hot pursuit, he flees to the young mother's front yard, setting the stage for what Arlene Croce termed the dance's penultimate "motiveless malignity." The Ballet Mistress directs three women in an

eerie "Garland Dance," and then the two Kops, the Private Eye, the Crook, the Stooge, and a dancer who has stolen a comrade's wages are knifed to death in a methodical, ritualized massacre. In a last, gratuitous death, the baby is slaughtered as well, rocketing the mother into "The Dance of the Chosen Maiden," pilfered from the format of the Nijinsky original. For the closing scene before a mirror, the dancers all revive for a frenetic dance rehearsal as the curtain falls. Is this a demonic celebration of an archetypal American violence or Taylor's deathless apotheosis of the dancer's discipline?

"The ambiguities are just a reflection of the time," Taylor shrugs from his overstuffed chair, slicing himself another piece of coffee cake. "Though I suppose I have a bit of a split personality myself," he adds. "It can come in handy in the theater." Riding a creative crest since his retirement from the stage, Taylor has not retreated from the gothic darknesses that have always inspired an important part of his repertory. And yet an undefinable sweetness in his character has contributed to works of a wholly unambiguous temper, among the most joyful experiences anywhere in the dance world.

"The main thing about choreography," Taylor will tell you, "is to keep people from bumping into one another," but he has successfully navigated bodies to Bach, Scriabin, Debussy, Beethoven, and many other classical composers; after viewing the seminal *Aureole* (1962), to music by Handel, Edwin Denby praised Taylor as "the first American choreographer since Robbins who took the trouble to teach himself the continuous clarity of a well-made ballet." Rudolf Nureyev saw an early performance of this masterwork at the Spoleto Festival in Italy and began practicing its steps before he met their maker; he would dance the work in Mexico City in 1964, the first of many appearances with the Taylor company. Fifteen years later, Mikhail Baryshnikov joined the company for *Airs,* to music by Handel, and brought the ballet into the repertory of American Ballet Theatre in 1981. Taylor is pleased that his work has been performed by the Pennsylvania Ballet, the Royal

Aureole, with Nicholas Gunn (foreground). "The more Taylor danced and choreographed," Edwin Denby wrote in the early 1960s, "the more a powerful and complexly fluid dance momentum engaged him. His gift defined itself as one not for anti-dance but for pro-dance." (© 1976 Susan Cook)

Danish Ballet, the Netherlands Dance Theatre, the Paris Opéra Ballet, the Grands Ballets Canadiens, Ballet Rambert in England, and Bat Dor in Israel; more companies request his dances than he can possibly provide. And yet he remains defensive about his modern pedigree, preferring the license it gives him to create his own rules.

No company performs his work better than his own collection of nymphs and satyrs, bruisers and androgynes, moving with a ritual flow, a tribal sense of energy that seldom requires absolute positions in space. Skipping, prancing, slumping, and leaping sideways across the stage, Taylor's dancers move in big muscular runs, lumbering slides, and ground-skimming leaps quite contrary to the gravity-defying lift of the ballet. The buoyant exuberance of his style combines the speed, momentum, and kinetic logic of classicism with the floor-bound energy and active torso of the Graham technique, reflecting Taylor's own strengths as a dancer—and even his years as a competitive swimmer. A widely acclaimed soloist with the Martha Graham company during the late 1950s, Taylor was the recipient of a special Balanchine solo during Graham's shared evening with the New York Ballet in 1959. "We called him 'The Geek,'" Kirstein later recalled; Taylor's body twined and twitched "like a fly caught in a glass of milk," as Balanchine described it; the solo had to be dropped from the City Ballet repertory because no one else could master it. Taylor's subsequent choreography has drawn on the full resources of the contemporary performer, portraying dancers as vermin and heroes, beasts and victims—even freeing them from the tyranny of gender roles, with women suddenly muscling men through the middle of some variation. "Down with choreography, up with dancers," Taylor has written. "Audiences expect a veritable miracle in the shape of a human being, which is what a good dancer is."

By its very nature a temporary art, Taylor's choreography seems a veritable conundrum of time to a man who can look at his surviving repertory—more than half his eighty works are lost, presumably for the duration—and scarcely recognize it as his own. "That's the nicest thing about dance," he suggests—"it's *erasable*." He actually seems to prefer this distance from his own past and the history of the world. He has developed no "school" or technique; many former dancers, including Twyla Tharp and Laura Dean, have gone on to their own choreographic careers, but none reflects his singular obsessions. And yet Taylor has acquired a vast audience, including balletomanes as well as those who instinctively distrust ballet, in part because of his ability to celebrate the art of dancing with a special ebullience, conviction, and daring—a *gameness* that gives his works their special feeling of celebration. Certainly the Paul Taylor Dance Company isn't chic enough to appeal to fashionable audiences; it lacks the high seriousness and aesthetic purity to attract an avant-garde crowd. But the company has performed in three hundred American cities and fifty-three foreign countries, and is the only contemporary dance company to come even close to selling out City Center for nearly a decade running.

·　　·　　·

Circumstance as much as choice contributed to Paul Taylor's consuming need for independence, his confusion of the immediate and the temporary, and his complex relationship to tradition. Born in Pittsburgh on July 29, 1930, he began his schooling in Massachusetts but lived most of his early life in Washington, D.C., and his mother's ancestral Virginia, staying for extended periods with his sister and an isolated farm family, at an Episcopal boarding school, and a military academy. With three children from a previous marriage, Taylor's mother divorced his physicist father when he was four and worked constantly to support her family. In terms of strength, Taylor recalls, "She'd give Martha Graham a run for her money."

Taylor showed an early talent for drawing and, over his mother's objections, entered Syracuse University on a partial art scholarship. Working in the school cafeteria for extra money, he noticed that the swim team seemed especially well fed, so one afternoon he went to the pool to try out for the team. A natural athlete who had excelled on his prep school football squad, Taylor received a swimming scholarship and quickly became a champion sprinter. "I loved swimming and I loved competitions," Taylor recalls. "I also learned a lot about getting nervous before a performance."

The art department at Syracuse, meanwhile, was "teaching everybody to paint like Matisse," and Taylor didn't like it. Restless, he discovered some dance books about the Ballets Russes and Martha Graham, which led him in the summer of 1951 to answer an ad in a dance magazine for a job as chauffeur at a school in Bar Harbor, Maine. Taylor returned to Syracuse that fall determined to become a dancer. Practicing in the athletic dormitory hall, he won a work scholarship the following summer to Connecticut College, where his first sight of Martha Graham was of "this creature dressed entirely in red crossing a lawn." Graham took one look at Taylor in class and murmured to an assistant, "I want him." When the summer ended, Graham gave Taylor her phone number in New York City and told him to call if he was ever in town.

After a trip to Washington for a crash course in ballet, he descended on New York City in the fall of 1952. Auditioning for the Juilliard School, he showed up wearing socks—it seemed to him a smart compromise between ballet slippers and bare feet. The chairperson of Juilliard's dance division, Martha Hill, accepted him without hesitation: "He couldn't do anything wrong."

Taking a $12 a month apartment in Hell's Kitchen, Taylor plunged into modern dance and ballet classes on a partial scholarship at Juilliard during the day, studying at the Graham school in the evenings. Supporting himself for the next several years doing odd jobs and dancing in television commercials and Broadway shows—in one audition, managing to break his nose attempting a backflip for Jerome Robbins—Taylor took to the Graham style like a second skin: "It felt like what dancing should be." By 1953, he had left Juilliard and was understudying parts for the company, and two years later became a full member.

"There was an odor of friction that Martha worked best by," Taylor recalls. "If things went smoothly, she'd stir them up. She was never dull. Only now do I consider how remarkable it was that she was still dancing in her early fifties, or however old she was. [She was approaching sixty.] At that point, there was little movement invention. Martha would give us some idea of the direction she wanted, and we'd fiddle around and find it. I loved working with her—even though half of it was about not tripping over the costumes."

With modern dance somewhat set in its ways, Taylor joined a small New York avant garde attempting to define new directions for the future. Studying at the Metropolitan Opera Ballet School, he became involved with Dance Associates, a loosely knit group of experimentalists guided by James Waring, a choreographer, teacher, and dedicated outsider who believed that dance "is any movement without an object in mind." Taylor was learning deaf-signing to communicate with a new friend, and Waring exploited this skill in *Three Pieces for Solo Clarinet* (1954), the first solo ever created especially for Taylor's gifts. Through his new friendships, he also met a number of young New York visual artists, and later worked with Robert Rauschenberg and Jasper Johns on a series of window dressings for midtown department stores. Sharing Taylor's interests in collage and the use of everyday materials for art-making, Rauschenberg would assemble set designs for Taylor's dances into the 1960s; every few years a mysterious artist named George Tacit would contribute work as well. Years later, Taylor finally admitted that Tacit was one of his own alter egos.

Merce Cunningham was ten years Taylor's senior, a choreographer with a growing reputation in avant-garde circles. Attracted by Cunningham's movement ideas and shared background with Martha Graham, Taylor traveled to Black Mountain College in the summer of 1953 and ended up joining Cunningham's fledgling company, shaving his beard to dance Off Broadway at the Theatre de Lys that fall. Taylor was to have appeared in *Dime a Dance,* a work that included "a little waltz, a little foxtrot, and a running dance—all kinds of things," says Cunningham. It was developed in "open form," a method of composition that separated choreography from its realization: Audiences drew cards to determine which sequences were danced. The problem was that the audience never drew Taylor's card.

"I asked Merce, 'Do I have to leave it up to chance that I get to *dance?*'" Taylor recalls. "Merce said, 'Well, *yes.*' So I left."

In 1954, at last ready for his first concert on his own, Taylor shared a bill with Waring at the Henry Street Settlement House, presenting *Jack and the Beanstalk,* a comic work with a balloon set by Rauschenberg. "Mostly beatniks saw it," Taylor says. His works over the next several years remained impenetrable to outsiders; a 1956 concert was "without passion, point, or purpose," according to at least one critic. What most threw audiences was the absence of psychological tension. Taylor was creating pure dance fantasies under his own motto: "If you wanna send a message, try Western Union." *Four Epitaphs*— now called *Three Epitaphs,* the oldest surviving work in the Taylor repertory—was a pure choreographic joke, featuring four unpleasant-looking creatures decked in Rauschenberg's dark body stockings and mirrored headgear, slumping, scuffling, and grinding their shoulders to scruffy New Orleans jazz. Poignant, miserable, and hilarious at once, *Four Epitaphs*'s good-natured insult to the divinity of man had an even more unsettling emotional impact than it does today. "You didn't know whether to laugh or cry," Rauschenberg declared.

In 1957 Taylor performed his famous *Seven New Dances,* an anticipation of some of the more radical experiments that overtook the dance world

Three Epitaphs, with costumes by Robert Rauschenberg, "a masterpiece of nonsensical hilarity," wrote one of Taylor's early mentors, Louis Horst. (© 1978 Jack Vartoogian)

in the 1960s. The single performance at the 92nd Street YM-YWHA "caused most of the audience to leave soon after it began," a later program noted, "the Y management not to rent him their hall again, and Louis Horst, one of his mentors, to publish a celebrated review which consisted of three square inches of blank space." In *Epic* Taylor wore a business suit and walked across the stage to a complicated system of counts, performing tight, deliberate, everyday gestures to the sound of a taped voice: "At the tone, the time will be . . .," and so on. In *Duet* he stood smoking a cigarette while a woman sat at his feet gazing calmly into the audience for several minutes, to a random sound score by John Cage. "Does nothing lead to something?" asked *Dance Magazine* prophetically. "Paul Taylor," wrote Terry, "seems determined to drive his viewers out of their minds."

Under the influence of John Cage, Taylor was attempting his own redefinition of dance performance—exposing himself without the support of a style, exploring intuition and sur-

reality, and discovering a sense of stillness that would serve him throughout his career. Still touring the world in the mythic psychodramas of Martha Graham, Taylor in his own work had reached a kind of zero point: Convinced that the subject of dancing is the human body in motion and repose, he began to think that the austerity of *Seven New Dances* was a wrong direction. He *liked* the physicality of modern dance and ballet; while remaining opposed to applied psychology in dance, he began to realize that some degree of individual inflection simply could not be avoided. "I realized that no matter how scientific or abstract you get—I used to keep little dictionaries of movement—you can't escape meaning. I realized that when the girl walked away from the other girls, she wasn't just walking—she was leaving."

With *Aureole,* choreographed in New York City during the hot summer of 1962, Taylor began to discover an even more traditional impulse. Romantic in form and feeling, the work was everything that modern dance at the time

Orbs, with Paul Taylor. (© Herbert Migdoll)

was not. Danced to the music of Handel, *Aureole* was extravagantly praised in *The New York Times* as a nineteenth-century *ballet blanc* after its first performance at the American Dance Festival in Connecticut. Taylor still considers this description a vile misrepresentation, but with his first unqualified success, he was free to leave the Graham company and embark entirely on his own career. Resenting the facility with which he had made it, he followed *Aureole* with more absurdist studies, dance lampoons, and bizarre movement experiments. But recognition continued: international State Department tours, a pilot grant from the newly formed National Endowment for the Arts, and enough money to pay his dancers regular salaries.

In 1966, he presented his first full-evening ballet, *Orbs,* a neoclassical ceremony of the four seasons choreographed to Beethoven's late string quartets. A homage to the formal obligations of classicism, with extended passages of both comic mime and pure dance, *Orbs*'s subject was nothing less than the cyclical nature of human existence—typically viewed by the choreographer as "changes that just happen." *The New York Times*'s critic heralded the performance "a major event,"

but many progressive viewers were either shocked or dismayed. "I couldn't accept the idea," Marcia Siegel has written, "that a modern dance choreographer would deliberately relinquish the obligation to search for new movement or new forms. . . . If he betrayed insiders, he opened up modern dance to an entirely new audience which had found the art esoteric or difficult before."

In the midst of these new triumphs, Taylor was forced to cope with serious health problems. In Germany, in 1970, he finally saw a doctor "who told me I had ulcers on top of ulcers, the worst he'd ever seen," Taylor recalls. But he went ahead anyway with plans for a three-act magnum opus, a dance history of the founding of America as seen through the Book of Genesis. Completed in 1973, after two years of work, *American Genesis* was nearly Taylor's Waterloo. Six dancers and one stage manager withdrew during its making; nearly everyone involved agreed that the piece didn't work, and the critics would second the opinion.

On stage, opening night at the Brooklyn Academy of Music, Taylor finally collapsed, five minutes before the closing curtain. "The next

Esplanade, with a leaping Lila York. (© 1977 Jack Vartoogian)

thing I knew I was being carried off. I didn't know how ill I was. I thought I could just take a couple of pills and make it through." The media reported a case of flu and exhaustion, but outraged doctors told Taylor he'd had hepatitis for at least twelve months. Taylor somehow managed to finish that season, but his career as one of the great dancer-choreographers of the 1950s and 1960s was over. A brief, unspectacular comeback bid in 1974 ended quickly, and he finally admitted to himself that he hadn't enjoyed performing in years.

The end of a choreographer's performing career can be a traumatic moment for any company; for Taylor it meant a surge of creativity that has continued into the present, yielding the bulk of the repertory for which he is known today. In 1975, *Runes* harkened back to the hermetic ritualism of early modern dance, while *Esplanade,* one of his greatest creations, anticipated a postmodern blend of the classical and the everyday. Inspired by a girl Taylor saw running for a bus on Houston Street near his home, *Esplanade* has its dancers running, walking, crawl-

ing, and sliding across the floor in complex geometric patterns accompanied by a joyous Bach score—the last two movements the same that Balanchine had chosen for *Concerto Barocco.* The company sold out two weeks at New York's City Center, without hype or guest artists or the choreographer himself. His ulcers continued to plague him—in 1976 he choreographed *Polaris* without getting up from his chair—but the Paul Taylor Dance Company had established itself as one of America's most important dance institutions.

In 1976, however, a South American tour was suddenly canceled: The enormous expense of a second successful City Center season had left the company $50,000 in debt, forcing it to disband. "An indictment of our society," *The New York Times* declared, and the National Endowment provided an emergency challenge grant of $17,500, nearly matched during a one-week benefit in Washington hosted by First Lady Betty Ford. The Taylor company was saved but, like nearly every dance group in America, continues to survive by the skin of its teeth. Television loomed as an important medium for exposing the company to the public, but Taylor was hesitant about the prospect—"trepidatious," to use his own neologism. As Emile Ardolino recalls, "He didn't much like the idea of putting his dances into that little box."

Nevertheless, Taylor had participated in a CBS "Camera Three" experiment in the early 1970s, and when he was offered the chance to present *Esplanade* and *Runes* on *Dance in America* in 1977/78, he accepted, although he made it evident that he was not enormously interested in the business of translating dances for the screen.

Quick, vivid crosscutting was required to capture *Esplanade*'s baroque architecture; successive takes of the dangerous slides across the floor were held to a minimum to reduce the risk, with the camera held close to the floor so that the movement seemed to swell into the camera and fill the screen. Sometimes the restricted viewpoint of the camera augmented the dance's surprise: When Carolyn Adams raced exultantly across the space, the camera followed her; when she leaped high into the air, her momentum carried Elie Chaib into the frame to catch her, and not a moment too soon. *Runes,* lit by a full moon rising slowly above the horizon, presented an easier challenge. The camera did not alter the nature of Taylor's primitive rites, as shamans become victims, then celebrants in a flow of acrobatic shapes and archaic imagery—presenting an illusion of timeless change with the same passion that Taylor had mastered in the theater.

Although the choreographer was pleased with the first program, he decided that he needed the immediacy of a live audience for the next two programs, and so both were recorded live onstage at the American Dance Festival in North Carolina: *Aureole, Three Epitaphs,* and *Big Bertha;* then *Le Sacre du Printemps (The Rehearsal)* and *Arden Court.* "You get an energy and a continuity in live performance," says Ardolino, who directed both shows and edited the first with Taylor's help and suggestions. "But you can't possibly get all the camera angles you need, even with five cameras. The dance becomes more of an event than anything else. You gain some-

thing, and you lose something." Without the kind of precise camera work possible under studio conditions, some important moments of dancers in live performance are shaping a dance from moment to moment, benefiting from the emotional and physical feelings generated by the dance as it was made to be experienced in the theater.

After it was all over, the choreographer breathed a sigh of relief and presented Ardolino with one of the many shell boxes he enjoys constructing during his stays on Long Island. And thanked him for how well he'd "boxed" his dances.

·   ·   ·

Taylor recently received his third speeding ticket in eighteen months, threatening his ability to hold a license, so he drives more cautiously these days. "I'd be very happy on a desert island," he murmurs, crashing up a winding moonlit drive to an odd-looking shingled contemporary house hidden in the woods between vast potato fields and Long Island Sound. Somewhere he'd read a complaint about the lack of social life on the north fork of Long Island and figured that it might be a good place not to think about dance.

After starting a fire in the stone fireplace, he tentatively offers to read from his memoirs-in-progress. His editor, Robert Gottlieb, "told me to write about my inner life, but all that did was get me depressed," he mutters, rustling through an untidy stack of papers. "I'm trying to be Nabokov in this, and I'm trying to be five years old. But what I like about autobiography is the invention. I was amazed I could go backward in time. I always thought I didn't want to remember anything."

Apologetically, with frequent pauses, he peers through half-glasses to read in a flat monotone. The digressive text abounds with neologisms and florid metaphors: A Mexican shoreline was littered with "explosive nature's flotsam garlands"; when the company danced *Aureole* in Mexico City with ghastly sunburns, the theater curtain was "hemorrhaging with modernist magenta lozenges." A chapter on Twyla Tharp, who spent nine months with the company in 1963, dwells mysteriously on a dog sucking exhaust pipes in a midwestern parking lot. "All my friends get it," he explains sheepishly.

The subject of his former avant-garde associates remains a tender one. A 1968 feature in *The New York Times Magazine* spoke of "the cold war in modern dance" between its two leading practitioners, Merce Cunningham and Taylor. Although Taylor respects Merce and considers him a friend, he feels little affinity with his work. "Merce had gotten stuck and gone into retreat," Taylor remarks of the early days, "and John Cage got him out of it with chance operations, so he wouldn't have to make any decisions. Unfortunately, they kept going on it. John is the brains—Merce the instinct. He's a powerful dramatic dancer. He tells other people to just do the movement, but you watch Merce." His own pursuit of an idiosyncratic "superhuman" virtuosity, his haymaking sense of humor, cheerful perversity, and good-natured love of Americana—"I feel American," he says, "although I've never felt particularly legal"—have tended to distance him from the contemporary avant garde. Nevertheless, he wonders about his reputation among the younger postmodernists, more directly influenced by Cunningham's work than his own. "I was caught between generations in modern dance," he says, a little defensively. "I never felt it was my job to categorize myself. But it's true, my work did change. I've always done what I've wanted to see. I don't know what other people want to see."

In the morning he walks along the frozen, snow-covered beach, where the irrepressible Deedee—age seventy in dog years—dashes like a pup to catch a thrown stick. Taylor speaks of the original settlers who came to this forbidding shore, then ruminates about whatever meaning his work might contain.

"I've always thought of art as a kind of complicated game, not a museum or a graveyard," he says, watching chunks of ice sloshing against a shingle. "It should be fun in some deep way. It's not that work has to be new. But it should have some kind of fresh attack." After pointing out the rock where his company skinny-dips during the summer, he continues, "It's about

order," weighing his words as if he may not have a chance to change them. "It's as simple as that. It's a kind of religion. There are all kinds of order. There can be ordered chaos, too."

By early afternoon, he drives back into the sky-scraping crisis center of New York City, to prepare for work on Monday morning. As he noted in his book: "A dance is like a snowy mountain to climb, and yet it's not ours to conquer. The audience goes home and the wind blows the footprints away. It's a habit, an addiction."

.   .   .

Wandering into Taylor's cramped rehearsal studios one afternoon a few months later, I blunder into the middle of a flight of men hurtling in from the wings, arms raised in archaic half-circles, muscular torsos twisted to stage front like a herd of Cretan bulls noticing something dangerous to their left. David Parsons sidesteps me with an amused grin. I skitter to a seat in the narrow viewers' space, where Taylor—the filter of a lit cigarette pressed firmly against his cheek—smiles wanly at my clumsiness. He has lost a tooth snorkeling over a reef in the Indian Ocean, and looks a little like a scurvy pirate. Although the studio is not warm, salty rings of perspiration stain the underarms of his dark-plaid shirt; the dancers, of course, are sweating profusely, because nobody marks through a dance at a Taylor rehearsal. "We're all a little guarded in our states of mind," he warned ruefully before suggesting the visit. "We're working very hard, and now we're trying to keep friction to a minimum."

Taylor is no longer as close to his company as in the days when he danced and toured with them, a contemporary in age, but they seem a remarkably contented group, ready to get on with whatever the choreographer has in mind. "Everybody in the company has a different relationship with Paul," says one former dancer. "There's a great deal of intimacy and a great deal of battle." "If I didn't have a company, I wouldn't choreograph," Taylor once told an acquaintance. "What would you do?" the person inquired. "I'd either garden or die," Taylor an-

An essay in masculine prowess: Christopher Gillis, Elie Chaib, Robert Kahn, Daniel Ezralow, and David Parsons in Taylor's *Arden Court*. (© 1981 Lois Greenfield)

swered. "So you're sort of like God," the acquaintance decided. The response apparently struck a strange chord, for the choreographer nearly fell out of his chair laughing.

Currently the company is running the virtuosic *Arden Court,* danced to the baroque music of the eighteenth-century composer William Boyce. One of Taylor's most spectacular works, an essay in masculine prowess, its rampant heroism glorifies the muscular energy of six aspirant supermen: Elie Chaib, Christopher Gillis, Robert Kahn, Tom Evert, David Parsons, and Kenneth Tosti. Suddenly dancer Carolyn Adams is wafted in like a black-gold cherub from a baroque cartouche.

"That looks dumb," Taylor announces when the section is completed. Apparently the choreography has eroded over the past few days, and he's a little annoyed. "I think it needs to look a little more *insane.*"

"That preparation really should look brutal," he tells a new company member, referring to him as What's-his-name. "Don't separate the jump from the turn so much. And the leg unfortunately isn't to that corner." The dancer tries the move again, without success. "*No.* You have to go really deep into that lunge." Taylor seems permanently welded to his chair, but lumbers up to demonstrate the movement with surprising buoyancy and speed, turning in the air, tucking his legs under himself, then spinning around into a huge lunge almost level to the floor, his rear leg stretching in the opposite direction from where the dancer had gone. The dancer gets the picture. "He'll be doing that when he's sixty," mutters Daniel Ezralow.

They attempt the section one more time, and Taylor laughs at flubs and fudges that weren't funny a few minutes ago. Afterward, Bettie de Jong, now rehearsal mistress after nearly twenty

Paul Taylor in rehearsal with dancer Linda Kent. (©
1983 Johan Elbers)

years with the company, gives corrections while
Taylor fusses with the tape recorder. One dancer
can't seem to understand a certain move. "It's a
Graham move," De Jong explains. Taylor glances
around for a second; this is a description he is
loath to adopt. "A *distortion* of a Graham move,"
he says firmly. "This is why we need a school."

He seems slightly embarrassed by the disorder of the dance, too dumbfounding in such
close quarters for an outsider to tell much about.
The company runs *Esplanade* next, racing and
sliding dangerously across the dirty wooden floor.
Taylor watches Ruth Andrien with visible anxiety. She is recovering from a back injury and
insists she is all right, but Taylor has told her to
take it easy, with little effect. Afterward, he gives
more notes: "No fifths or pointed feet," he says.
"Too many habits. And in the line, that position
has to be more distorted and clearer. Those 'little agonies' aren't there. It's not the form—you

have to have more tension." This correction does
not register, so Taylor tries a different approach.
"Now some of you girls still have your periods," he suggests. A few of the "girls" snicker,
while others glare in mock disgust. "I'm not
saying this is about cramps," Taylor continues.
"I just want to fire your imaginations." Once
again, the correction takes hold; the movement
acquires a new, more immediate reality. The
magic of the Taylor metaphor.

Paul Taylor is not entirely "a lonely figure
on an isle of artistic isolation," as he urges in his
memoirs. Extraordinarily removed from the
winds of mood, rumor, and fashion, he nonetheless has a craft, a studio, and a group of individuals eager to help him scratch what he calls
the "throbbing fermentation of my latest itch."
It is essentially a secret adventure.

"Dance is such a fragile amorphous thing
that it becomes very hard to define," Taylor explains. "The success of my dancers is built around
a very real situation. They really like each other.
There are these mutual feelings of admiration and
dependence that you can't teach. I've never
thought of the stage as a place for realism, but
when things are real in this way it's better than
anything I can think of."

The company finishes the day's work with
Dust, a dance Taylor has privately dedicated to
the courage of the handicapped. Susan McGuire,
formerly with the Martha Graham Dance Company, performs a long, balletic passage with a
typical Taylor twist: Her right arm dangles use-
lessly, as if the nerves were cut. Afterward, she
kneels by Taylor's chair to discuss a few problems.

"That was lovely, Susan," he tells her finally.

She returns his look and smiles. "You made
it," she replies.

TWYLA THARP AND DANCERS

· GETTING THERE ·

Winter, 1979. Twyla Tharp and Dancers have moved uptown to American Ballet Theatre's West Sixty-first Street studios to prepare their first New York season in almost two years. Lunch hour has just begun, and two women have stripped off their sweat-soaked dance gear to stand nude, like guests at a Fellini cocktail party, smoke low-tar cigarettes and ponder their dry clothes. Other dancers are talking madly beneath the barres; they suddenly rise to coach themselves with icy derangement through a series of shuffles, slides, and scattershot lifts that sends them sprawling half the length of the studio in a matter of seconds.

They're shouting the counts out loud and a little gaga: *"One and two and go and go, GO!"* France Mayotte dashes diagonally across the space while Tom Rawe attempts to extricate himself from a maze of bodies in time to catch her under the armpits and swing her around. Unfortunately he's a split-second late and smashes her in the chest, sending a chain reaction of disaster down the line. *That's* the lift that's been gumming the works. Standing in February sunshine streaming through the skylight, the two naked women turn away and start throwing on their dry clothes.

"Okay, guys, I got it," says Rawe gamely, rubbing his hands together. The dancers return to the far wall and run the sequence to perfection

this time, with a relaxed, calibrated air, like classical virtuosos just horsing around, dreaming up movement as they go along. What audiences in the theater will ultimately see, of course, are people careening along at the highest reaches of *fun,* dancing with a casual exhilaration and freedom extraordinarily in tune with the times.

Satisfied, the dancers gather their things and head off to lunch, efforts unobserved by the choreographer, who has sequestered herself in a broom closet to study videotapes of their unfinished dance, *Chapters & Verses*—shaping up as an impressionistic history of the disco generation from the Mickey Mouse Club to the theme-and-variation jackboot of nightclub purgatory. It is her very first attempt to create a "story-dance," an unfashionable hybrid she would have scoffed at attempting a decade earlier; work began last summer, and at this point in the choreographic process, she's thrown away more movement than she's kept.

"Teeny, toRRid TwYla," Tharp scrawled in the program notes for her 1976 New York season, ". . . lives to tell the terrible TRUTH/tracing TRAGEDY to Travesty/teasing traditION through trickly torrents twisting, traipsing, trysting, THRUSTING . . ."—fidgeting now before the blue glow of a video screen, rehearsing the past for some clue, some key to the present dilemma. A certain rest-

A rehearsal of *Chapters & Verses* at the old American Ballet Theatre studios on 61st Street (left to right): France Mayotte, Chris Uchida, Tom Rawe, and Tony Ferro. (© 1978 Don Perdue)

Twyla Tharp in *Sue's Leg.* (© Herbert Migdoll)

lessness and an uncompromising perfectionism have dominated Tharp's progress throughout her career, beginning with her earliest unaccompanied movement studies in the 1960s and continuing through the addition of music, humor, characterization, partnering, and set design in the 1970s. Polishing every insight gathered along the way, she developed a formal mastery that allows her company to cut loose with an expenditure of energy unequaled by any choreographer in the world save Balanchine. By revealing how contemporary dancers feel about themselves, she has successfully confounded the distance between classicism and pop dancing, modernism and popular entertainment; by discovering how popular culture can nurture a higher order of imagination, she has assembled a repertory of dances embodying what Tom Wolfe calls "the hog-stomping baroque exuberance of American civilization."

Now Tharp's latest expansion of possibility may actually be an intimation of her childhood, when her only contacts with the outside world were the attractions at her parents' drive-in theater near San Bernardino, California—four movies and ten cartoons a week, from M-G-M movie musicals to Daffy Duck. Working on her

France Mayotte (foreground) in "3-5-0-0" from the *Hair* dances, presented near the Lincoln Memorial in Washington, D.C. *Hair* inspired Twyla Tharp's new "desire for grandeur." (Courtesy Twyla Tharp Dance Foundation)

own video and film projects since the mid-1960s, she had to wait until the mid-1970s to collaborate on a major Hollywood picture: *Hair* (1978), director Milos Forman's ironical tribute to the 1960s counterculture, with one dance sequence shot before thirty thousand people at the Washington and Lincoln Memorials in Washington. Although most of Tharp's contribution was edited out of existence, the experience moved her toward a new "desire for grandeur," as she baldly puts it, quickening her curiosity about how movement and gesture can convey a story. For the first time since a lecture that accompanied the second half of *The Bix Pieces,* she is allowing her dancers the luxurious consolation of the Spoken Word. With *Chapters & Verses,* Tharp has placed herself at the threshold of a three-year, three-part odyssey toward a new dance-theater form that will provide her with the greatest challenges of her artistic career.

As she explains it: "You just reach a place where you begin to want *more.*"

·　　·　　·

Lunch hour has ended, and with the dancers warming up at the barres, Tharp suddenly bursts through the swinging doors—poker-faced, cross, and ten minutes late, limping urgently, dressed in a stretched gray T-shirt, striped leg warmers trailing a few yards of blue wool, and a tattered pair of beige-gray "Woolworth sauna" rubber pants patched at the crotch with a maze of yellow gaffer's tape. She resembles nothing so much as a martyr in a medieval painting.

Approaching forty, Tharp finds it more and more difficult to prepare herself physically for another New York season. A brazen, totally unsentimental woman, Tharp believes in having the highest possible expectations for herself, but at the moment she has more irons in the fire than she can possibly handle. Flinging herself into a canvas chair, she consults her clipboard, and some sort of ozone falls through the air: The rehearsal is fifteen minutes behind schedule. Dancers are already pulling up their socks over their jazz shoes and diving into place along the far wall. "When you dance with Twyla," Shelley Washington later explained, "you make yourself totally available to Twyla all the time."

"Everything okay?" the choreographer calls out at last.

The company's senior member, Rose Marie Wright, nods affirmatively, the stage

(From left): Shelley Washington, Rose Marie Wright, John Carrafa, Tony Ferro, Jennifer Waye, and Tom Rawe in Tharp's *Baker's Dozen*. (© 1985 Brownie Harris)

manager throws on the tape recorder, and the air suddenly fills with the dreamy jazz piano of Willie "the Lion" Smith, performed by Dick Hyman. The dance is *Baker's Dozen,* and the wintry sun-drenched studio at ABT transforms itself into a Newport lawn party in the long ago.

In the opening section, "Echoes of Spring," six couples coast across the floor in turn, dancing with an innocent, casual friskiness, as if showing off for themselves alone. Tharp knew next to nothing about partnering until the mid-1970s, but now her dancers urge one another on to larger and more acrobatic ballroom effects: William Whitener and Christine Uchida, both formerly with the Joffrey Ballet, accelerate into hair-raising catches, off-balance supports, and classical leaps and turns that take a new measure of the ballroom form. Raymond Kurshals and

his partner, then Richard Colton and guest artist Sara Rudner, a longtime Tharp dancer with her own company now, dart on and off the floor and exchange partners, until finally the two men are left alone with Rudner. Colton eyes Kurshals politely, walking in a circle around him, and Kurshals backs away meekly into a barre.

Caging the dance in progress, the choreographer settles down, her fierce mood subsiding into a humane and sensible scrutiny. She enjoys dramatizing the divisions between sections of a dance; in "Tango à la Caprice," the company works in threesomes, as if Kurshals, seeking to join a duet, had had a good idea. The partnering grows sharper, denser, with arching kicks executed with the suave straight-backed arrogance of flamenco. Soon the trios pass into foursomes and frozen tableaux that melt away into one sumptuously ordered rout after another. The eye moves with an easy rhythm through all this, following the state and surge, noting what the choreographer intends it to see: The underlying structural clarity of the dance is what allows Tharp to breathe new life into the familiar. Along with such traditional procedures as unison movement, canon, counterpoint, theme and variation, she systematically tears dance phrases apart and puts them back together in entirely different shapes, altering their direction and attack, tossing in steps from older works, and even piling unrelated phrases of movement on top of one another—all without compromising the integrity of the music's shifts from ragtime to swing. "You don't have to know about structure," was Tharp's caustic explanation to one interviewer. "That's my business, and there are few people I would expect to look at something maybe twice and see what the design is." Her choreography succeeds because every moment is set forth as valid and necessary, renewing the reality of very concrete, natural processes. "Nearly all the movement has something very specific in mind," says Jennifer Waye. "Like *this* movement is about getting to the floor, except it's an *en dehors* attitude turn."

The dancers plunge into a series of eccentric character dances, including a Chaplinesque fox-trot, while a corps of eight passes upstage in a swooping glide that has appeared throughout the dance as a motif. Waye and Washington seem not to want to leave the floor, but are finally lofted out by more dancers who sweep across the front of the studio. Colton is the last dancer left, catching Uchida as she flies through the air from the wings. Tossing her offstage, he lazes his way to the center of the stage, then pops six or seven wistful pirouettes while sinking to the ground, where he sits on his heels and wiggles his hips, a dreamy Lothario remembering some palmy moment on a parquet dance floor. Colton is enjoying himself, and the company improvises a few admiring hoots and whistles. Then Tom Rawe stumbles after him in an inimitable impersonation of a Fitzgeraldian drunk, and a wedge of dancers drives across the space behind, spilling soloists and couples like so much penny-ante overflow from some fabulous celebration in the next studio; indeed, dancers from ABT are watching through the doorway window. The solos continue while the company crosses and recrosses the space, until everyone gathers in tableau for a kind of group portrait, a few kneeling in front, the rest posing with hands on hips or leaning jauntily against a neighbor. Only Christine Uchida stands apart from the group. They turn around for another shot, more impromptu this time, glancing over their shoulders as if caught by a camera's flash. It's an image of a sane community: sublime in its ordinariness, decent, hardworking, willing and able to laugh at itself.

Tharp first began choreographing to music by Willie "the Lion" eight years ago, while quite pregnant, in a farmhouse attic in upstate New York. Now *Baker's Dozen* has evolved into a tribute to her extended family of solo performers, the title alluding to the twelfth role being danced by either Sara Rudner or Tharp herself. *Baker's Dozen* bathes in an America of champagne, midnight swims, sudden spats, and makings-up to music at a pavilion by the sea; Tharp has taken the measure of an innocence lost, mourned, and only distantly remembered, but recovered anyway—and it is this quality of nostalgia without illusions that gives the dance its contemporary feeling.

The dancers are reshaping themselves into a final wedge, preparing to sweep off the floor in that oddly syncopated swooping glide. Earlier, there had been a few rumbles of indecision about the irksome rhythm; now the group makes a total shambles of its final cakewalk. Tharp has been watching silently, but now she crosses her elbows over her chest, tugs at her ears, and shrieks like a bat. "Hey, you guys, don't work on something to get it wrong! We're getting very good at that!"

The tape recorder is turned off, and Rose Marie Wright labors for a minute with the dancers to mend the rhythm problem. But there's no time to work the solution into the dance, for the rehearsal schedule says it's time for a run-through of the still-unfinished *Chapters & Verses*—the casual elegance of Willie "the Lion" replaced by the straining brass of an Edwin Franko Goldman march.

Flouncing onstage like a bunch of barnstorming circus kids, the company executes a series of intentionally clichéd acrobatic stunts, full of thwarted climaxes and dumb virtuosity. Have these children run away? The music shifts abruptly into Robbie Robertson and The Band's rock classic, "The Shape I'm In," with a troupe of snot-nosed, unruly children bullied through calisthenics by a surly drill instructor, played by Tom Rawe. *"Sound off, three-four,"* Rawe bellows. Tharp's dancers are *talking,* but they have the attention span of six-year-olds. Mugging ferociously, punching each other in the shoulders, they raise their hands for attention—*"May I go to the bathroom please? I gotta go bad!"* Another band of overgrown, hormone-engorged little monsters thud and prance across the space to The Mickey Mouse Club March, segueing into a solo for William Whitener accompanied by Mouseketeer Jimmy singing *Now it's time to say good-bye, to all our family.* . . . "With its slopping spine and arms, its wide épaulés braced against turned-in legs, it looks like a satire of Paul Taylor," Arlene Croce would later write, "and it may be a personal memento of the year that Twyla Tharp spent in Taylor's company before forming her own group—a memento of her artistic adolescence."

This explosion of noise and vulgar antics ends with a portion of "Street from the Night Before," an original disco tune with a big-band overlay, commissioned from composer John S. Simon. Flowing, sensuous, almost Quaaluded movement is laid over three crossing of the space, developing over twelve minutes and finally degenerating into a vicious brawl. The acting becomes wildly overblown, almost operatic in scale, the angry arguments a new way of showing the origins of a movement impulse: *"I'm gonna slug you in the mouth, so watch."* In the center of it all, Rawe dances a melting love duet with Rudner, a feminine figure in red. The section finally degenerates into a writhing orgy, spilling across the floor to a dazed disco beat.

A few chapters of a never-to-be-completed novel, *Chapters & Verses* presents only shards of a rudimentary story, weaving together various popular dance styles from a contemporary adolescence with Tharp's new perception of "those crazy people who walk down the street talking to themselves. Fascinating. I love them." But *Chapters & Verses*'s comic patchwork also touches upon certain aspects of the choreographer's own life, redreaming the social experiences of her youth: the miscarriages of love, the costs of enforced discipline, the ambition to escape the past only to rediscover it on stage, and most important, how families are lost and found in America. Over the next two years, Tharp will expand these themes, bringing her formidable rage and carpentry, a lusting intelligence, and a nearly Faustian ambition to bear on nothing less than her own comic-tragic vision of contemporary America. From the beginning, she resolutely refuses to view her new investigations as a departure.

"The perverse thing is thinking that it's possible to get away from yourself," she says. "The further you go, the closer you come back. Sometimes in trying to change too much you cease to utilize the strongest lessons you have at your disposal. The best thing, the most sensible, obviously the *sanest* thing to do is to become that which you understand the most."

Tharp leans back in her chair, relaxing for a few minutes before the final run-through of the afternoon—*Electric Blues,* her featured dance from *Hair* adapted for the stage. The dancers are resting against the mirrors, stretching, massaging one another's shoulders, not exactly aflame with excitement about the coming season; pressure and hard work are constants with the Tharp company. The choreographer, who considers her group a model of social arrangements, joins warmly in their easy mirth, mentioning how much she's looking forward to dancing *Baker's Dozen*—"if I'm still alive."

When the *Electric Blues* rock music breaks

"Street from the Night Before" from *Chapters & Verses*. (© 1979 Jack Vartoogian)

out, she hauls herself out of her chair and begins jogging, stiffly at first then with limber grace, around the edge of the studio floor. Three men run onto the floor tossing a football, and she keeps bumping into them. Fed up, she hassles them with a few missed punches. Suddenly they have her by the arms and ankles and launch her straight above their heads. Tharp screams—she has never much liked being lifted—then screams again, more reasonably, when the men let go and catch her a few inches off the floor. She's forgotten her own choreography, her rubber sweat pants are creeping down her thighs, but the music reaches the guitar bridge and Tharp is sucked again into the lunatic machinery: passed between legs, over shoulders, chucked like a sack, and perched on someone's thighs for an enormous loop-the-loop eight feet in diameter, originally choreographed with Tharp wearing a crash helmet. When the machine is through, it spits her across the floor and Twyla executes one of her classic pratfalls, legs flailing in a paroxysm of outraged dignity.

But suddenly she's up and spinning coolly in place—the tomboy jogger transformed by an onstage costume change into an indestructible dancing Siva, god of creation and destruction.

From hard rock to ancient India, from the dance floors of Newport to discos and a lawn in Central Park, Tharp remains radically skeptical of the idea that any work of art can be truly new, original, private. Nevertheless, by dancing "*a little bit differently* every day," as Tom Rawe once put it, she has found her own reasons for everything she does—because "art," she once wrote, "is the only way to run away without leaving home."

· · ·

Born in Portland, Indiana, on July 1, 1941, the first child of Quaker parents, Tharp began her "buckshot education" in the arts with ear training, reportedly before the age of one. In the years before leaving home, she studied ballet, tap, acrobatics, baton twirling, drums, viola, violin, piano, painting, music composition, and harmony—her mother's way of preparing her for any eventuality. Faced with a curriculum that would have crushed all but the most irrepressible spirits, Tharp developed a sense of the American *Weltanschauung* unique among her contemporaries, along with a discipline and paradoxical defiance of convention that must have been her best means of psychic survival. It would take years before she learned to use everything she knew. Meanwhile, she says without evident remorse, "I feel I was cheated out of a childhood in some ways."

Named, legend has it, after the local "Pig Queen" at the county fair, Twyla claims she picked her own birthdate: "July 1. Middle-of-the-roader. Dead center of the year. *The only place for an extremist to be.*"

Tharp tells the story of her artistic development in a rush of words and images. "I went through a gruesome experience when I was about four," she says, "in a piano contest against kids who were mostly older than I was. In order to get through it quicker, I forgot my repeats, because I'd been promised that if I just got through it I would get a Milky Way bar. The pressure of playing piano in a competition as a teeny kid was worse than almost anything else could ever be. That was what I got from my first piano teacher, Miss Brown of Muncie, Indiana. . . . I was a very silent child. I didn't talk much because I didn't trust it. I liked music. I believed those drives and sentiments and feelings. By the age of five, I was practicing the piano a couple of hours a day."

At age eight, Twyla moved with her family to San Bernardino—"the end of the earth" she calls it—where she lived in a separate wing of a big house, attended school, and worked at the family drive-in, breaking twenties at the refreshment stand while still in elementary school, then working as a carhop as a teen-ager. Forever after, she says, she has seen the world in two dimensions. She continued the dance lessons begun in Indiana, at some point even studying Gypsy and flamenco dancing with Rita Hayworth's uncle. Certain days were planned to the last detail: fifteen minutes for tambourine dancing, twelve minutes for toe-tap, eleven minutes for handstands, ten minutes for grand jeté . . . With a tiny plastic phonograph, she made up her own dances. "I've always seen dances in my head," she says. "I thought everyone did. I guess not everyone does. I think actually everyone does; they just don't pursue it to the degree that I have."

"When I was fourteen, I started studying with these people in Fontana whose names were Milada Miladava and her sister, Feola Miraz. Now these ladies were actually former Ballet Russe de Monte Carlo dancers, trained at the Paris Opéra, if you can believe it, and Milada was a relatively well-known dancer who'd been in all the Ballet Russe movies and the *Gaîté Parisienne.* They were both very beautiful and were actually very good dancers. They referred me after a while to a lady named Collenette in San Marino, where my mother started driving me twice a week for the next four years. On schooldays, we'd be driving back from five-thirty class and I'd do my homework by the light from the glove compartment." She would graduate as her high school's valedictorian and cheerleader. The other kids considered her "weird," but she had no sense of their standards; frankly, she was developing her own.

"Collenette was British, one of Pavlova's seven baby ballerinas," Tharp continues. "She had a tremendous sense of form and dignity. You did *not* wear pointe shoes until you were in the fifth class, and you were put in rows according to who did the best—there was no futzing around. If you could do four pirouettes, you went to the front, if you could do two you went to the back. Nothing about being nice: 'Oh, it's your turn today, dear, go to the front row.' This is very useful to learn in this country; I'm very grateful. . . . Apart from Balanchine and having the opportunity to grow up around him, like Edward Villella did, one could not have done much better than to have the sort of lineage I had."

With her superb academic record, Tharp enrolled as a pre-med student at nearby Pomona College, with vague plans to become a psychiatrist. ("I made up things I was going to be," she recalls. "That was only to cover my tracks.") But by the end of her freshman year, she decided that she had to escape from home, from family, from whatever unforgiving engines had driven her through her endless lessons. In 1961, she enrolled at Barnard College, three thousand miles away in New York, still without the intention of becoming a professional dancer. She took her first modern classes at Barnard, dropping out the day her teacher told her to "make a sunrise"; she also realized, studying at various ballet studios around town, that she was not destined to become a ballerina.

"I couldn't bear the attitude," she explains. "I couldn't understand the fact that ballet was *about* going through certain conventions—the word *convention* in itself takes care of it. Ballet had become like the decorative art on Greek temples: just remnants of a past that nobody really understood anymore."

Nevertheless, Tharp threw herself into ballet as well as modern dance classes around the city during her years at Barnard—sometimes as many as two or three a day, first at the Graham studio, then with Merce Cunningham and Carolyn Brown (after an ad in *Dance Magazine* caught her eye), and later with Alwin Nikolais, Erick Hawkins, and the jazz teacher Luigi. By the time she graduated from Barnard in 1963, with a degree in art history, the freedom and insights of the modernists had begun to recast her instincts: She received permission to miss her graduation ceremonies to travel with the Paul Taylor Dance Company on her first important professional engagement.

Tharp made a swift impression in the Taylor company with her matter-of-fact bravado, her comedic strength, her sexy, vulnerable arrogance, and a formidable technique. "She was a tough and sassy dancer who could buffalo her way through anything," Taylor recalls. If she learned anything from Taylor's audacious physicality, his faith in human oddity, and occasional sardonic wit, she has trouble acknowledging it. "You learned from Paul by watching him dance," she says. "I loved to watch him when he was still working with the Graham company, which was where I first saw him. I was taken by the way he looked, and found out that he was doing his own choreography. I was definitely attracted to him as a dancer, not as a choreographer."

At a postperformance party during a London tour, she struck up a conversation with a certain well-placed dance critic, passing along her negative thoughts about a new work in the repertory. Taylor, who can read lips, eavesdropped from across the room. Tharp claims she was handed her walking papers the next day. Taylor insists that "when we got back to America, I told her she should think about whether she really wanted to stay with us. She went away for a while and came back, a little too quickly, and said she would. Then she quit again, two days before the start of a Broadway season. Later she came to us and said she wanted to go on unemployment and that I'd fired her. Well, I couldn't agree to that. So whenever I see her now, she says, 'You fired me!' and I say, 'You quit!' "

Whatever the truth of the matter, Tharp was clearly too uncompromising to survive in anyone's company but her own. "There was a body that wanted to move around," she explains. "But it wasn't particularly contented with any of the ways it was presented with. So it went off to find what felt right."

·   ·   ·

Tharp's first piece of choreography initiated her calculated instincts for doing something completely and correctly before moving on. *Tank Dive,* performed for an audience of twelve at the Hunter College art department in 1965, lasted only four minutes: "I didn't know shit from Shinola about choreography," she says today. Setting out to master her craft, Tharp moved downtown to begin pouring out four or five dances a year, discarding them after each performance, and thinking of her newly formed company of women as just "a bunch of broads doing God's work."

Working at the Judson Church because the space was free, she felt a wariness bordering on contempt for her contemporaries' lack of formal discipline; yet her own concentration on the formal qualities of concrete physical processes was very much a part of 1960s postmodernism. The first reviews were uniform in their adjectives:

cool, cerebral, beautiful, yes, waging the vanguard battle for the serious values of high art. But also blunt, emotionless, enigmatic, executed with faintly belligerent expressions, as if to say, "There's no way we can do this except through the body, but I wish to God there were," Tharp herself later suggested. "Twyla Tharp's main concern in choreography," wrote Don McDonough, "is to throw lines of movement across and through space and thereby establish a zone of human mastery over the real estate that is our environment." Her own memory of those days is similar: "My God, the first five years, nothing but *form,*" she says. "Horizontals and verticals, that was *it.* Post-lentils-and-beans."

Beginning with *Generation* (1967), Tharp's rogue structuralism began to relax somewhat. A twenty-eight-minute quintet "written" for a large open space, the dancing came in cascades of freewheeling, thrown-away movement that seemed to liberate the individual expressiveness of performers. Her formalism was still formidable, but with her unusual gift for generating energy and commitment in rehearsals, Tharp was beginning to "make visible and public the ways, usually confused, involuntary, and secret, in which people behave toward one another," as Dale Harris later wrote. Choreography seemed the soundest way to end her long separation from other people. "I didn't know how much I minded not having known other kids until I started trying to be a married person," Tharp recalls, referring to a marriage near the end of her college years that ended in divorce not long afterward. "Then I realized it had been a disaster. I didn't know how to talk to anybody."

By the end of the decade, Tharp was scoring dances for larger and larger groups of people, working in nontheatrical spaces like museums and art galleries, and leaving increasing room for improvisation and hazard. In *Medley* (1969), originally created at the American Dance Festival in Connecticut and later performed on the Great Lawn in Central Park, Tharp laid aside her prolific notes and charts to "choreograph chaos," augmenting her company of six women with sixty nondancers dressed in street clothes.

By 1970 this drift outdoors culminated in a major change in her life. Accompanied by her second husband, Robert Huot, a painter who had worked with her as a designer since 1965, she moved to a 250-acre farm in upstate New York to have a baby.

Tharp's "bucolic experiment" in rural living, removing her from the pressures and distractions of her rising recognition in the world of experimental dance, resulted in a new clarity of purpose. Rose Marie Wright and Sara Rudner, her two most important dancers, traveled upstate during the summer, and Tharp produced a spartan masterpiece, *The Fugue*—the oldest work still in repertory, and Tharp's "doctorate" in structure. Based on twenty twenty-second movement variations performed in silence, except for the amplified sound of the dancers' feet slapping the stage, it was as close as she would ever come to pure logic in movement. Only later would she discover her trio was a canon, not a fugue—but other than that, Tharp insists, "It's perfect."

"Okay, now what?" Tharp asked herself aloud. With looser joints, a lower center of gravity, and new warm feelings due to her pregnancy, she began horsing around to a favorite record by the jazz pianist Jelly Roll Morton and his Red Hot Peppers. The result, *Eight Jelly Rolls* (1971), marked the beginning of work "filled with feelings and references to all the old guys," and set Twyla Tharp off on her spectacular rise.

In her opening moment, Rose Marie Wright cast a lean, impenetrable look into the audience, as if to say, "Well, you're here, so you might as well watch," then launched herself into a slinky, sexy, shuffling, shadowboxing jazz solo. The deadpan neutrality and casual concentration on the mechanics of movement remained from Tharp's earlier dances, but when Tharp and Rudner emerged behind Wright, twitching and cavorting the length of the stage and vanishing into the wings, something new was happening: *Eight Jelly Rolls* was unmistakably fun to do and fun to watch, with sensuous bouts of lyricism and reckless comic horseplay perfectly matching Jelly Roll Morton's shifting landscape of bluesy depression, mayhem, and happiness. Tharp placed recognizable characters on stage, dancing in elegant halter faux-tuxedos, showing up too early and diving back into the wings, taking on one another in zany dance competitions, stealing scenes until somebody finally hauled them out of the lights. With her sidesplitting caricature of a falling-down drunk, created on the day she actually went into labor, Tharp revealed herself in one stroke as the finest comedienne in American dance. Stumbling onstage to "The Smokehouse Blues," she performed a series of magnificent pratfalls, followed by epic struggles to regain her feet and join a chorus of six damsels languishing behind her. Accessible yet deeply satisfying, *Eight Jelly Rolls* represented Tharp's break with the 1960s avant garde, but for the choreographer the dance was an act of re-attachment—a reconciliation with the past and the beginning of her true direction.

Later that same year, in a suite of five dances, Tharp consciously celebrated her deepening realization of the continuity of past and present, and the potential riches of her monstrous education. Choreographed to Haydn but ultimately performed to music by the early jazz cornetist Bix Beiderbecke, *The Bix Pieces* was a dance literally about remembering—all the way back to her earliest tap and baton lessons in San Bernardino. "It seems to me that art is a question of emphasis," a lecturer announced during the course of the dance. "That aesthetics and ethics are the same. The inventiveness resides first in choice and then in synthesis—in bringing it all together. That this action is repeated over and over again, the resolution somehow marvelously altered each time." *The Bix Pieces* demonstrated Tharp's new perception of how few fundamental concepts of dance there truly are; that dance steps from classical ballet and tap-dancing are profoundly related, and can be combined and recombined in nearly infinite variety. In addition, *The Bix Pieces* had "a kind of bedrock that no one could understand," Tharp later explained, "such as the fact that the five dances were cyclical and were in a rondo form and that my father had just died and my son had just been

Eight Jelly Rolls. The statuesque Rose Marie Wright, a former dancer with the Pennsylvania Ballet, appears at extreme left. The beneficiary of an almost photographic memory for movement, Wright could faithfully reproduce even the most unruly dancing, helping Tharp explore her vision of the trained dancer as "being like those toys that are in a dozen pieces, connected by strings." "Rose is facts," says the choreographer. "Rose is the truth." (© 1974 Tony Russell, courtesy the Twyla Tharp Dance Foundation)

born and all this kind of stuff which you wouldn't know from dancing but which makes obvious and absolute sense."

With *The Raggedy Dances,* assembled in 1972 to music by Scott Joplin and Wolfgang Amadeus Mozart, Tharp continued to fashion entirely personal intersections of ballet, jazz, spunk, spit, and a little of the old soft-shoe. Abandoning the purely formal aspirations of her generation, absorbing lessons from whenever and wherever she liked, she began to create a fusion of styles that meant nothing less than a new kind of contemporary classicism.

·   ·   ·

In 1973, a new work for the City Center Joffrey Ballet set the world of dance on its ear. Coproduced with the Twyla Tharp Foundation, *Deuce Coupe* placed a pack of hotdogging adolescents dancing to fourteen bubble-gum surf-rock tunes by the Beach Boys against a backdrop painted live in performance by the United Graffiti Artists of New York. What was happening on the subways of Manhattan, Brooklyn, the Bronx, and Queens and on the boardwalks of Venice, California, was right there on the City Center stage: After years of dopey rock ballets, *Deuce Coupe* represented the fantasies of a generation confirmed, showing ballet dancers moving to the same music contemporary youth danced to on a hot Saturday night. Tharp's no-holds-barred sock-hop may have seemed a mere embrace of novelty or a rude surge of energy from below—even an attack on the ballet's doddering irrelevance in a world of subway vandalism and rock assault. But through it all a pristine ballerina executed an alphabet of ballet steps from *ailes de pigeons* to *voyagé arabesque,* as a lingering image of the resplendent orderliness as well as the more ludicrous attitudinizing of the ballet. The ballerina was Tharp's way of showing audiences how classicism was the basis of everything they saw—the bedrock of her dancers' training and of her own attempt to shatter convention and reconceive it in contemporary terms. Celebrating the cult of youth, *Deuce Coupe* was popular art in the best sense—open, unpretentious, immediately gratifying—and it immediately made Twyla Tharp the darling and the brat of the dance world of the 1970s.

After *Deuce Coupe II,* a new version "customized" for the Joffrey alone, and *As Time Goes By,* a fresh interpretation of Haydn's Farewell Symphony, Tharp returned to her own company to fashion a new work to the music of Chuck Berry *(Ocean's Motion). Sue's Leg,* aired on *Dance in America* in 1975, was her celebration of the music of Fats Waller and the dance of the American 1930s—the Big Apple, marathon and ballroom dancing, Busby Berkeley–style production numbers, even the bump and grind. Evoking the extravagant frivolity of a vanished decade with feints and starts, lunging pratfalls, and ants-in-the-pants pile-ups, *Sue's Leg* established a continuity between generations—demonstrating how dance can make the past not only seem new, but valuable. Tharp was opening a

continent of energy and expression, but the following year, she set her sights on the heart of the dance establishment, sending American Ballet Theatre off the deep end with *Push Comes to Shove,* an astute report on the condition of the company and of all American ballet.

Push opened in front of a closed curtain, with Martine van Hamel, Marianna Tcherkassky, and Mikhail Baryshnikov performing a shuffling, sinuous trio with a derby hat to Joseph Lamb's "Bohemian Rag." In a second opening, the curtain parted and the music shifted to Haydn's Eighty-second Symphony, "The Bear," with the Russian bear, Baryshnikov, dancing in all his glory, interspersing daring off-balance turns and leaps with disco dancing and the casual, fingers-through-the-hair distraction of a man rehearsing for his life. Tcherkassky and soloist Kristine Elliott then led a corps de ballet through an episode of classical ballet gone berserk, with dancers mixing in the wrong formations, reshaping predictable images from the grand ballets of the nineteenth century, then dropping them completely to stroll nonchalantly to another part of the stage. Van Hamel and Clark Tippet performed a goofy, competitive pas de deux with the corps in the background exchanging courtly greetings, then clawing at one another in the air until Baryshnikov returned for an orgy of choreographed bowing. The disorganization of the corps, the rivalry between stars, Baryshnikov's astounding virtuosity, and the conflict between ABT's dramatic, theatrical tradition and its new concentration on the classics had been laid bare by an experimental artist who simply looked at what was before her and acknowledged it as the subject of the dance.

According to at least one critic, the thirty-four-year-old choreographer was an amateur, a pervert, a nihilist who transformed ballet dancers into spastics making up their own steps as they went along. *Push Comes to Shove* was indeed a mighty ballet for the great unwashed, an avant-garde ballet for the masses, but Tharp insisted it was not a travesty. Her rebellion against the decorum of classical style had absorbed the past without destroying it, drawing out her own ver-

Marianna Tcherkassy, Mikhail Baryshnikov, and Martine van Hamel in *Push Comes to Shove,* performed by American Ballet Theatre. "You probably have to be born here to do it," Baryshnikov has said in admiration of Tharp's dances. (© 1981 Jack Vartoogian)

sion of the resources of a classical company: naturalness, virtuosity, and supreme musical craftsmanship. More than any other contemporary choreographer, Tharp knew what artistic freedom was worth, answering not only to the timelessness of ballet but also to the needs and perceptions of her own era. Beyond a few disgruntled reviews, *Push Comes to Shove* met with a salvo of critical as well as popular acclaim, moving Tharp to the forefront of contemporary choreographers for the ballet—even though she wanted no part in certain of its conventions. On the opening night of *As Times Goes By,* she had thrown a bouquet of flowers back into the audience.

Internationally hailed as a liberating personification of American youth, Tharp's own company became one of the most popular and controversial dance troupes in the world, and Tharp herself a "herald of a new age," Arlene Croce announced. Continuing to range across a variety of American dance genres, Tharp appeared with Baryshnikov in a duet, *Once More, Frank,* to the "swinging sounds" of Frank Sina-

tra; choreographed to Mozart and in silence, *Mud* was danced in pointe shoes and Adidas; the jubilant *Cacklin' Hen* was Tharp's version of an old-fashioned country hoedown; *After All* was assembled on ice for Olympic gold-medalist skater John Curry; and *Give and Take* was a genuflection to the muse of Balanchine, although Balanchine reportedly didn't like it much. The full-throttle energy of her dancers, the high, unfettered artfulness of her formal strategies, and the verisimilitude of her Americanism were thrilling, even if Tharp had given herself no heavy themes to stagger under; with her garrulous knack for churning up hurricanes of witty movement, her cool, seductive showmanship and constant flanking maneuvers, some people considered her achievement little more than an adolescent revolt. Walter Sorrell concluded his massive study of world dance, *Dance in Its Time* (1980), with a brief description of Tharp's work as "the glamour and superficiality of a vitality going nowhere. It seems as if she were the living proof of the deadness of the past era."

Increasingly stung by attacks on her work

as merely trendy and crowd-pleasing, Tharp responded with voodoo defiance, dividing her company into a "red" team and a "blue" team, so that one could tour while the other stayed home to develop new choreography. She understood the ultimate seriousness and validity of what she was after—to excel absolutely and to please absolutely—but the accusations of immaturity struck a nerve. By the end of the 1970s, Tharp had entered the fateful condition of an artist seeking some higher moral stature, succumbing to the Faustian temptation to make some encompassing statement about her generation and her time. Her growing interest in dramatic narrative and the mystique of the "masterpiece" held out the promise of another phase of work during the fifth decade of her life—a shift in interests as radical as the advent of humor, character, and popular dance styles in the 1970s.

·   ·   ·

The decade ended with a major success at the Brooklyn Academy of Music: Kudos were heaped on the elegant *Baker's Dozen,* which Tharp considered a predictable response. The playful fragmentation and nascent violence of *Chapters & Verses,* like the *Hair* dances, required a less familiar effort from audiences than her wisest, most heartfelt entertainment. Nevertheless, Tharp knew that her first attempt at storytelling was only partially realized; even Arlene Croce, ordinarily her most eloquent champion, noted "a glib, super-Broadway style I have never before associated with Twyla Tharp."

Still, Tharp persisted with far riskier plans to construct an evening-length dance-theater piece with words. Audiences awaiting the rebirth of *South Pacific* would be kept waiting, for the piece would evolve into something entirely new: a "dansical," involving an original score, a constant stream of dancing and mime, and a spoken text to parallel them both. How to make words coexist with movement without falling into redundancy or apology? She produced a first draft herself, grandly titled *Life in America,* then a second, by some logical Tharpian declension, called *Complaints.* Tharp's text showed her flair for do-

mestic observation—one wag dubbed it "danced Updike"—but the material needed restructuring and a tighter verbal focus. A writer was needed.

Tharp's agent suggested playwright Thomas Babe, a favorite at Joseph Papp's New York Shakespeare Festival, who was fluent in a range of styles, from the harsh urban violence of his *Prayer for My Daughter* to the period evocativeness of his Civil War–era *Rebel Women.* Tharp found the prospect of dealing with someone else's strong feelings and perceptions daunting—"because I have always, for good or bad, felt great commitment about what I do," she later acknowledged, "and feeling the same degree of commitment about what somebody else does is a whole other problem." But Thomas Babe seemed "levelheaded" and Tharp decided to take a chance on the first major collaboration of her career.

An affectionate camaraderie quickly developed between the two collaborators, who seemed no less fresh for vying at the threshold of their fortieth birthdays. Both are divorced—Tharp's second marriage ended after six years—and the single parent of a young child, facing the impossibility of the family as it is traditionally conceived. Leaving behind their youth, they had become recognized artists facing up to the burden of posterity and the need to create works that might truly last. In their collaboration, they have chosen to address the issues of family and family life, of a woman unfit for life as an adult, and to see it all from the point of view of a child. The choreography incorporated "The Hard Circus" from *Chapters & Verses,* with its exuberant child's vision of circus show biz, and the chafing disco orgy from "The Street" section, condensed and reworked to produce Tharp's first true fugue.

When We Were Very Young finally shaped itself into a story told by a father to his young daughter about his own mother, Jane, and his bittersweet recollections of her suffering, brutality, and death at the age of forty—all set against his longings for the family to exist as perfectly as it does in a home movie. Green thoughts from a greener shade: The text became a kind of radio play, with a child actress and Babe himself reading from a platform high above the stage. The "dansical" traces Jane's mock-picaresque adventures in a world of chance, domination, and submission, her fugitive sexuality and drinking, and boisterous rows that finally are not all that comical. It is an image of the American dream of childhood turned nightmare; a monstrous vision of Mom, Dad, and the two kids; a litany of mis-alliances and thwarted desire, layering fantasy and history. The title was borrowed from a child's book by A. A. Milne, with a recurring motif the poem "Disobedience," about a middle-aged mother who goes down to the end of the town and is never heard from again. *"James James Morrison Morrison Weatherby George Dupree, took good care of his mother, though he was only three. . . ."* A fanatical Red Army chorus of dancers recites these words in brisk cadence as a kind of glue for the action of the dance. Tharp liked the poem because "it seems to make growing up the ultimate and cardinal sin." The tension between childhood and adult constraint, and the mature acceptance of this perilous condition, found new expression in her interpretation of the role of Jane, which she and Sara Rudner would perform on alternate nights—"if I'm still alive," she says again.

A few weeks before the opening, Twyla Tharp was making very confident noises in a *Dance Magazine* interview: "The new piece represents a culmination, and if this does not turn out to be a developed and full and matured person performing in this new piece I will be very disappointed, because I have spent a lifetime getting here."

The success of the rest of the repertory—including the new *Brahms' Paganini,* a brilliant chamber exercise in neoclassical virtuosity by the contemporary Paganini of choreographers—kept the Tharp Foundation from going to the cleaners on Broadway. But *When We Were Very Young* proved an enormous miscalculation, and the critics dined on it. Nailed by the brutality of her high ambitions, Tharp's reach had exceeded her

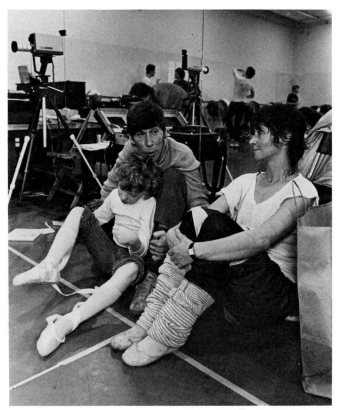

Thomas Babe, his daughter, Kirisa, and Twyla Tharp at a rehearsal for their collaboration, *When We Were Very Young.* (© 1980 Johan Elbers)

grasp: With its surprisingly literal and distracting approach to words and movement; its sentimentalization of defeat, hysteria and petulant anger; and its morass of nostalgic values, *WWWVY* presented characters unmatched to the grisly situations Tharp and Babe had concocted for them. John S. Simon's undistinguished music, Babe's confusing, jocular-avuncular script, and the furious mime sequences for father, mother, and two siblings never found an illuminating focus. Critic Tobi Tobias called the whole thing "tediously like the eternal kvetch."

Still, many of its actual dance sequences were enormously imaginative, and audiences applauded. As the thirty-nine-year-old mother at the turning point of her life, Twyla Tharp "played a part that fits the way she looks and dances," Croce acknowledged. "The hell-bent

Twyla Tharp and Raymond Kurshals in *When We Were Very Young*. (© 1983 Martha Swope)

energy, the comic, hardboiled defensiveness, the quizzical temperament, and the beautiful, sexy legs were accommodated in the role of a furious child-woman whose motor races all the way to destruction. Accommodated but not released.'' Attempting to stand in the middle of the road of life in the image of her own mother, who had inaugurated so much of Tharp's sense of herself, Twyla/Jane went down to the edge of the stage— the edge of the world—and leaped into the or-

chestra pit, never to be seen again. "That", she said later, " was a very deep pit."

· · · ·

Eighteen months later, Twyla Tharp's seventy-eight-minute intermissionless apocalypse, *The Catherine Wheel* (1981), opened on Broadway as her longest, most ambitious work to date, and the greatest rock ballet ever made. The Dantesque moment of self-awareness in the middle of the journey had coalesced into an image of

The beginning of trouble in *The Catherine Wheel:* A pineapple flies in from the wings and boffs Tom Rawe on the head during a dance with his bride, Jennifer Waye. (© 1981 Johan Elbers)

perplexed and calculating terror, the creation of two artists with no time for nostalgic reminiscences: THE NUCLEAR FAMILY MEETS THE NUCLEAR BOMB blared the banner headline of the *Soho Weekly News,* above a glamorous Richard Avedon portrait of Tharp and her new collaborator, rocker David Byrne, gazing coolly into the camera, cheek-to-cheek but not quite touching. Tharp has risen phoenixlike from the fiasco of her first Broadway show to plunge headfirst into the nuclear nightmare of the 1980s.

The constraints of adulthood and the desire for artistic maturity had been transformed by *The Catherine Wheel* into the reality of martyrdom. Tharp's new heroine, Saint Catherine of Alexandria, was tortured to death on a spiked wheel in A.D. 307, although a few legends claim that the wheel exploded at her touch, killing her infidel torturers. A Catherine wheel is a firework similar to a pinwheel; a Catherine wheel republic is in constant revolution; Catherine wheels are the tumbling cartwheels performed on Saint Catherine's Day, a Catholic feast for unmarried women dropped from the liturgical calendar in 1969. All of these themes find echoes in the dance, which links some invidious threat to Tharp's continuing comic nightmare of the All-American Horrible Family. But the hell-fired *Catherine Wheel* is at its heart a mysterious allegory about a pineapple—at various times an Edenic fruit, a bomb, a prize, a torture device, a housewarming gift, a bribe, a philosopher's stone, a sacrificial offering, and the MacGuffin of a mystery story—a thing to be sought after, shunned, bought and sold, devoured, pillaged, used as a weapon. "It's a little like interleaving the *National Enquirer* with *The Golden Bough*," Croce suggested.

The Catherine Wheel's raw and delirious Grand Guignol returns to the quintessential cartoon characters from *WWWVY:* The bull-headed, lecherous father, again played by Tom Rawe, and the ambitious, brutal, and brutalized mother, Jennifer Waye, Rawe's partner in real life, open their honeymoon with a bashful ballroom number. Then the pineapple flies in and boffs Rawe in the head, turning the marriage into Saturday night wrestling at the Olympic Auditorium. They are swiftly joined by two klutzy, moronic offspring, versions of earlier characters from *Chapters & Verses,* again performed by Raymond Kurshals and Katie Glasner; a pert, hysterical housemaid played by Shelley Washington; and a cute, fuzzy dog, also Dad's future sexual victim and murderer, played by Christine Uchida. The family ruckuses that follow exfoliate into a kind of dance-theater of cruelty, the performers miming greed, lust, rage, and horror with a psychic and visual charge at once fascinating and repelling. After Mom teaches her kids how to dance, she takes them to town in a Rumba line, where she attempts to sell her daughter to a naïve, dreamy poet played by John Carrafa. Pursuing his own disembodied ideal of perfection, the poet is more interested in pineapples than in virginal flesh—or Mom's flesh either, for that matter. While the pineapple grows bigger and bigger through each imbroglio, satisfying no one, a feminine figure in red, Sara Rudner, weaves in and out of the action as the Leader, understanding and lamenting the horror of it all. At age forty, Tharp has taken herself out of the dance, just as Jane, approaching forty, disap-

peared off the edge of the stage. Mention the word *retirement,* however, and her hair stands on end.

Santo Loquasto's set is filled with Leonardo-like wheels and circles, and a forest of twenty-four vertical poles that descend to obstruct the chorus of blindfolded, black-and-red-clad dancers who accompany the Leader through darkness and light, sometimes appearing as ghostly shadows on a scrim. After the final appalling family combat has littered the stage with great chucks of pineapple, the chorus appears with brooms to sweep the floor clean; Mom and Dad reappear to perform a brief history of social dancing—Two-step, Charleston, Lindy, Twist, and Frug—through the constant interruptions of the kids, who want their own cuddles and knockdowns. The Leader attempts to impale the bundled shards of pineapple on the heavenly machinery, where they belong, and Loquasto's suspended rack with clanging spikes descends; but the chorus prevents her, and the machine, like the torture device in Kafka's *Penal Colony,* nearly crushes her under its weight, seeking to inscribe some unintelligible lesson on her skin. The Leader finally "repents," dancing in great circles with a golden pineapple mounted on a wheel, opening the ground for the final "Golden Section"—with the company decked out in gold lamé, careening before a golden wall, through some of the most dangerous and spectacular choreography Tharp has ever created.

The glory of Tharp's anger and the astounding complexity of her allegory, with its interlocking systems of meaning that the dancers find endlessly amusing, finally aren't the point. Ceaseless dancing, a blazing river of it, is blasted along by the extraordinary rhythmic energy and inventiveness of David Byrne's music and lyrics. Byrne was a painter before his band, Talking Heads, began appearing in New York clubs in the mid-1970s with a clean, structural sound and coruscating lyrics dealing with occasions of urban life and the more paranoid manifestations of Middle America. More recently, through sound collaborations with the English experimental art-rocker Brian Eno and a growing fas-

The heavenly machinery descends in shadow play during *The Catherine Wheel*. (© 1981 Martha Swope)

Sara Rudner, one of the great dancers in the world, in *The Catherine Wheel*. Like Carolyn Brown for Merce Cunningham and Carolyn Adams and Bettie de Jong for Paul Taylor, Rudner has contributed immeasurably to the development of Tharp's work through her adventurousness and extraordinary naturalness as a performer. "Twyla has learned that I'll do all the crying and she can do all the thinking," Rudner says. (© 1981 Johan Elbers)

cination with polymetric rhythms from Africa, Latin America, and the Near East, as well as Afro-American funk, Byrne has begun to explore music for its possible role in community building. Whether Byrne's score "will one day be ranked alongside *Le Sacre du Printemps, Romeo and Juliet,* and *Appalachian Spring* is open to question," noted *The New York Times,* but the question has been raised.

Tharp's own vision of community has undergone a change as well: Her desire to respond directly to the abrasions of the world, to act out all that is feared and sought after, has uncovered an impulse to horrify and excite through an idiomatic American violence; violence has become her way of reflecting on the world, a meditation on what has been lost. From the large-spirited *Baker's Dozen* only two years earlier, Tharp has come to create Bruce Springsteen's *Short Stories,* which may or may not end with a rape and murder—"where everything is brutal, violent, where everyone takes advantage of everyone else and there is no future at all," as she remarked in an interview with the *Los Angeles Times.* What had happened?

"A lot of things. Disasters in my life. You don't want to know . . . I'm not speaking politically now. I'm speaking in terms of manners. I miss a lot of the old-fashioned conventions: the simple pledges; the real honesty; the getting married; the staying married; the meaning it; then doing what you mean. It used to be that people really stood by their word. These days, when someone says something, chances are they don't know what they're talking about.

"Sometimes I think it's just I'm getting older," she continues, "and that the way I look at people has changed. But I don't think so. I think that societal conventions have altered radically in the last thirty years. I am not politically active because, while political action may change the course of people's lives, so does art. I don't have time for political revolution . . . In some ways being an artist is a much more powerful position to be in. I am, in fact, dealing with real world problems. I'm dealing with morality in those dances."

The fury of Tharp's vision disguised a quest not unlike Saint Catherine's—who wanted to be "the most perfect, the best spokesperson, the purest," Tharp would tell *Dance in America* audiences; she was "ultimately martyred for her ideal of abstract perfection." Not long after *The Catherine Wheel*'s premiere, Tharp tells an interviewer, "I have this overriding belief that there is a right way of doing things, and that one reaches a state of grace when one functions in the most direct fashion. Once in a while I feel that I've done the best that I could possibly do and sometimes more: That it's the best that can be done. It's a notion of God that simply means there is an order apart from oneself. There is a *right* way."

"I ultimately believe," Tharp almost shouts, "that things can be powerful and effective and moving and ambitious and that people will respond positively, and I think my faith in that allows me to do what is obviously risky and emotionally devastating—which it is. We've had a lot of timid stuff recently, you know," she growls. "Real *repressed.*"

Audiences flood into the Winter Garden, but *The Catherine Wheel* production expenses will nearly break the foundation. One night a deranged woman climbs over the orchestra pit and onstage during the middle of the dance for an unforeseen contretemps. Dressed in a large overcoat, she carried a barbeque fork in her hand, which she has used to slash two ushers on her way into the theater. Now she is drifting toward the dancers. Tharp hurries onstage from the house; the sound operator is off his headset and wandering the auditorium, so there is no way to stop the music tape. Vaguely aware of the strange woman, the dancers continue, and the audience naturally assumes she's part of the show. Finally Tharp, the house manager and the stage manager venture onstage to try to talk to her, but she brandishes the fork; her eyes are glazed over. Twyla is prepared to tackle the woman if she makes a move—or better, to back her into the same pit that accepted Jane the year before. After a full five minutes, someone manages to bring down the curtain, and the woman is removed by

"The Golden Section" from *The Catherine Wheel,* with Richard Colton, Jennifer Waye, and Keith Young in the foreground. (© 1981 Johan Elbers)

the police and taken to Bellevue Hospital. No one ever learned whether or not she had intentionally chosen *The Catherine Wheel* as her target.

A shard of the violence and insanity of "real life" had passed through Tharp's fun-house mirror and onto the stage before the dance could enter "The Golden Section," in which icy terror finally surrenders to Tharp's exorbitant craftsmanship. Some critics described the final dance as nothing more than a sustained showstopper, an abstract divertissement out of keeping with the rest of the evening. But for Tharp the coda is a glittering auto-da-fé, a holocaust of willed and urgent hope that places her company beyond the firestorms and millennialist fantasies of the present to harness the energy of the sun, which is the power of the atomic bomb and the force binding all of nature. To airy, eerie whistles and pulsing congas and bass, dancers flee in straight lines across the space, detonating phrases of movement with unbroken fierceness: split leaps, daring snatches out of the air, bodies as barriers instantly overcome, reckless unison gestures, dead arched drops between legs, pinwheels made out of women's bodies turning noiselessly in the air. Through such limb-risking partnerships, "The

Golden Section" proposes Tharp's alternative to the disorder and violence of American life: Her hunger for functioning in the most direct fashion has led her to transcend ordinary human emotions through the expression of ensemble craft—her only real alternative to the corrosive forces of marriage, family, and middle-class life in general.

The Catherine Wheel is the anthem of an artist's search for grace under pressure, preparing a *physical,* nonabstract union with some higher principle of order. A flawed, infuriating masterpiece, *The Catherine Wheel* becomes a kind of cautionary fable of disciplined energy that refuses to gaze at terror from afar. "The Golden Section" is its racked and tortured Judgment Day, thrusting its dancers beyond individual fantasy and emotion into shared myth—into history, or its end.

·　　·　　·

In 1982, Tharp decided to create a television version of *The Catherine Wheel* impossible to achieve in live performance.

"The Broadway production wasn't clear enough," Tharp had told Dale Harris of *Ballet News.* "It failed to do justice to the dancers; their acting didn't get across to the audience in the way I wanted it to, in the way it does now. One of the most important things I got from the chance to put *The Catherine Wheel* on television was the opportunity to reexamine the piece with fresh eyes."

The seventy-four-minute television version was shot in twelve days—on film, rather than video tape, so that the most sophisticated lighting design could be used. The symbol of the pineapple, the confusing source of *The Catherine Wheel's* familial disruptions, was often portrayed in animations that gave sharper focus to its myriad meanings; but *Dance in America's The Catherine Wheel,* opening on a meadow outside an English church overlooking the sea, also included a new figure devised for television: Saint Catherine herself. Portrayed by a computer-generated model that is nothing more than a bundle of thin white lines in the shape of a human body, Catherine descends from the heavens to inspire the Leader's pursuit of perfection. In clarifying the stage production, Tharp moved beyond video technology into the "soul of a new machine."

The Catherine model was developed by a computer-graphics artist, Rebecca Allen, working at the New York Institute of Technology in Westchester County, New York—the only laboratory in the world where research into state-of-the-art technology for three-dimensional computer animation continues daily. Allen's unique system for animating the human figure, a kind of machine for generating video/computer puppetry, makes it possible to manipulate a figure on screen and view it from any point on a 360-degree sphere. "Once you program a body into this machine," says Tharp, "you can completely control and dictate its movements. It can do anything, both humanly possible and inhumanly possible." But finally she was "more interested in Sara than I am in computers": The presence of a computer-Catherine freed the Leader to fulfill a clearer role in the action, struggling heroically against the chorus to return the pineapple's monstrous, solipsistic energy to the machinery it came from.

What Tharp discovered in the course of developing *The Catherine Wheel* for television was that all along the dance had needed things that only television could do—furious shifts in perspective, fast and slow motion, animation ghost-overs, and stop-action freezes. *Dance in America's* video version forces audiences into a more exhilarating confrontation with the drama, clarifying and even simplifying its logic in a fashion that seems literally to explode the dancers' bodies on the screen.

Tharp's explorations of rage and outrage could seemingly go no further, but the choreographer found a way. With a pounding, thudding electric guitar score by Glenn Branca, *Bad Smells* (1982) accosted audiences with brutal images of primitive destruction, its dancers flailing and grimacing through some night of the living dead—their bodies captured onstage by a camera operator and projected live on a screen overhead. Then suddenly the violence was tamed: the sensational *Nine Sinatra Songs* (1983), assembled as a kind of emotional buffer against the fury of the Branca score, appeared to mark the beginnings of a new era in the career of Twyla Tharp.

A series of duets danced under a huge mirrored ball in gorgeous evening wear designed by Oscar de la Renta, the Sinatra dances had as their subject "couples, love, marriage, and off into the sunset!" declared the choreographer. In the Age of Reagan, they became the greatest popular success in the history of the company. No parody of America's traditional images of modern romance: *Nine Sinatra Songs* smacked of a born-again conversion to the lost manners of the social revolution, but its studied suavity and well-groomed violence reflected Tharp's continuing desire to communicate complex dramatic meanings directly to audiences. As Balanchine knew better than anyone, emotion and character in dancing are more than a matter of mere storytelling; as Edward Villella told *Dance in America* audiences, only a master storyteller can do without a plot. Tharp has learned this lesson the hard way—the way she learns everything—and returned to pure dance works with a richer sense

Twyla Tharp in *Fait Accompli*. "You might say *Fait Accompli* is kind of farewell," says the choreographer, " . . . a kind of giving up of life." (© 1984 Beatriz Schiller)

of theatrical possibility, newly committed to the transgression and inclusion of everything.

As a formal craftsman rivaled only by Jerome Robbins and Paul Taylor among living American choreographers, Tharp has continued deliberately to explore every imaginable dance convention; inevitably, she has even reapproached ballet with new fascination and respect. The romantic *Once Upon a Time* (1983), set to music by the Imperial composer Glazunov, was assembled for Baryshnikov and four very young dancers at ABT; the stunning *Bach Partita* for thirty-six stars and members of the corps became a full-blown homage to Balanchine and her first purely neoclassical ballet. "It's funny," said the choreographer, "but I chose not to do this ballet for twenty years." For her own company, she assembled another dance that invited audiences to share her new trust of neoclassical style: Bereft of her signature bumps and shimmies and shuffles, *Telemann* was nearly a *ballet blanc,* and some people could hardly believe it. In late May 1984, ABT took the unusual step of honoring Tharp with her own evening of work; a few weeks later, Tharp and Jerome Robbins shared the stage of the State Theater for *Brahms/Handel,* danced by the New York City

Ballet. Twyla Tharp had indisputably arrived as the leading ballet choreographer of her generation.

Then suddenly *Fait Accompli* appeared, a dance obsessed with death: what it is like to die, and more important, to struggle against dying with ruthless intensity. Beneath a battery of blazing lights designed by Jennifer Tipton, Tharp's company moves in and out of darkness, executing duets, quartets, octets with frenetic precision, punctuating the air with tense, karate-like blows. Joggers pass through roiling fumes, clutching their throats and gasping for breath; voices drift through the driving synthesizer-and-percussion score by David van Tiegham, reporting airline disasters and urban catastrophes. Lines of dancers appear and reappear, repeating unison phrases at double, then quadruple speeds; poses are struck, held, shaken out, held, and shaken out again.

Tharp had read accounts of executions and concentration camps, studying as well the powers of totems to ward off evil; now the second half of the dance presents the choreographer herself, as lean and defiant at age forty-three as she was twenty years earlier—after five months of daily running, push-ups, calisthenics, and even boxing lessons before her morning barre—taking on eight men in a series of nonstop duets *in extremis*. As in *Electric Blues* five years before, Tharp is pretzeled, tossed, succored, and abused, hoisted, arced, launched, and rolled across the stage for minutes without touching the ground. And finally she is alone, dancing a brilliant solo that seems to recapitulate every idea she has ever had. The physical pain and psychic suffering of a career has arrived at its end—for *Fait Accompli* is Tharp's last dance for herself, a professional death, an angry giving up of life.

She stands at center stage like Petrouchka, the straw puppet, patting her heart and catching the gesture with her free hand before it can be fully extended. As the stage empties of dancers for the last time, Tharp cups her hands into imaginary binoculars and peers across the stage at the audience. Then she shudders, shakes, and grunts, as if to say, "I've given you every drop of my blood," as if gathering all her rage, intelligence, and mettle to cast against the world. Then her shoulders fly up to her ears and she turns, gliding in a slow-motion run downstage, where footlights suddenly brighten—as if to show us, the audience, what she has been seeing all along, and to reaffirm, as her entire career has done, the imaginative link between the theater and the world.

And what could she possibly do next?

"I'm not going to talk about it," says the choreographer. "I'm going to do it."

VIDEOGRAPHY

CITY CENTER JOFFREY BALLET
January 21, 1976

Producer: Emile Ardolino
Director: Jerome Schnur
Editor: Girish Bhargava
Lighting: Ralph Holmes

Olympics (excerpt): choreography by Gerald Arpino, music by Toshiro Mayuzumi

Principal dancer: Russell Sultzbach

Parade (excerpts): choreography by Léonide Massine, music by Erik Satie, set and costumes by Pablo Picasso

Principal dancer: Gary Chryst

The Green Table (excerpt—The Chinese Conjurer): choreography by Kurt Jooss, music by Frederic Cohen, set and costumes by Hein Heckroth, masks by Hermann Markard

Principal dancer: Christian Holder

Remembrances (excerpts): choreography by Robert Joffrey, music by Richard Wagner, set by Rouben Ter-Arutunian, costumes by Willa Kim

Principal dancers: Francesca Corkle, Jan Hanniford, Paul Sutherland

Trinity: choreography by Gerald Arpino, music by Alan Raph and Lee Holdridge

Principal dancers: Christian Holder, Gary Chryst, Dermot Burke, Pamela Nearhoof, Donna Cowen, Starr Danias, Robert Thomas

Includes on-camera appearances by Léonide Massine, Kurt Jooss, Robert Joffrey, and Gerald Arpino.

SUE'S LEG
Remembering the Thirties
March 24, 1976

Producer: Merrill Brockway
Director: Merrill Brockway
Writer: Arlene Croce
Editor: Glenn Jordan
Film editor: Muriel Balash
Lighting: Jennifer Tipton

Sue's Leg: choreography by Twyla Tharp, music by Fats Waller, costumes by Santo Loquasto

Principal dancers: Twyla Tharp, Rose Marie Wright, Kenneth Rinker, Tom Rawe

Includes documentary material on social dancing of the 1930s.

MARTHA GRAHAM DANCE COMPANY
April 7, 1976

Producer: Emile Ardolino
Director: Merrill Brockway
Writer: Nancy Hamilton
Editor: Girish Bhargava
Lighting: Ralph Holmes

Frontier: choreography by Martha Graham, music by Louis Horst, set by Isamu Noguchi

Principal dancer: Janet Eilber

Lamentation: choreography by Martha Graham, music by Zoltan Kodály, costumes by Martha Graham, after designs by Edythe Gilfond

Principal dancer: Peggy Lyman

Appalachian Spring: choreography by Martha Graham, music by Aaron Copland, set by Isamu Noguchi, costumes by Martha Graham

Principal dancers: Yuriko Kimura, Tim Wengerd, David Hatch Walker, Janet Eilber

Diversion of Angels: choreography by Martha Graham, music by Norman dello Joio, costumes by Martha Graham

Principal dancers: Peggy Lyman, Peter Sparling, Takako Asakawa, David Hatch Walker, Elisa Monte, Tim Wengerd

Adorations: choreography by Martha Graham; music by Mateo Albeniz, Domenico Cimarosa, John Dowland, Girolamo Frescobaldi; set by Leandro Locsin; costumes by Halston

Principal dancers: Takako Asakawa, Jessica Chao, Mario Delamo, Janet Eilber, Diane Gray, Eivind Harrum, Bonnie Oda Homsey, Peggy Lyman, Susan McGuire, Daniel Maloney, Peter Sparling, David Hatch Walker, Tim Wengerd, Henry Yu

Cave of the Heart (excerpts): choreography by Martha Graham, music by Samuel Barber, set by Isamu Noguchi, costumes by Martha Graham

Principal dancer: Takako Asakawa

Host: Gregory Peck

Includes on-camera statements by Martha Graham.

PENNSYLVANIA BALLET
June 2, 1976

Producer: Emile Ardolino
Director: Merrill Brockway

Writer: Tobi Tobias
Editor: Girish Bhargava
Lighting: Ralph Holmes

Grosse Fugue (excerpt): choreography by Hans van Manen, music by Ludwig van Beethoven, set by Jean-Paul Vroom, costumes by Hans van Manen

Principal dancers: Dane LaFontsee, Edward Myers, Jerry Schwender, Janek Schergen

Concerto Barocco (second movement): choreography by George Balanchine, music by Johann Sebastian Bach

Principal dancers: Joanne Danto, Gregory Drotar, Gretchen Warren

Madrigalesco (excerpt): choreography by Benjamin Harkarvy, music by Antonio Vivaldi, set by Nicholas Wijnberg

Principal dancers: Alba Calzada, Edward Myers, Marcia Darhower, Jerry Schwender

Adagio Hammerklavier (excerpt): choreography by Hans van Manen, music by Ludwig van Beethoven, set and costumes by Jean-Paul Vroom

Principal dancers: Michelle Lucci, Lawrence Rhodes

Concerto Grosso (excerpt): choreography by Charles Czarny, music by George Frederick Handel, costumes by Joop Stokvis

Principal dancers: Karen Brown, Tamara Hadley, Mark Hochman, David Jordan

Includes documentary material on the Pennsylvania Ballet and an on-camera statement by Barbara Weisberger.

AMERICAN BALLET THEATRE
December 15, 1976

Producer: Emile Ardolino
Director: Merrill Brockway

Writer: Tobi Tobias
Editor: Girish Bhargava
Lighting: Ralph Holmes

Billy the Kid: choreography by Eugene Loring, music by Aaron Copland, set by Jac Venza, costumes by Jared French

Principal dancers: Terry Orr, Marianna Tcherkassky, Frank Smith, Clark Tippett

Les Patineurs: choreography by Sir Frederick Ashton, music by Giacomo Meyerbeer, set by William Mickley, costumes by Cecil Beaton

Principal dancers: Fernando Bujones, Karena Brock, Kristine Elliott, Nanette Glushak, Charles Ward

Host: Paul Newman

THE MERCE CUNNINGHAM DANCE COMPANY
An Event for Television
January 5, 1977

Producer: Emile Ardolino
Director: Merrill Brockway
Writer: Merce Cunningham
Editor: Girish Bhargava
Lighting: Ralph Holmes

Minutiae: choreography by Merce Cunningham, music by John Cage, set by Robert Rauschenberg, costumes by Remy Charlip

Solo: choreography by Merce Cunningham, music by John Cage, costumes by Mark Lancaster

Westbeth: choreography by Merce Cunningham, costumes by Jasper Johns

Septet: choreography by Merce Cunningham, costumes by Remy Charlip

Antic Meet: choreography by Merce Cunningham, costumes by Robert Rauschenberg

Scramble: choreography by Merce Cunningham, set and costumes by Frank Stella

RainForest: choreography by Merce Cunningham, music by David Tudor, set and costumes by Andy Warhol

Sounddance: choreography by Merce Cunningham, set and costumes by Mark Lancaster

Video Triangle: choreography by Merce Cunningham, costumes by Mark Lancaster

Principal dancers: Karole Armitage, Karen Attix, Ellen Cornfield, Merce Cunningham, Morgan Ensminger, Meg Harper, Catherine Kerr, Robert Kovich, Chris Komar, Charles Moulton, Julie Roess-Smith

Includes on-camera statements by Merce Cunningham.

DANCE THEATRE OF HARLEM
March 23, 1977

Producer: Emile Ardolino
Director: Merrill Brockway
Writer: Tobi Tobias
Editor: Girish Bhargava
Lighting: Ralph Holmes

Forces of Rhythm (excerpts): choreography by Louis Johnson; music by Rufus Thomas, Donny Hathaway; set by David Hays; costumes by Zelda Wynne

Bugaku (excerpt): choreography by George Balanchine, music by Toshiro Mayuzumi, set by David Hays, costumes by Zelda Wynne

Principal dancers: Lydia Abarca, Paul Russell

The Beloved: choreography by Lester Horton, music by Judith Hamilton, costumes by Zelda Wynne after Lester Horton

Principal dancers: Gayle McKinney, Roman Brooks

Holberg Suite (excerpt): choreography by Arthur Mitchell, music by Edvard Grieg, costumes by Zelda Wynne

Principal dancers: Homer Bryant, Virginia Johnson, Paul Russell

Dougla (excerpt): choreography by Geoffrey Holder, music by Geoffrey Holder, costumes and projections by Geoffrey Holder

Principal dancers: Melva Murray-White, Ronald Perry, Gayle McKinney, Roman Brooks

Includes documentary material on Dance Theatre of Harlem, with statements by Arthur Mitchell.

PILOBOLUS DANCE THEATRE
May 4, 1977

Producers: Emile Ardolino, Judy Kinberg
Director: Merrill Brockway
Writer: Elizabeth Kendall
Editor: Girish Bhargava
Lighting: Ralph Holmes

Monkshood's Farewell: choreography by Pilobolus, music by Robert Dennis, drawings by Edward Gorey, costumes by Malcolm McCormick

Ocellus: choreography by Pilobolus, music by Moses Pendleton and Jonathan Wolken

Ciona: choreography by Pilobolus, music by Jon Appleton

Untitled: choreography by Pilobolus, music by Robert Dennis, men's costumes by Malcolm McCormick

Principal dancers: Robby Barnett, Alison Chase, Martha Clarke, Moses Pendleton, Michael Tracy, Jonathan Wolken

Includes documentary material on Pilobolus.

TRAILBLAZERS OF MODERN DANCE
June 22, 1977

Producers: Merrill Brockway, Judy Kinberg

Director: Emile Ardolino

Writer: Elizabeth Kendall

Editor: Girish Bhargava

Lighting: Ralph Holmes

A documentary on the American modern dance pioneers from Isadora Duncan to Martha Graham, ending in 1932

Five Brahms Waltzes in the Manner of Isadora Duncan: choreography by Sir Frederick Ashton, music by Johannes Brahms, costumes by Paul Dan

Principal dancer: Lynn Seymour

Spear Dance Japonesque (excerpts): choreography by Ted Shawn, reconstructed for the Joyce Trisler Danscompany by Klarna Plinska; music by Louis Horst

Principal dancer: Clif de Raita

Soaring: choreography by Ruth St. Denis and Doris Humphrey, reconstructed by Klarna Plinska; music by Robert Schumann

Principal dancer: Nancy Colahan

Étude: choreography by Isadora Duncan, music by Alexander Scriabin

Principal dancer: Annabelle Gamson

Mother: choreography by Isadora Duncan, music by Alexander Scriabin

Principal dancer: Annabelle Gamson

Polonaise: choreography by Ted Shawn, reconstructed by Norman Walker; music by Edward MacDowell

Principal dancers: David Anderson, Daniel Ezralow, Michael Deane, Donlin Foreman, Clif de Raita, Tim Wengerd

CHOREOGRAPHY BY BALANCHINE: PART I
with Members of the New York City Ballet
December 14, 1977

Producer: Emile Ardolino

Director: Merrill Brockway

Writer: Arlene Croce

Editor: John Godfrey

Lighting: Ralph Holmes

Tzigane: choreography by George Balanchine, music by Maurice Ravel, set by William Mickley, costumes by Joe Eula

Principal dancers: Suzanne Farrell, Peter Martins

Divertimento No. 15 (andante movement): choreography by George Balanchine, music by Wolfgang Amadeus Mozart, set by William Mickley, costumes by Karinska

Principal dancers: Tracy Bennett, Merrill Ashley, Maria Calegari, Susan Pilarre, Stephanie Saland, Marjorie Spohn, Victor Castelli, Robert Weiss

The Four Temperaments: choreography by George Balanchine, music by Paul Hindemith

Principal dancers: Bart Cook, Merrill Ashley, Daniel Duell, Adam Lüders, Colleen Neary

Host: Edward Villella

CHOREOGRAPHY BY BALANCHINE: PART II
with Members of the New York City Ballet
December 21, 1977

Producer: Emile Ardolino

Director: Merrill Brockway

Writer: Arlene Croce

Editor: John Godfrey

Lighting: Ralph Holmes

Jewels: choreography by George Balanchine, set by William Mickley, costumes by Karinska

Emeralds (excerpts): music by François Felix Fauré

Principal dancers: Karin von Aroldingen, Gerard Ebitz, Merrill Ashley

Rubies (excerpt): music by Igor Stravinsky

Principal dancers: Patricia McBride, Robert Weiss

Diamonds (excerpt): music by Peter Ilich Tchaikovsky

Principal dancers: Suzanne Farrell, Peter Martins

Stravinsky Violin Concerto: choreography by George Balanchine, music by Igor Stravinsky, set by William Mickley, costumes by Karinska

Principal dancers: Kay Mazzo, Bart Cook, Peter Martins, Karin von Aroldingen

Host: Edward Villella

SAN FRANCISCO BALLET: ROMEO AND JULIET
June 7, 1978

Producers: Emile Ardolino, Judy Kinberg
Director: Merrill Brockway

Writer: Tobi Tobias
Editor: Girish Bhargava
Lighting: Ralph Holmes

Romeo and Juliet: choreography by Michael Smuin, music by Sergei Prokofiev, set and costumes by William Pitkin

Principal dancers: Diana Weber, Jim Sohm

Host: Richard Thomas

THE PAUL TAYLOR DANCE COMPANY
November 29, 1978

Producer: Emile Ardolino
Director: Charles S. Dubin

Writer: Paul Taylor
Editor: John Godfrey
Lighting: Ralph Holmes

Esplanade: choreography by Paul Taylor, music by Johann Sebastian Bach, costumes by John Rawlings

Runes: choreography by Paul Taylor, music by Gerald Busby, set by Gene Moore, costumes by George Tacit

Principal dancers: Bettie de Jong, Carolyn Adams, Nicholas Gunn, Monica Morris, Elie Chaib, Lila York, Ruth Andrien, Linda Kent, Robert Kahn

CHOREOGRAPHY BY BALANCHINE: PART III
with Members of the New York City Ballet
November 29, 1978

Producers: Emile Ardolino, Judy Kinberg
Director: Merrill Brockway

Writer: Arlene Croce
Editor: Girish Bhargava
Lighting: Ralph Holmes

Chaconne: choreography by George Balanchine, music by Christoph Gluck, set by Peter Harvey, costumes by Karinska

Principal dancers: Suzanne Farrell, Peter Martins

Prodigal Son: choreography by George Balanchine, music by Sergei Prokofiev, set and costumes by Georges Rouault

Principal dancers: Mikhail Baryshnikov, Karin von Aroldingen, Shaun O'Brien

Host: Edward Villella

CHOREOGRAPHY BY BALANCHINE: PART IV
with Members of the New York City Ballet
March 7, 1979

Producers: Merrill Brockway, Judy Kinberg
Director: Emile Ardolino

Writer: Arlene Croce
Editor: Girish Bhargava
Lighting: Ralph Holmes

Ballo della Regina: choreography by George Balanchine, music by Giuseppe Verdi, set by Ralph Holmes, costumes by Ben Benson

Principal dancers: Merrill Ashley, Robert Weiss

The Steadfast Tin Soldier: choreography by George Balanchine, music by Georges Bizet, set and costumes by David Mitchell

Principal dancers: Patricia McBride, Mikhail Baryshnikov

Elegie (from Tchaikovsky Suite No. 3): choreography by George Balanchine, music by Peter Ilich Tchaikovsky, set by Peter Harvey, costumes by Nicolas Benois

Principal dancers: Karin von Aroldingen, Sean Lavery

Tchaikovsky Pas de Deux: choreography by George Balanchine, music by Peter Ilich Tchaikovsky, set by Peter Harvey, costumes by Karinska

Principal dancers: Patricia McBride, Mikhail Baryshnikov

Allegro Brillante: choreography by George Balanchine, music by Peter Ilich Tchaikovsky, set by Peter Harvey, costumes by Karinska

Principal dancers: Suzanne Farrell, Peter Martins

Host: Edward Villella

THE FELD BALLET
May 16, 1979

Producer: Judy Kinberg   Writer: Tobi Tobias
Director: Emile   Editor: Girish Bhargava
    Ardolino   Lighting: Ralph Holmes

Excursion (excerpt): choreography by Eliot Feld, music by Samuel Barber

Principal dancer: Christine Sarry

Intermezzo (excerpts): choreography by Eliot Feld, music by Johannes Brahms

Principal dancers: Christine Sarry, Eliot Feld, Helen Douglas, Edmund LaFosse, Linda Miller, Gregory Mitchell

Danzon Cubano: choreography by Eliot Feld, music by Aaron Copland

Principal dancer: Edmund LaFosse

The Real McCoy (excerpts): choreography by Eliot Feld, music by Ira Gershwin, costumes by Rouben Ter-Arutunian

Principal dancers: Michaela Hughes, Eliot Feld

La Vida (excerpt): choreography by Eliot Feld, music by Aaron Copland

Principal dancer: Alfonso Figuera

Santa Fe Saga (excerpt): choreography by Eliot Feld, music by Morton Gould

Principal dancer: Gregory Mitchell

Half Time: choreography by Eliot Feld, music by Morton Gould, costumes by Willa Kim

Principal dancers: Helen Douglas, Michaela Hughes, Christine Sarry, Kenneth Hughes, Jeff Satinoff

Includes documentary material with on-camera appearances by Aaron Copland, Morton Gould, and Eliot Feld

MARTHA GRAHAM DANCE COMPANY
Clytemnestra
May 30, 1979

Producers: Emile   Editor: Girish Bhargava
    Ardolino, Judy   Lighting: Ralph Holmes
    Kinberg
Director: Merrill
    Brockway

Clytemnestra: choreography by Martha Graham, music by Halim El Dabh, set by Isamu Noguchi, costumes by Halston

Principal dancers: Mario Delamo, Peggy Lyman, Yuriko Kimura, George White, Jr., Diane Gray, Bert Terborgh, Tim Wengerd, Elisa Monte, Peter Sparling, Lucinda Mitchell, Janet Eilber, Christine Dakin

Host: Christopher Plummer

TWO DUETS WITH CHOREOGRAPHY BY JEROME ROBBINS AND PETER MARTINS
February 20, 1980

Producers: Emile   Writer: Tobi Tobias
    Ardolino, Judy   Editor: Girish Bhargava
    Kinberg   Lighting: Ralph Holmes
Directors: Emile
    Ardolino
    (Other Dances)
    Emile Ardolino,
    Kirk Browning
    (Calcium Light Night)

Other Dances: choreography by Jerome Robbins, music by Frédéric Chopin, set by Rouben Ter-Arutunian, costumes by Santo Loquasto

Principal dancers: Natalia Makarova, Mikhail Baryshnikov

Calcium Light Night: choreography by Peter Martins, music by Charles Ives, set by Steve Rubin

Principal dancers: Heather Watts, Ib Andersen

Includes rehearsal footage and on-camera statements by Jerome Robbins and Peter Martins

DIVINE DRUMBEATS:
Katherine Dunham and Her People
April 16, 1980

Producers: Merrill   Writer: Glen Berenbeim
    Brockway,   Editor: Girish Bhargava
    Catherine   Lighting: Ralph Holmes
    Tatge
Director: Merrill
    Brockway

Rites de Passage: choreography by Katherine Dunham; music by Paquita Anderson, Georges

Auric, Katherine Dunham; costumes by John Pratt

Principal dancers: Norman Davis, Doris Bennett, Pearl Reynolds

Narrator: James Earl Jones

Includes an on-camera appearance by Katherine Dunham and documentary material about her career

BEYOND THE MAINSTREAM
May 21, 1980

Producers: Merrill Brockway, Carl Charlson	Writer: Faubion Bowers
	Editor: Girish Bhargava
	Lighting: Ralph Holmes
Director: Merrill Brockway	

A documentary on some of the more prominent postmodern choreographers

Line-up (excerpt): choreography by Trisha Brown, music by Gordon Lightfoot

Glacial Decoy (excerpt): choreography by Trisha Brown, projections and costumes by Robert Rauschenberg

Principal dancers: Trisha Brown, Russell Dumas, Elizabeth Garren, Lisa Kraus, Nina Lundborg, Stephen Petronio

Contact Improvisation

Principal dancers: Steve Paxton, Danny Lepkoff, Nina Martin, Lisa Nelson, Nancy Stark Smith, Randy Warshaw

Trio A: choreography by Yvonne Rainer

Principal dancers: Frank Conversano, Bart Cook, Sara Rudner, with documentary footage of Yvonne Rainer

Chair (excerpt) and *The Matter* (excerpt): choreography by David Gordon

Principal dancers: David Gordon, Valda Setterfield

Light (Stone Fields (excerpts): choreography by Kei Takei

Principal dancer: Kei Takei

Dance: choreography by Laura Dean, music by Laura Dean

Principal dancers: Laura Dean, Angela Caponigro, Paul Epstein, Peter Healey, John Proto, Patty Shenker, Perry Souchuk, David Yoken

THE AMERICAN DANCE FESTIVAL: PILOBOLUS
May 21, 1980

Producer: South Carolina Educational Television (Sidney J. Palmer)	Writer: Elizabeth Kendall
	Editor: Randy Brinson
	Lighting: Ralph Holmes
Director: Emile Ardolino	

Walklyndon: choreography by Robby Barnett, Lee Harris, Moses Pendleton, Jonathan Wolken

Principal dancers: Robby Barnett, Jamey Hampton, Michael Tracy, Jonathan Wolken

Momix: choreography by Moses Pendleton, music by Ardie Wallace and the Sugar Hill Gang

Principal dancer: Moses Pendleton

Alraune: choreography by Alison Chase, Moses Pendleton; music by Robert Dennis; costumes by Malcolm McCormick

Principal dancers: Alison Chase, Moses Pendleton

Molly's Not Dead: choreography by Alison Chase, Moses Pendleton, Robby Barnett, Jonathan Wolken; music by Walt Michael, Tom McCreesh, Tom Campbell; costumes by Kitty Daly

Principal dancers: Robby Barnett, Allison Chase, Jamey Hampton, Michael Tracy, Jonathan Wolken, Georgiana Holmes

Includes documentary material and interviews with Pilobolus members and Charles Reinhart, director of the American Dance Festival

NUREYEV AND THE JOFFREY BALLET IN TRIBUTE TO NIJINSKY
March 9, 1981

Producers: Emile Ardolino, Judy Kinberg	Writer: Dale Harris
	Editor: Girish Bhargava
	Lighting: Ralph Holmes
Director: Emile Ardolino	

Petrouchka: choreography by Michel Fokine, music by Igor Stravinsky, set and costumes by Alexandre Benois

Principal dancers: Rudolf Nureyev, Denise Jackson, Christian Holder, Gary Chryst

La Spectre de la Rose: choreography by Michel Fokine, music by Carl Maria von Weber, set and costumes by Léon Bakst

Principal dancers: Rudolf Nureyev, Denise Jackson

L'Après-midi d'un Faune: choreography by Nijinsky, music by Claude Debussy, set and costumes by Léon Bakst

Principal dancers: Rudolf Nureyev, Charlene Gehm

Includes documentary material on Nijinsky and the Diaghilev era and on-camera statements by Rudolf Nureyev and Robert Joffrey

LIVE WITH THE SAN FRANCISCO BALLET: THE TEMPEST
March 30, 1981

Producers: Emile Ardolino, Judy Kinberg
Director: Emile Ardolino

Writer: Cobbett Steinberg
Lighting: Ralph Holmes

A co-production with KQED, San Francisco

The Tempest: choreography by Michael Smuin, music by Paul Seiko Chihara after Henry Purcell, set by Tony Walton, costumes by Willa Kim

Principal dancers: Evelyn Cisneros, Tomm Ruud, Attila Ficzere, David McNaughton

Host: Gene Kelly

Includes an intermission feature on the creation of the ballet

L'ENFANT ET LES SORTILEGES
(The Spellbound Child)
May 25, 1981

Conceived for television by George Balanchine in collaboration with Kermit Love

Producers: Emile Ardolino, Judy Kinberg
Director: Emile Ardolino

Editor: Girish Bhargava
Lighting: Ralph Holmes

L'Enfant et les Sortilèges: choreography by George Balanchine; music by Maurice Ravel; design concept, puppets, models, and costumes by Kermit Love; production design supervised by David Mitchell

Principal dancers: Christopher Byars, Francis Sackett, Alexia Hess, Julie Kirstein, Mel Tomlinson, Susan Freedman, Karin von Aroldingen

Singers: Karen Hunt, Gary Glaze, Emily Golden, Elizabeth Pruett, Jane Shaulis, William Stone, Dan Sullivan, Carl Tramon, Ruth Welting

Puppeteers: Richard Ellis, Bruce Edward Hall, J. J. Kroupa, Roman Paska, Jim Rowland, Bryant Young

PAUL TAYLOR:
Three Modern Classics
January 11, 1982

Producers: Emile Ardolino, Judy Kinberg
Director: Emile Ardolino

Writer: Holly Brubach
Lighting: Ralph Holmes

In association with the University of North Carolina Center for Public Television

Aureole: choreography by Paul Taylor, music by George Frederick Handel, costumes by George Tacit

Principal dancers: Carolyn Adams, Elie Chaib, Lila York, Ruth Andrien, Robert Kahn

Three Epitaphs: choreography by Paul Taylor, American folk music, costumes by Robert Rauschenberg

Principal dancers: Linda Kent, Thomas Evert, Susan McGuire, Cathy McCann, Daniel Ezralow

Big Bertha: produced by South Carolina Educational Television, choreography by Paul Taylor, music from the St. Louis Melody Museum Collection of Band Machines, set and costumes by Alec Sutherland

Principal dancers: Bettie de Jong, Thomas Evert, Monica Morris, Carolyn Adam

Includes a retrospective of Paul Taylor's career

PAUL TAYLOR:
Two Landmark Dances
April 12, 1982

Producers: Emile Ardolino, Judy Kinberg
Director: Emile Ardolino

Writer: Holly Brubach
Lighting: Ralph Holmes

In association with the University of North Carolina Center for Public Television

Le Sacre du Printemps (The Rehearsal): choreography by Paul Taylor, music by Igor Stravinsky, set and costumes by John Rawlings

Principal dancers: Bettie de Jong, Ruth Andrien, Christopher Gillis, Elie Chaib, Carolyn Adams, Lila York

Arden Court: choreography by Paul Taylor, music by William Boyce, set and costumes by Gene Moore

Principal dancers: Carolyn Adams, Elie Chaib, Lila York, Robert Kahn, Susan McGuire, Thomas Evert, Christopher Gillis, Daniel Ezralow, David Parsons

BOURNONVILLE DANCES,
with Members of the
New York City Ballet
May 24, 1982

Producers: Judy Kinberg, Edward Villella
Director: Edward Villella

Writer: Tobi Tobias
Editor: Girish Bhargava
Lighting: Ralph Holmes

Ballabile from *Napoli:* choreography by Auguste Bournonville, music by Holger Simon Paulli, set by David Mitchell, costumes by Ben Benson

Principal dancers: Lisa Hess, Daniel Duell

Pas de deux from *Kermesse in Bruges:* choreography by Auguste Bournonville, music by Holger Simon Paulli, set by David Mitchell, costumes by Ben Benson

Principal dancers: Heather Watts, Helgi Tomasson

Pas de trois from *La Ventana:* choreography by Auguste Bournonville, music by Hans Christian Lumbye, set by David Mitchell, costumes by Ben Benson

Principal dancers: Lourdes Lopez, Stephanie Saland, Robert Weiss

Pas de deux from *William Tell:* choreography by Auguste Bournonville, music by Gioacchino Rossini, set by David Mitchell, costumes by Ben Benson

Principal dancers: Darci Kistler, Ib Andersen

Pas de deux from *Flower Festival in Genzano:* choreography by Auguste Bournonville, music by Edvard Helsted, set by David Mitchell, costumes by Ben Benson

Principal dancers: Merrill Ashley, Peter Martins

Tarantella from *Napoli:* choreography by Auguste Bournonville, music by Holger Simon Paulli, set by David Mitchell, costumes by Ben Benson

Principal dancers: Lisa Hess, Daniel Duell

Includes documentary material on Auguste Bournonville

THE GREEN TABLE,
with the Joffrey Ballet
December 13, 1982

Producer: Judy Kinberg
Director: Emile Ardolino

Writer: Tobi Tobias
Editor: Girish Bhargava
Lighting: Ralph Holmes

The Green Table: choreography by Kurt Jooss, staged by Anna Markard, music by Frederic Cohen, set and costumes by Hein Heckroth, masks by Hermann Markard

Principal dancers: Philip Jerry, Gary Chryst, Beatriz Rodriguez, Valmai Roberts, Carole Valleskey, James Canfield, Jerel Hilding, Mark Goldweber

Includes a documentary on the life and career of Kurt Jooss

BALANCHINE CELEBRATES STRAVINSKY
February 14, 1983

Producers: New York City Ballet— Barbara Horgan, in association with Lincoln Center

Director: Emile Ardolino
Writer: Nancy Goldner
Lighting: Ralph Holmes

Agon: choreography by George Balanchine, music by Igor Stravinsky

Principal dancers: Heather Watts, Mel Tomlinson

Variations: choreography by George Balanchine, music by Igor Stravinsky

Principal dancer: Suzanne Farrell

Persephone: choreography by George Balanchine, music by Igor Stravinsky, set by Kermit Love

Principal dancers: Karin von Aroldingen, Mel Tomlinson

Persephone: Vera Zorina

Singers: Joseph Evans, members of the New York City Opera

THE CATHERINE WHEEL
March 28, 1983

Producer: British Broadcasting Company—Alan Yentob
Director: Twyla Tharp

Editor: Dave King
Lighting: Jennifer Tipton

The Catherine Wheel: choreography by Twyla Tharp, music by David Byrne, set and costumes by Santo Loquasto

Principal dancers: Sara Rudner, Jennifer Way, Tom Rawe, Katie Glasner, Raymond Kurshals, Shelly Washington, Christine Uchida, John Carrafa, Richard Colton

THE MAGIC FLUTE
with Members of the New York City Ballet
April 25, 1983

Producer: Judy Kinberg
Director: Merrill Brockway

Writer: Holly Brubach
Editor: Girish Bhargava
Lighting: Ralph Holmes

The Magic Flute: choreography by Peter Martins, music by Riccardo Drigo, set by David Mitchell, costumes by Ben Benson

Principal dancers: Heather Watts, Ib Andersen

Introduced by Peter Martins

SAN FRANCISCO BALLET: A SONG FOR DEAD WARRIORS
January 16, 1984

Producer: Judy Kinberg
Director: Merrill Brockway

Writer: Holly Brubach
Editor: Girish Bhargava
Lighting: Alan Adelman

A co-production with KQED, San Francisco

A Song for Dead Warriors: choreography by Michael Smuin, music by Charles Fox, costumes by Willa Kim, projections by Ronald Chase

Principal dancers: Evelyn Cisneros, Antonio Lopez, Vane Vest

Followed by a docudrama on Richard Oakes and the American Indian takeover of Alcatraz, Smuin's inspiration for the ballet; Smuin appears on-camera

A CHOREOGRAPHER'S NOTEBOOK:
Stravinsky Piano Ballets
by Peter Martins
February 13, 1984

Producer: Judy Kinberg
Director: Merrill Brockway

Writer: Holly Brubach
Editor: Girish Bhargava
Lighting: Ralph Holmes

Eight Easy Pieces: choreography by Peter Martins, music by Igor Stravinsky, costumes by Santo Loquasto

Principal dancers: Stacy Caddell, Susan Gluck, Roma Sosenko

Tango: choreography by Peter Martins, music by Igor Stravinsky, costumes by Ben Benson

Principal dancers: Heather Watts, Bart Cook

Piano Rag Music: choreography by Peter Martins, music by Igor Stravinsky, costumes by Ben Benson

Principal dancer: Maria Calegari

Concerto for Two Solo Pianos: choreography by Peter Martins, music by Igor Stravinsky, costumes by Ben Benson

Principal dancers: Heather Watts, Ib Andersen, Jock Soto

Includes Peter Martins speaking on-camera about his beginnings as a choreographer under the guidance of George Balanchine

AMERICAN BALLET THEATRE:
Don Quixote
March 5, 1984

Producer: National Video Corporation—RobinScott

Director: Brian Large
Lighting: Jennifer Tipton

Don Quixote: choreography by Mikhail Baryshnikov after Petipa and Alexander Gorky, music by Ludwig Minkus, set and costumes by Santo Loquasto

Principal dancers: Mikhail Baryshnikov, Cynthia Harvey, Frank Smith, Victor Barbee, Richard Schafer

BALANCHINE, PARTS AND II
May 28, 1984, and June 4, 1984

Producer: Judy Kinberg
Director: Merrill Brockway

Writer: Holly Brubach
Editor: Girish Bhargava

A documentary retrospective on the career of George Balanchine

BARYSHNIKOV BY THARP
with American Ballet Theatre
October 5, 1984

Producer: Don Mischer
Directors: Don Mischer, Twyla Tharp
Writers: Twyla Tharp, Peter Elbling

Editors: Kevin Fernan, Mark West
Lighting: William Klages

The Little Ballet: choreography by Twyla Tharp, music by Alexander Glazunov, costumes by Santo Loquasto

Principal dancers: Mikhail Baryshnikov, Elaine Kudo, Amanda McKerrow, Nancy Raffa

Sinatra Suite: choreography by Twyla Tharp, songs performed by Frank Sinatra, costumes by Oscar de la Renta

Principal dancers: Mikhail Baryshnikov, Elaine Kudo

Push Comes to Shove: choreography by Twyla Tharp, music by Joseph Lamb and Franz Josef Haydn, costumes by Santo Loquasto

Principal dancers: Mikhail Baryshnikov, Elaine Kudo, Susan Jaffe, Robert La Fosse, Cheryl Yeager

AN EVENING OF DANCE AND CONVERSATION WITH MARTHA GRAHAM
December 14, 1984

Producer: Denmarks Radio—Thomas Grimm

Director: Thomas Grimm
Editor: Kim Toftum
Lighting: Ib Mortenson

Errand into the Maze: choreography by Martha Graham, music by Gian-Carlo Menotti, set by Isamu Noguchi, costumes by Martha Graham

Principal dancers: Teresa Capucilli, Larry White

Cave of the Heart: choreography by Martha Graham, music by Samuel Barber, set and costumes by Isamu Noguchi

Principal dancers: Takako Asakawa, Donlin Foreman, Jacqulyn Buglisi, Jeanne Ruddy

Acts of Light: choreography by Martha Graham, music by Carl Nielsen, costumes by Halston

Principal dancers: Peggy Lyman, George White, Jr., Christine Dakin, and Company

Includes on-camera statements by Martha Graham

AMERICAN BALLET THEATRE AT THE MET
February 22, 1985

Executive Producer: National Video Corporation— Robin Scott

Director: Brian Large
Lighting: David K. H. Elliot

Les Sylphides: choreography by Michel Fokine, music by Frederic Chopin, sets and costumes by Alexandre Benois

Principal dancers: Marianna Tcherkassky, Cynthia Harvey, Cheryl Yeager, Mikhail Baryshnikov

Triad: choreography by Kenneth MacMillan, music by Sergei Prokofiev

Principal dancers: Amanda McKerrow, Robert La-Fosse, Johan Renvall

Paquita: choreography by Natalia Makarova after Petipa, music by Ludwig Minkus, costumes by Theoni Aldredge

Principal dancers: Cynthia Gregory, Fernando Bujones

THE TAYLOR COMPANY:
Recent Dances
March 29, 1985

Producer/director: Société Radio Canada— Pierre Morin

Editor: Claude Faucher
Lighting: Jean-Guy Corbeil

Mercuric Tiding (excerpt): choreography by Paul Taylor, music by Franz Schubert, set by David Gropman, costumes by Cynthia O'Neal

Snow White: choreography by Paul Taylor, music by Donald York, set and costumes by Gene Moore

Sunset: choreography by Paul Taylor, music by Edward Elgar, set and costumes by Alex Katz

Dancers: Cathy McCann, Christopher Gillis, Lila York, Linda Kent, Susan McGuire, David Parsons, Kenneth Tosti, Thomas Evert, Kate Johnson, James Karr, Raegan Wood, Douglas Wright, Sandra Stone, Elie Chaib, Karla Wolfangle

Includes on-camera interview with Paul Taylor by Holly Brubach

THE SAN FRANCISCO BALLET IN CINDERELLA
December 1985

Producer: Judy Kinberg
Directors: Emile Ardolino, Michael Smuin

Lighting: Alan Adelman

A co-production with KQED, San Francisco, in association with the San Francisco Ballet

Cinderella: choreography by Lew Christensen and Michael Smuin, music by Sergei Prokofiev, sets and costumes by Robert Fletcher, with additional costumes by Sandra Woodall

Principal dancers: Evelyn Cisneros, Alexander Topicy, Vane Vest, Tomm Ruud

Host and Hostess: Kermit the Frog and Miss Piggy

Amberg, George. *Ballet: The Emergence of an American Art*. New York: Mentor Books, 1949.

Anderson, Jack. *Dance*. New York: Newsweek Books, 1974.

_____. *The One and Only: The Ballet Russe de Monte Carlo*. New York: Dance Horizons, 1981.

Balanchine, George, and Mason, Francis. *101 Stories of the Great Ballets*. Garden City, N.Y.: Doubleday, 1975.

Banes, Sally. *Terpsichore in Sneakers: Post-Modern Dance*. Boston: Houghton Mifflin, 1980.

Beaumont, Cyril. *The Ballet Called Swan Lake*. London: Wyman & Sons, 1952.

Bentley, Toni. *Winter Season: A Dancer's Journal*. New York: Random House, 1982.

Brown, Jean Morrison, ed. *The Vision of Modern Dance*. Princeton: Princeton Book Co., 1979.

Buckle, Richard. *Diaghilev*. New York: Atheneum, 1979.

_____. *Nijinsky*. New York: Avon Books, 1975.

Cage, John. *Silence*. Middletown, Conn.: Wesleyan University Press, 1973.

Chujoy, Anatole. *The New York City Ballet*. New York: Knopf, 1953.

Cohen, Selma Jeanne. *Dance as a Theater Art*. New York: Dodd, Mead, 1974.

_____. *Doris Humphrey: An Artist First*. Middletown, Conn.: Wesleyan University Press, 1972.

Copeland, Roger, and Cohen, Marshall, eds. *What Is Dance?* New York: Oxford University Press, 1983.

Croce, Arlene. *Afterimages*. New York: Knopf, 1977.
_____. *Going to the Dance*. New York: Knopf, 1982.

Cunningham, Merce. *Changes: Notes on Choreography*. New York: Something Else Press, 1968.

De Mille, Agnes. *America Dances*. New York: The Macmillan Company, 1980.

Denby, Edwin. *Dancers, Buildings and People in the Street*. New York: Popular Library, 1965.

_____. *Looking at the Dance*. New York: Horizon Press, 1949.

Duncan, Isadora. *The Art of the Dance*. New York: Theater Arts Books, 1928.

_____. *My Life*. New York: Liveright, 1955.

France, Charles, ed. *Baryshnikov at Work*. New York: Knopf, 1979.

Franks, A. H. *Twentieth-Century Ballet*. London: Burke, 1954.

Gautier, Théophile. *The Romantic Ballet*. Translated by Cyril Beaumont. Reprint. New York: Arno Press, 1980.

Goldner, Nancy. *The Stravinsky Festival of the New York City Ballet*. New York: Eakins Press, 1973.

Gordon, Suzanne. *Off Balance: The Real World of Ballet*. New York: Pantheon Books, 1983.

Gruen, John. *The Private World of Ballet*. New York: The Viking Press, 1975.

_____. *The World's Great Ballets*. New York: Harry N. Abrams, 1981.

Guest, Ivors. *The Dancer's Heritage: A Short History of Ballet*. London: Dancing Times, 1977.

_____. *Fanny Elssler: The Pagan Ballerina*. London: A. & C. Black Ltd., 1970.

Haggin, B. H. *Ballet Chronicle*. New York: Horizon Press, 1970.

Haskell, Arnold. *Ballets Russes: The Age of Diaghilev*. Worcester and London: Trinity Press, 1968.

Highwater, Jamake. *Dance*. New York: A. & W. Publishers, 1978.

Hodgson, Moira. *Quintet: Five American Dance Companies*. New York: William Morrow, 1976.

Jowitt, Deborah. *Dance Beat*. New York: Marcel Dekker, 1977.

Kendall, Elizabeth. *Dancing: A Ford Foundation Report.* New York, 1983.

_____. *Where She Danced.* New York: Knopf, 1979.

Kirstein, Lincoln. *Blast at Ballet: A Corrective for the American Audience.* New York: Marstin Press, 1938.

_____. *The Book of the Dance: A Short History of Classical Theatrical Dancing.* Garden City, N.Y.: Doubleday, 1942.

_____. *Movement and Metaphor.* New York: Praeger, 1970.

_____. *Nijinsky Dancing.* New York: Knopf, 1975.

_____. *Thirty Years: The New York City Ballet.* New York: Knopf, 1978.

Kochno, Boris. *Diaghilev and the Ballets Russes.* New York: Harper & Row, 1970.

Krokova, Rosalyn. *The New Borzoi Book of Ballets.* New York: Knopf, 1956.

Livet, Anne. *Contemporary Dance.* New York: Abbeville Press, 1978.

Lloyd, Margaret. *The Borzoi Book of Dance.* New York: Knopf, 1949.

Magriel, Paul. *Chronicles of the American Dance.* Reprint. New York: Da Capo Press, 1978.

Martin, John. *American Dancing.* Reprint. New York: Dance Horizon, 1966.

_____. *The Modern Dance.* Reprint. New York: Dance Horizon, 1968.

Makarova, Natalia. *A Dance Autobiography.* New York: Knopf, 1979.

Martins, Peter, and Cornfield, Robert. *Far from Denmark.* Boston and Toronto: Little, Brown, 1982.

Maynard, Olga. *American Modern Dancers: The Pioneers.* Boston: Little, Brown, 1965.

_____. *The American Ballet.* Philadelphia: Macrae Smith, 1959.

Mazo, Joseph. *Prime Movers.* New York: William Morrow, 1977.

McDonough, Don. *The Complete Guide to Modern Dance.* Garden City, N.Y.: Doubleday, 1976.

_____. *Martha Graham.* New York: Popular Library, 1973.

_____. *The Rise and Fall and Rise of Modern Dance.* New York: New American Library, 1970.

Nijinska, Bronislava. *Early Memoirs.* New York: Holt, Reinhart & Winston, 1981.

Payne, Charles. *American Ballet Theatre.* New York: Knopf, 1978.

Percival, John. *Modern Ballet.* New York: Harmony Books, 1970.

Reyna, F. *A Concise History of Ballet.* New York: Grosset & Dunlap, 1965.

Reynolds, Nancy. *Repertory in Review: 40 Years of the New York City Ballet.* New York: Dial Press, 1977.

Ruyter, Nancy Lee Chalfa. *Reformers and Visionaries: The Americanization of the Art of Dance.* New York: Dance Horizons, 1979.

Sachs, Curt. *World History of the Dance.* New York: W.W. Norton, 1965.

Shawn, Ted, with Poole, Gray. *One Thousand and One Night Stands.* New York: Doubleday, 1960. Reprint. New York: Da Capo Press, 1979.

Shelton, Suzanne. *Divine Dancer: A Biography of Ruth St. Denis.* Garden City, N.Y.: Doubleday, 1981.

Sherman, Jane. *The Drama of Denishawn Dance.* Middletown, Conn.: Wesleyan University Press, 1979.

Siegel, Marcia. *At the Vanishing Point: A Critic Looks at Dance.* New York: Saturday Review Press, 1972.

_____. *The Shapes of Change: Images of American Dance.* Boston: Houghton Mifflin, 1979.

_____. *Watching the Dance Go By.* Boston: Houghton Mifflin, 1977.

Smakov, Gennady. *Baryshnikov: From Russia to the West.* New York: Farrar, Straus & Giroux, 1980.

Sorrell, Walter. *Dance in Its Time: The Emergence of an Art Form.* Garden City, N.Y.: Anchor Press/Doubleday, 1981.

Spencer, Charles. *The World of Serge Diaghilev.* New York: Penguin Books, 1974.

Stearns, Marshall, and Stearns, Jean. *Jazz Dance: The Story of American Vernacular Dance.* New York: Schirmer Books, 1979.

Steinberg, Cobbett, ed. *The Dance Anthology.* New York: New American Library, 1980.

Stevens, Franklin. *Dance as Life: A Season with American Ballet Theatre.* New York: Avon Books, 1976.

Stewart, Virginia, and Armitage, Merle. *The Modern Dance.* New York: Carnegie Corporation, 1935. Reprint. Brooklyn, N.Y.: Dance Horizon, 1970.

Taper, Bernard. *Balanchine.* New York: Collier Books Macmillan, 1974.

Terry, Walter. *The Dance in America.* New York: Harper & Row, 1956; revised 1971.

INDEX

Page references for illustrations are in **boldface** type.